2002 Report

Economic and Social Progress in Latin America

Beyond Borders

The New Regionalism in Latin America

Distributed by the Johns Hopkins University Press for the Inter-American Development Bank

Washington, D.C.

ACKNOWLEDGMENTS

The Research Department, under the direction of Guillermo Calvo, and the Integration and Regional Programs Department, under the direction of Nohra Rey de Marulanda, were responsible for the preparation of this Report. Robert Devlin, Antoni Estevadeordal and Ernesto Stein, with the collaboration of Mauricio Olivera, coordinated the interdepartmental team in charge. The principal authors are as follows:

Chapter 1:	Robert Devlin, Antoni Estevadeordal and Ernesto Stein
Chapter 2:	Robert Devlin and Antoni Estevadeordal
Chapter 3:	Robert Devlin, Antoni Estevadeordal and Marcos Jank
Chapter 4:	Roberto Echandi and Carolyn Robert
Chapter 5:	Arturo Galindo, Alejandro Micco and César Serra
Chapter 6:	Alberto Barreix, John Strong and Juan José Taccone
Chapter 7:	José Luis Machinea and Josefina Monteagudo
Chapter 8:	Eduardo Fernández-Arias, Ugo Panizza and Ernesto Stein
Chapter 9:	Ernesto Stein and Ugo Panizza
Chapter 10:	Ernesto Stein, Christian Daude, Stephen Meardon and Eduardo Levy Yeyati
Chapter 11:	Ernesto López-Córdova and Mauricio Mesquita Moreira
Chapter 12:	Suzanne Duryea, Raymond Robertson with Werner Hernani

Other contributors to the chapters were Manuel Agosin, Alberto Barreix, Mario Berrios, Cesar Calderón, Andrew Crawley, Alberto Chong, Daniel Chudnovsky, Edgardo Demaestri, Kenroy Dowers, Ramón Espinasa, Paolo Giordano, Jaime Granados, Jeremy Harris, Peter Kalil, Andrés López, Stephen Meardon, Alejandro Micco, Eric Miller, Josefina Monteagudo, Guillermo Ordoñez, Magdalena Pardo, Andrew Powell, Fernando Puga, Fernando Quevedo, Ennio Rodríguez, Ricardo Rozemberg, Gilles St. Paul, Matthew Shearer, Kim Staking, Kati Suominen, Gustavo Svarzman, Luiz Villela, and Masakazu Watanuki. Eduardo Lora provided helpful comments, suggestions and advice. Chapter 11 benefited from data provided by the Instituto Brasileiro de Geografía e Estatística (IBGE) and by Mexico's Instituto Nacional de Estadística, Geografía e Informática (INEGI). We also thank Bank personnel who participated in internal discussion workshops on the background papers for this Report, and who provided comments during revisions.

Research assistants were Lucio Castro, David Colin, Megan Dooley, Rosa Finch, Ian Fuchsloch, Virgilio Galdo, Reuben Kline, Josefina Posadas, Alejandro Riaño, and Ricardo Vera. The IDB Publications Section handled the editing and design. Madison Boeker and John Dunn Smith provided additional editorial support. María de la Paz Covarrubias and Martha Skinner provided general administrative assistance.

The opinions expressed in this Report are those of the authors and do not necessarily reflect the views of the Inter-American Development Bank or its Board of Executive Directors.

PREFACE

Since independence, the nations of Latin America and the Caribbean have repeatedly pursued an agenda of regional integration in one form or another. Initiatives have varied in terms of their objectives, ranging from monumental political unions to simple agreements for the free trade of goods. However, while efforts to "get together" with neighbors seem to be one of the defining features of the region's history, the goal has always been elusive. Regional initiatives have repeatedly fallen victim to factors such as political and military conflict, skewed distribution of benefits among partners, inappropriate design and implementation, macroeconomic instability and economic crisis, or the physical obstacles of nature.

After the disappointing performance of the early post-war economic integration initiatives, the near collapse of regional trade during the crisis of the 1980s, and the shift to a more open market-based development strategy, regional economic integration appeared to have become a relic of the past. To the surprise of many, however, regional integration initiatives reappeared in the 1990s, and in new and robust forms.

The regionalism of the 1990s emerged as an integral component of the structural reform process in Latin America, complementing and reinforcing the modernization policies pursued unilaterally and adopted as part of the region's participation in the multilateral liberalization emerging from the Uruguay Round. The structural reforms have changed the face of development policy and the regional initiatives designed to support it. Indeed, the regional integration of the 1990s so dramatically parted ways with the early post-war experience that it has been coined the "new regionalism."

This new regionalism has emerged as a result of more favorable conditions on different fronts. The move to more external openness and market-based activity has unleashed new global trade and investment opportunities and provided incentives for new regional approaches to commercial relations. Improved macroeconomic management has made the Latin American economies more resilient. Democracy has fostered social participation, pacified borders, and increased the disposition to cooperate and integrate with other countries, including the industrialized democracies of the North that also are increasingly looking South for regional partners. Meanwhile, the launch in Doha of new World Trade Organization negotiations promises that regional initiatives will be accompanied by stronger multilateral rules. In this new setting, regional integration can create an enabling environment for further liberalizing reforms, encourage productive transformation, and foster the cooperation that will more readily generate net benefits for all.

During the 1990s, regional integration has made progress on several fronts. Market access for the trade of goods within the subregions has been substantially liberalized. Functional cooperation in areas such as regional infrastructure, security and protection of democracy is also without historical precedent. Moreover, regional economic integration and cooperation with northern industrialized countries—politically inconceivable only 15 years ago—are now advancing on multiple fronts that encompass the major regional markets of the world.

Despite these gains, of course, many challenges remain. Important strategic issues for the Latin American countries and their potential industrial country partners are posed by such matters as parallel initiatives for deepening integration in the subregions, widening the scope of the integration process to include integration with industrialized countries, and tying this process into the potential synergies from the multilateral negotiations in Geneva. Existing subregional agreements that have the necessary political leadership and economic relevancy should redouble efforts to move forward in their common market objectives. Or, absent these conditions, they should consider other more limited but still valuable alternatives, such as preserving and perfecting free trade areas. At the same time, the region must fully exploit the new opportunities to support structural reform and development by integrating with major industrialized regions, as well as with the entire world under the umbrella of the Doha Development Agenda. In pursuing these goals, countries need to take into account the increased demand for participation by civil society, and develop mechanisms to ensure that the fruits of regionalism, and the globalization of which it is part, are more equally distributed. Meanwhile, industrialized countries have a responsibility to provide market access to overly protected sectors in which Latin America has a comparative advantage, facilitate sustainable agreements by supporting trade-related capacity building, and be vigilant of the special problems that smaller economies encounter in regional and multilateral liberalization.

Since its founding, the Inter-American Development Bank has been, in the words of its first President Felipe Herrera, the "Integration Bank." That vocation remains strong today and is expressed in the Bank's Corporate Strategy for attaining economic growth and reducing poverty in Latin America. Regional integration stands as one of the four central pillars of that strategy, along with competitiveness, modernization of the state, and social development.

The new regionalism clearly can support the overarching objective of development. The 2002 Report on *Economic and Social Progress in Latin America* attempts to contribute to this endeavor by examining some of the advances and shortcomings of the process and proposing a future agenda to build on the promising developments of the 1990s. The Report is not meant to be the last word on a topic that generates much discussion. But it will give readers a better understanding of the state of regional integration in Latin America and the Caribbean, as well as provide food for thought regarding the future direction of policy.

Enrique V. Iglesias
President
Inter-American Development Bank

CONTENTS

ROAD MAP TO THIS EDITION

The 2002 *Economic and Social Progress Report* begins with a **summary and agenda** in terms of regional integration in Latin America and the Caribbean (Chapter 1). Where does the region stand and where is it going? The focus is on the interaction between current subregional integration schemes, the new agenda launched in Doha for multilateral trade talks, North-South initiatives such as the Free Trade Area of the Americas (FTAA), and inter-regional agreements with the European Union and Asia. Following this overview, the remainder of the book is divided into three parts.

Part I focuses on different **dimensions of regional integration**. Chapter 2 analyzes the merits, objectives and instruments of what has been deemed the "new regionalism" in Latin America in the 1990s. While trade integration and related market access issues have been the focus of much attention (Chapter 3), other dimensions are examined that may be equally important: the institutional requirements necessary to make regional integration agreements run smoothly (Chapter 4), financial integration (Chapter 5) and the integration of infrastructure (Chapter 6). The chapters focus on the main effects of integration in each of these areas, how much has been achieved, and what remains to be done.

Part II discusses important issues of **macroeconomic coordination**. Chapter 7 reviews the costs and benefits of different types of macro coordination, the obstacles that make coordination difficult, and experiences with coordination in Latin America. The focus then turns more closely to a particular type of coordination that warrants special attention: exchange rate and monetary policies. Chapter 8 discusses the potential for problems when countries bound by trade agreements have exchange rate disagreements, and Chapter 9 examines the deepest possible form of exchange rate coordination: the formation of currency unions.

Part III focuses on the **effects of regional integration** on foreign direct investment (Chapter 10), productivity (Chapter 11), and inequality (Chapter 12). A common theme is whether different types of regional integration agreements (North-South, South-South) produce different impacts. Throughout, the authors try to derive lessons from the experiences of Latin America and other regions that can shed light on the potential consequences of regional integration agreements with industrialized countries. Such agreements—among them the FTAA—have become increasingly important to Latin America and will play a critical role in the future of the region.

Chapter 1

REGIONAL INTEGRATION: SUMMARY AND AGENDA

The 1990s witnessed a resurgence of interest in regional integration throughout the world. Europe, which had steadily advanced in regional integration during the post-war era, began the decade by implementing an ambitious Single European Market and closed it by launching the euro. North America established a comprehensive free trade area through the North American Free Trade Agreement (NAFTA), which was built on the U.S.-Canada free trade area of the late 1980s. The Southeast Asian countries went beyond their long tradition of regional cooperation by expanding the Association of Southeast Asian Nations (ASEAN) into a free trade area. In Africa, there were some 15 mostly new regional integration agreements (RIAs), and in Latin America and the Caribbean, some 30 have emerged since 1990.

As the 1990s progressed, there was growing evidence of regional integration initiatives aimed at linking developed and developing economies. Latin America is a case in point. Mexico's joining of NAFTA marked the beginning of efforts in the region to negotiate reciprocal free trade with industrialized markets. The launching of the Free Trade Area of the Americas (FTAA) at the end of 1994 aimed to link the region with the United States and Canada to create the world's largest free trade area by 2005. At the same time, two countries signed bilateral free trade agreements with Canada and a number of other negotiations are under way with Canada and the United States as well. Meanwhile, Chile and Mexico signed free trade agreements with the European Union (EU). Along with Peru, the same two countries participated in the Asian-Pacif-

ic Economic Cooperation (APEC), involving most of Southeast Asia, Japan, Australia, New Zealand and North America. Other agreements are in various stages of negotiation.

Why the resurgence of regional integration? There are many reasons, but the overarching motive appears to be the search for additional policy tools to manage insertion into an increasingly globalized and competitive world economy. There is substantial evidence that successful countries deploy policies that can proactively harness the forces of globalization for economic growth and development, while those countries that distance themselves from these same forces lag behind. In effect, regional integration initiatives represent a third tier of trade policy reform, which aims to complement and reinforce the unilateral and multilateral liberalization undertaken as part of the structural reform process that has been underway since the mid-1980s. Seen in this light, regional integration is an integral part of the structural reform process itself.

The process has brought challenges as well. As we move into the 21st century, the regional dimension has become a more important component of the overall national policy package, and the stakes have become higher. During the 1990s, trade grew significantly among regional partners, creating in many cases economic interdependencies among neighbors for the first time in modern history. Yet a number of the agreements—particularly in South America—have encountered difficulties as they have been rocked by unstable international capital flows, macroeconomic instability, political uncertainty and broken momentum or backsliding on regional commitments. Economic problems in one country now can spill over faster to other countries in the region not only through financial contagion but also via trade shocks in neighboring economies. Clearly, the easy stage of integration is now over; the subregions will need renewed political leadership and a redoubling of efforts if they are to achieve their deep objectives of a common market.

Moreover, looming over all the current regional integration agreements is the reality of a successful FTAA process, the negotiations of which cover a broad and complex trade agenda that is now in the intense final lap towards 2005. A major question is how countries will manage the articulation of their FTAA negotiations with their strategically important subregional objectives, negotiations with Europe, and the Doha Development Agenda negotiation in Geneva, also scheduled to finish in 2005. Among the myriad of existing agreements, which ones will have sufficient economic and political relevancy to coexist with the FTAA? Another complex issue is how countries will mobilize the capacity and technical skills to effectively participate simultaneously in so many strategically important negotiations and implement their results. These are questions of monumental proportion because the results of negotiation on all these fronts will effectively regulate the bulk of external trade and investment of the countries involved over the coming decades.

The importance of these agreements and future negotiations has not been overlooked by the private sector and civil society, which want to be heard regarding the process of negotiations that will affect them. This democratic demand will require developing channels of communication that permit the public's voice to be heard but protect public authorities from being "captured" by interest groups. Persisting with economic liberalization through regional integration— not to mention the unilateral or multilateral opening— will require more than ever domestic consensus building, particularly in the current context in which liberalizing reforms are being called into question by different sectors of the population.

One of the potential benefits of North-South agreements like the FTAA is that they can serve as an anchor for the developing country members. Teaming with industrialized partners awards credibility to regional commitments and energizes structural change

through trade and investment commitments. NAFTA has provided to some extent this type of umbrella to Mexico during difficult times in the hemisphere; the FTAA and comprehensive agreements with the EU raise the prospects of other umbrellas being extended to the rest of the region.

The opportunity for an ambitious FTAA agreement must not be lost. Recent passage of trade promotion authority in the United States, even though a far from perfect mandate from the standpoint of many regional trade partners, now sets the stage for finishing the negotiation. The negotiations of such a complex agreement among 34 countries with a heterogeneous economic profile and varying geopolitical interests will be extremely difficult. However, the negotiations provide a significant vehicle for the region to pursue reforms and liberalization that have slowed or stalled in subregional agreements, effectively creating a new floor for trade and investment with neighbors and the rest of the hemisphere. For the United States and Canada, it is an opportunity to acquire a bigger productive platform for their firms to compete internationally. At the same time, it presents an opportunity to counteract protectionist tendencies in those sectors that have lost their comparative advantage, but in which Latin American countries are competitive and desperately in need of market access to promote sustained economic recovery and poverty reduction. And for the two parties there is the challenge of developing an FTAA institutional architecture that protects every country's rights and obligations and promotes balanced outcomes among partners with very different capacities.

An advancing FTAA, however, should not cause countries to lose sight of simultaneous opportunities to tighten commercial relations with the EU, as well as to look to new markets in Asia. In addition to the benefits that can be derived from cooperation and trade agreements with these regions, it is a way to advance further in the process of open regionalism, and an important component of progress toward global free trade.

Finally, the regional integration agenda cannot prosper without a vibrant multilateral system that regulates world trade and the regional agreements that are increasingly part of it. Completion of a comprehensive Doha Development Agenda in Geneva is essential to provide a better foundation for subregional agreements and advance some critical areas of their extraregional agendas, including those in the FTAA and agreements with the EU. But the synergy is not one way, since regional agreements are pushing liberalization forward in areas that are still a distant frontier in the multilateral system. Working together, the two levels of integration can serve to strengthen the global economy and make it more prosperous for everyone.

TAKING STOCK OF THE NEW REGIONALISM OF THE 1990s

Regional integration is a means to an end and not an end in itself. Hence it would be surprising if regional policy consistently moved in a direction contrary to an overall development strategy of a particular country. Regional economic integration usually begins with some type of trade agreement and can progressively expand into a wider scope of collective economic policy as well as cooperation in noneconomic areas, and even evolve into some forms of political union.

The classic levels of regional economic integration, ranked by scope and deepness of commitments, are: (i) a simple free trade area in goods in which tariffs and other border measures are eliminated among partners; (ii) a more ambitious "second generation" free trade area liberalizing services and other areas of economic activity that impinge more directly on domestic policy as opposed to border measures per se; (iii) a customs union in which a free trade area is encircled by a common external tariff (CET) and a regional mechanism for tariff revenue collection and distribution; (iv) a common market that frees not only trade but factors of production, including labor movements; (v) a monetary union that adds a common currency, central bank and perhaps other forms of macroeconomic coordination; and (vi) an economic community or union that embraces collective agreements in most major areas of economic activity. The sequence that RIAs follow in their path toward deeper integration has in practice varied according to the case.

Since independence, the countries of Latin America have made any number of attempts to integrate both politically and economically. Efforts at economic integration have been especially strong in the post-war period. Early initiatives focused on development of regional free trade areas or common markets. These initiatives were inserted into the then-prevailing import-substitution industrialization (ISI) strategy and were aimed at staving off exhaustion of the model due to the small scale of domestic markets. Regional integration held the promise of creating scale economies through formation of a larger regional market. This market was to emerge through preferential tariff elimination among partners, which at the same time maintained or increased high barriers to extraregional imports and engaged in strong state intervention in economic activity, all of which were central features of the ISI strategy. The approach was controversial, in part because high levels of protection were considered to be a source of trade and investment diversion that was detrimental to the welfare of the countries involved, third parties, and the multilateral trading system. In any event, after a few years of apparent success, momentum faltered and the regional agreements fell into disarray.

The regional initiatives that emerged in the 1990s have been characterized as the "new regionalism." This is because the role of regional integration has changed dramatically with respect to the early post-war episode. The new regionalism is an integral part of an overall structural policy shift in Latin America towards more open, market-based economies operating in a democratic setting.

What are the motives behind the new regionalism? One is to reinforce market opening undertaken at the unilateral and multilateral levels. The formation of a regional market is also meant to create a more controlled and stable environment for firms to gain export experience—particularly in higher value-added goods that generally demand and spill over more knowledge-based skills—and to have an outlet for goods that face strong international protectionism. In addition to diversifying exports, the scale economies, attraction of foreign direct investment (FDI) and competition generated by a credible regional market are meant over time to dynamically raise productivity and develop international competitiveness. Regional integration also is being used as a geopolitical tool to fortify international bargaining positions and promote cooperation in achieving "neighborhood" objectives such as peace, democracy, the resolution of border-related problems, and the development of regional infrastructure. In what follows, we will take stock of the progress made with regards to regional integration in a wide variety of dimensions.

Support for Trade Liberalization

Trade liberalization has been a centerpiece of the structural reform process. Unilateral liberalization was particularly significant from 1985-95, after which Latin America also assumed the comprehensive disciplines of the Uruguay Round. As for regional integration, it has proven to be an important complement for lowering average levels of protection.

The many free trade area and common market agreements have generally involved the comprehensive elimination of tariffs on the trade of goods among partners, with relatively few exceptions. In effect, regional arrangements have established a managed policy environment based on reciprocity, within which countries have signaled their commitment to trade liberalization by going beyond that which was feasible or desirable at the unilateral and multilateral levels. Meanwhile, contemporary regional liberalization has avoided some of the pitfalls of the "old" regionalism, thanks to its working in tandem with the substantial process of unilateral and multilateral opening. Consequently, the authorities' commitment to regional liberalization has been more credible to the private sector than in the past and the risks of trade diversion have been substantially reduced. Moreover, regional liberalization has generally been sustained, even in the face of economic and balance of payment problems.

Regional integration to date has not been nearly as effective as a tool for liberalization in areas beyond goods. Most agreements affect goods only, and those that have assumed second-generation disciplines (services, intellectual property, investment, etc.) often have done so with only modest depth or content. The most advanced in this regard is NAFTA, where Mexico's liberalization has been comprehensive.

As tariffs have been eliminated, non-tariff measures have become the principal barrier to the trade of goods. Unilateral liberalization and the Uruguay Round eliminated most of Latin America's recourse to quantitative restrictions on imports (licenses and quotas). However, regional trade is still hindered by non-tariff barriers such as onerous customs procedures, technical standards, and other trade-related surcharges. There also is some evidence that stringent rules of origin have limited regional trade or caused exporters to bypass preferences altogether. Insufficient harmonization or lack of mutual recognition of regulatory frameworks also have limited full exploitation of the opportunities for regional trade. The economic payoff from effectively addressing these issues is high and would substantially reinforce the returns to tariff liberalization. However, the political economy of dismantling these obstacles is complex, and progress has generally been limited to date.

Forming Customs Unions

The four main subregional agreements of Latin America (Mercosur, the Andean Community, the Central American Common Market and the Caribbean Community) have all formally aimed at creating common markets or communities. Formation of a customs union is a necessary step in this direction. Since a customs union harmonizes the external tariff structure among partners and allows for a common collection of revenue, third party imports can enter the regional market via any country and then circulate without duty controls thereafter. In contrast, a free trade area (or an imperfect customs union) must administer (often complex) rules of origin to regulate access to preferences and avoid "trade deflection," i.e., the incentive for third party imports to enter the regional market through the lowest tariff partner country. Customs unions also promote leveraged bargaining through joint negotiations (as the countries' tariffs must move in tandem), which is not the case in a free trade area, where each country maintains sovereignty over tariff policy. On the cost side, customs unions are more demanding institutionally, even when imperfect, and countries lose independence in tariff policy and the ability to use it in response to shocks.

None of Latin America's subregions is close to being a true customs union. All have agreed to common external tariffs, but they are either in development (Central America and CARICOM), reformulation (the Andean Community), or have suffered serious unilateral perforations (Mercosur). Customs unions in the region have also been permissive regarding the ability of individual members to strike bilateral deals with third parties. Historically, Latin America has had great trouble forming a CET, much less a full-fledged customs union, and this has not changed under the new regionalism. One of the problems is the tension that has emerged between the larger market country—the tariff structure of which is typically a defining feature of a new CET—and smaller partner economies that favor lower tariffs to minimize the risk and cost of trade diversion. Fiscal dependency on tariffs and balance of payments problems have also eroded willingness to forgo autonomy in tariff policy. Meanwhile, none of the subregional customs unions have a formula and institutional structure to share tariff revenue.

The imperfect status of the region's customs unions has created precisely the type of costs that the system is supposed to eliminate. Time-consuming and costly border administration is still required to avoid trade deflection (close to half the time of international cargo transport by road in the Southern Cone is due to border delays). Important efficiencies in tariff revenue collection are forgone. And the potential for leveraged bargaining is undermined, as the ability to make credible group commitments is eroded by the possibility of unilateral actions.

Fostering Trade and Promoting Economic Transformation

Empirical evaluations to date suggest that, on balance, the regional liberalization of the 1990s has created trade. Some trade diversion is inherent in any regional integration initiative. However, trade diversion has been contained in most cases due to regional integration working in tandem with very substantial third party trade liberalization. It also should be remembered that not all trade diversion reduces welfare, as in the case when it improves the terms of trade or dynamically evolves into increased international competitiveness.

Measured from the standpoint of the growth of trade, many of the regional agreements have been economically relevant. In effect, regional preferences have reinforced the effect of unilateral liberalization in allowing neighboring markets to discover each other, particularly in the major subregions. But regional agreements and the awareness they create in the private sector have also sparked significant trade growth between distant and unfamiliar markets, with the Chile-Mexico free trade area being an example.

In terms of economic transformation, regional trade is substantially more laden with higher value-added manufactures than extraregional trade, and also displays significantly more specialization through intra-industry exchange. Hence, regional trade is contributing to export diversification in a region traditionally dependent on commodity exports. Mexico's participation in NAFTA is a good example: its export structure has evolved from petroleum to machines, thanks to integration into the production network of North American firms.

The opportunities afforded by the creation of a regional market are expected to increase productivity. For this to be important at the aggregate level, the regional agreement must affect a significant amount of overall economic activity and induce competition, trade and investment. Empirical estimates suggest that NAFTA has had significant productivity effects in Mexico. Similar work on Brazil suggests productivity gains have been more associated with unilateral external opening than with Mercosur as such. This is not surprising, since Brazil is by far the largest economy in Mercosur, and hence regional trade and investment are a relatively small share of that economy's total output. But another factor is that Mexico's integration has been with two major industrialized partners with different comparative advantages, allowing Mexico greater gains from trade, relatively more access to FDI and best practices, and access to a large and affluent market (all further magnified by geographical proximity).

The new regionalism is relatively young, and hence it remains to be seen to what extent regional trade becomes a platform for competitive international exports. If regional agreements just generate trade in goods that are competitive only in the regional market ("regional goods") due to preferences or other factors, countries may become excessively vulnerable to downturns in a partner country's economy.

Regional markets have served as an outlet for trade in goods that confront sizable levels of international protection (agriculture, food processing, textiles, steel, etc.) and in which the region has a comparative advantage. Notwithstanding numerous multilateral rounds of trade liberalization, industrialized countries have been resistant to liberalizing sectors that are sensitive to competition from developing countries. The Uruguay Round's elimination of the Multifiber Agreement in 2005 promises to bring relief in textiles. Advances in agriculture-related sectors remain modest, as important tariff peaks, sanitary measures, export subsidies and agricultural domestic support in the industrialized countries are major distortionary obstacles for Latin America to exploit its international comparative advantage. Eyes are now focused on the Doha Development Agenda in Geneva as a hopeful vehicle to open world markets to developing country agriculture-related exports, and to contain the antidumping activity that has often penalized successful export performance.

With the exception of NAFTA, cross-border trade in services has been more affected by unilateral and multilateral liberalization than formal regional integration as such. One reflection of this is that financial services integration in Latin America— for example in banking and equity markets—has largely involved de facto integration with the rest of the world and industrialized countries in particular. Foreign banks of industrialized countries now have a strong presence in most domestic financial markets and have been a major source of competition, modernization and credibility in the domestic banking systems in the region. Moreover, the same foreign banks have established subsidiaries and branches in almost all the countries of the region, creating potential for regional cross-border services. However, the potential opportunities for financial providers to operate at the subregional level will not be fully tapped until member countries adopt and implement financial integration protocols that exceed their commitments in the WTO.

Choice of Partners

The pursuit of regional agreements has been freewheeling. The initial wave at the beginning of the 1990s began with the launching, or renewal, of formal common market integration projects in the four subregions. These all involved countries that shared a common geographical area and a post-war history of attempts at economic integration. Parallel to this were initiatives by Chile, not a member of any group, which set out on its own to establish free trade areas with

immediate neighbors and distant countries alike. After joining NAFTA, Mexico set out to sign NAFTA-like agreements with most of Latin America. And since NAFTA, there has been an increasing propensity to link up with industrialized countries, something that would have been politically inconceivable before the new regionalism.

As discussed above, being part of a customs union has not been a barrier for individual countries negotiating bilaterally with other countries. Almost all the Andean Community members have at least one bilateral free trade area with another country, and some members of the Central American Common Market, CARICOM and Mercosur have also pursued their own bilateral agreements. These developments sometimes have been divisive to the group's cohesion and eroded the credibility of bloc negotiation.

The process may appear somewhat helter-skelter, but it does have its logic. The up side is that by pursuing multiple agreements, the countries have been confirming to the private sector their commitments to gradual liberalization (in the controlled and politically attractive setting of a reciprocal regional accord), creating new markets for their exporters, and reducing actual or potential trade diversion from existing preferential agreements. In fact, as the agreements expand their geographical coverage, they begin to approach multilateral proportions, and nearly eliminate trade diversion. For example, Mexico has free trade agreements with North America, Europe and almost all of Latin America, and is now pursuing free trade in Asia through APEC, and through a free trade area with Japan. There also has been a progressive tendency to upgrade to second-generation disciplines, albeit in many cases with cautious depth or content.

The biggest upgrade has been the growing interest in integrating with an industrialized market. Since the industrialized country in these instances already has a relatively liberal economic framework, the burden of adjustment falls mostly on the developing country partner. Nevertheless, theory and practice suggest that this can be a powerful tool in locking in liberalizing disciplines, providing incentives for modernization, reducing trade diversion, exploiting international comparative advantage, winning access guarantees to a major export market, generating a source of importation of technology and best practices, and attracting the industrialized country's foreign direct investors. Experience also has shown that negotiating an agreement with an industrialized country is an exercise in capacity building. Some countries that have negotiated free trade agreements of this type have seen their negotiating teams "graduate" to world-class levels and their domestic firms become less fearful of tackling international competition. Learning by doing seems to work here.

One of the downsides of these developments has been reduced transparency and increased transaction costs in world trade. A myriad of preferential agreements, all with different norms and coverage, have created a "spaghetti bowl" of administrative hurdles for trade in the hemisphere. Another issue that warrants attention is the increasing creation of "hub and spoke" trade where certain agenda-setting countries establish an extensive web of free trade areas in which they have free market access with many countries, but the same countries do not enjoy similarly favorable access conditions with each other. Chile and Mexico are hubs in the hemisphere, and Canada and the United States may also become hubs if the number of their agreements expands. In terms of the hemisphere, hubs and spokes are less efficient than a global FTAA. However, as will be discussed below, under certain conditions a growing envelope of hubs and spokes could be a building block for forming a welfare enhancing hemispheric agreement. But if overly leveraged with narrow commercial interests, the same strategy could perversely lead the way to a welfare reducing and unsustainable FTAA. In particular, in the FTAA, as well as in other extraregional initiatives, it is important to pay special attention to the specific needs of small economies, which, among other things, are vulnerable to insecure market access, and often lack the necessary institutional capacity to make the most of regional integration processes (see Box 2.5 in Chapter 2).

A related issue is the potential negative effects of the growing number of bilateral agreements on countries left out of a particular process (an issue of debate for Central America and the Caribbean before they gained non-reciprocal NAFTA parity with the United States).

All these issues are magnified by the fact that they are arising in most other parts of the world as well. Stating the balance of benefits and costs in a second best world is a difficult empirical exercise for individual countries and for the world community at large. In the meantime, opinions vary both at the theoretical and policy levels.

Attracting Foreign Direct Investment

Latin America's attitude toward foreign direct investment has evolved from early post-war skepticism into being much more receptive. Foreign firms are now generally viewed as potential sources of technology, export markets and best practices that reinforce the structural reform process. But there also is a similar view in other developing regions, which has increased competition to attract FDI, particularly from OECD countries.

Through much of the 1990s, Latin America experienced strong growth of FDI, which has become by far the main source of private foreign financing for the region. There are several reasons for this surge, including macroeconomic stability, the wave of privatizations and institutional reform, as well as regional integration.

Empirical work on a worldwide sample of countries presented in this volume confirms that regional integration does attract FDI when the host country becomes a member of an agreement or when there is significant extension of the market. These gains, however, can be unevenly distributed, especially when location is biased to larger market partners due to uncertain or uneven application of regional rules. The empirical work also finds that as source countries expand their participation in regional agreements, the existing FDI can be diverted or diluted.

At the same time that it contributes to attracting FDI, regional integration, by increasing the geographical area from which a multinational firm can supply the extended market, increases the scope of competition in incentives for the location of FDI. Incentives are warranted when investment projects generate positive externalities, and can lead to optimal outcomes in terms of the investment projects that are implemented, and in terms of their location. However, aggressive competition in incentives can also tilt the distribution of benefits unnecessarily in favor of the foreign firm. This has been an important source of contention in some subregions. Yet, subregional integration agreements have been slow to find mechanisms to coordinate the incentive schemes in order to help tilt the balance more in favor of the host countries.

Macroeconomic and Monetary Coordination

Crises in member countries and large swings in bilateral exchange rates can cause serious stress in the relationship between RIA partners. The current crisis in the Mercosur countries is a perfect example of this problem. Large exchange rate swings among the partners can generate protectionism in the countries that are hurt, defeating the purpose of the RIA; induce foreign investors to reconsider the location of their subsidiaries; prompt existing firms to relocate their investments toward the country that has gained in competitiveness; disrupt export flows, particularly in goods that are not easy to redirect to alternative markets; and weaken the partners' credibility regarding their own exchange rate commitments, and thus lead to contagion. For all these reasons, macroeconomic instability, and in particular significant exchange rate swings, have at times seriously eroded political commitment for regional integration agreements in their member countries.

The danger of contagion has led to an additional effect that has harmed the cohesion of regional integration agreements: the tendency of countries to differentiate themselves from their partners when these are affected by crises. These problems also have created periodic bouts of pressure to scale back an agreement from, for example, a customs union to a free trade agreement. In addition, they have provided incentives for ad hoc bilateral initiatives by adversely affected members.

It is hard to envision advancing toward deeper subregional agreements without dealing with these problems in some way. Unfortunately, advances have been modest. There have been some attempts to establish consultation mechanisms, macroeconomic targets or convergence criteria, and common databases to facilitate cross-country monitoring. But those efforts have fallen short of systematic coordination, to the detriment of stability and the deepening of the pacts. Moreover, financial cooperation is still quite limited, although the Andean countries have established a reserve fund (*Fondo Latino de Reservas*) that has

proven to be useful, most recently with the disbursement of financing to Bolivia.

Regional Institutions

The very top-heavy regional institutional structures inherited from the old regionalism have been reformed, and the new breed of agreements has tended towards scaled down intergovernmental arrangements. On the whole, neither approach has been fully satisfactory: the institutional architecture of the new regionalism appears to be too weak in the face of growing integration and interdependencies as well as the complexity of the agendas emerging in different forums. This is either because some needed institutions are missing, or because those that do exist are underfunded, have insufficient expert staffing, or lack relevance. Weak institutional environments also tend to discourage the full participation of smaller member states with less market power and capacities.

An especially important area is dispute settlement mechanisms. One of the main objectives of these judicial procedures, which represent an alternative to backroom diplomacy, is to make decisions more transparent and less dependent on the balance of power between the parties involved. Smaller markets obviously have a special interest in effective dispute settlement, but Latin America, often preferring diplomacy, has been sparse in its use of this approach and lacks effective methods of enforcement and compensation. Moreover, since there is little tradition of using such an approach, many countries lack domestic legal expertise in this area, which inhibits recourse to the mechanisms even when they do exist. This could be a real problem for the region in terms of the FTAA, in which dispute settlement mechanisms can be expected to play an important role.

Another key institution needing strengthening is technical secretariats, which provide member countries with access to homogeneous services and often serve as de facto "institutional memory" for integration processes.

Extraregional Initiatives

One generally bright spot to date has been the process of integration with industrialized countries. A very complex FTAA process has advanced steadily since its launch in 1994. Through disciplined organization, clear objectives, energetic participation, and technical, financial and logistical support from regional organizations, the FTAA has managed to stay on a track technically compatible with finishing the negotiation by the target date of 2005. While it remains to be seen whether the ultimate goal is achieved, the nearly eight-year old FTAA process has already generated a positive legacy through numerous beneficial externalities, ranging from creation of an unprecedented esprit de corps among hemispheric trade negotiators (and consequently a new forum to discuss bilateral issues), to the release and publication of much previously unavailable data and comparative studies of national and regional trade regulations. It has served as a learning laboratory for cutting edge negotiations and understanding complex trade issues and disciplines, including those of the WTO, and for creating important demonstration effects for the WTO itself in areas ranging from management of data reporting to transparency, participation, and articulation with civil society.

The recent EU agreements with Mexico and Chile are a notable sign of a maturing relationship: they were the European Union's first free trade agreements in the region as part of a general move from non-reciprocal to reciprocal agreements with Latin America. Moreover, they were based on a larger innovative concept that generates a "trade-cooperation nexus" through negotiation of a formal association agreement that integrates trade, cooperation and political dialogue. This integration of three areas of action that can make important contributions to development is backed by generous funding for cooperation and by formal medium-term programming exercises to support the allocation of resources. Also, when linking with subregional blocs, the EU focuses its cooperation on consolidating subregional integration. In the case of Mercosur, negotiations aim to achieve the EU's first inter-regional agreement between two customs unions. The negotiations have advanced, but the pace has been slowed by a number of factors, including European sensitivity to the liberalization of agriculture—where Mercosur is a world-class exporter—and serious economic problems in the Mercosur countries. The most recent EU-Latin America Summit established groundwork for eventual negotiation of reciprocal agreements with Central America and the Andean countries, while CARICOM is scheduled to begin negotiations this year for closure in 2008. As for APEC, after a promising beginning, this process seems to have lost momentum as a free trade exercise.

Regional Cooperation

Infrastructure

Increased border trade following the formation of regional agreements increases the demand for better integration in infrastructure. In Latin America, serious bottlenecks from increased trade need to be addressed. Road networks—a primary mode for cargo—need to be greatly improved, as does their servicing. Most other means of transportation need to be improved as well. Yet, to date, infrastructure connecting integrating countries has generally not been sufficiently developed. At the core of the issue is a problem of externalities. Regional infrastructure projects have costs and benefits that extend beyond countries' borders. The portion of the road that is built on one side of the border has benefits for the neighboring country. In the context of decentralized decision-making, these positive externalities will naturally result in underprovision of regional infrastructure. The key issue is how to make much needed regional projects happen, establish forms of coordinated decision-making that internalize the externalities, and at the same time overcome other political and regulatory risks that may arise due to the multi-country nature of the projects. Governments have responded to this challenge. The 12 nations of South America, through the Initiative for the Integration of Regional Infrastructure in South America (IIRSA), and Mexico with Central America through the Puebla-Panama Plan (PPP), have each launched unprecedented intergovernmental initiatives, with the support of regional organizations, to tackle coordinated regional infrastructure.

Geopolitics

Regional arrangements have also contributed to cooperation in terms of geopolitics. Mercosur and the Andean Community have democratic clauses and have used them to stave off threats to democracy in their subregions. Most border conflicts where there were military tensions have been resolved. The subregions also have grouped together to enhance their bargaining power, most notably in trade, where Mercosur, the Andean Community, CARICOM and, more recently, Central America, have negotiated in blocs.

Strengthening Institutional Capacity

Finally, the new regionalism has increasingly heightened the demand for technical assistance and financing in order to strengthen institutional capacity. North-South regional integration agreement negotiations as well as those in the WTO have been a special catalyst because of the asymmetric capacities between developed and developing countries, in particular the small economies, and the magnitude of the potential market opening.

In regional and multilateral forums, Latin American countries have identified at least two strategic priority areas. The first is increased capacity to effectively negotiate complex trade-related commitments and their implementation. The array of needs identified for negotiation is daunting, including training of negotiators, technical support for empirical evaluation of the impact of alternative liberalization scenarios and ex-post evaluation of the effects of regional agreements, and technical assistance for inter-country and inter-agency coordination, as well as for consultation mechanisms with the private sector and civil society. As for implementation, there is substantial need for institutional change and skilled personnel, especially when agreements have deep agendas.

The second priority area involves confronting the economic adjustments that are needed to manage costs and maximize benefits of agreements. To manage costs, two areas of immediate concern are fiscal reform to cope with lost tariff revenue, and developing efficient mechanisms to protect social sectors that lose ground as a result of integration. To maximize benefits, the areas of action are many, including education and training, customs modernization, industrial restructuring, identifying export markets, managing infrastructure, attracting FDI, and regulating financial markets.

The primary responsibility for carrying out institutional strengthening to confront the challenges of trade and integration agreements corresponds to the

individual developing countries. But organized North-South cooperation can help. Encouragingly, negotiations between developing countries and industrialized markets have served as a catalyst for this cooperation. For instance, more support for capacity building in the multilateral system contributed to the successful conclusion of negotiations in Doha. This has also become a major issue for the progress in the FTAA negotiations, is a central component in EU bilateral trade initiatives, and has been perhaps one of the more distinguishing features of APEC. Cooperation for institutional strengthening in the FTAA process is gaining steam and has focused on trade negotiation and implementation issues (often referred to as trade-related capacity building or technical assistance), and to a more limited extent on economic adjustment issues.

Equity Considerations

There is a widespread perception among economists, not to mention anti-globalization groups, that liberalization in developing countries has exacerbated inequality. In theory, this need not be the case. In fact, according to theory, integration with countries in the North should reduce wage inequality in the South, as goods produced in the North have a larger content of skilled labor, which should reduce the demand for skill in the South. On the other hand, integration (and in particular, integration with the North) brings about new technologies and foreign investments, which may increase the demand for skill, and thus increase wage inequality. The overall effect is ambiguous. In spite of widespread perceptions, the evidence from Latin America presented in this volume regarding changes in inequality suggests ambiguous results as well.

But even if integration led to increased inequality, should this discourage policymakers from pursuing regional and multilateral liberalization? The answer to this question is an emphatic no. First, integration brings about new technologies and foreign investment, both of which can be important ingredients for improvements in productivity and sustained growth. In the process, technology and FDI may increase the returns to skills, as new technologies and production processes of foreign firms may be more intensive in skilled labor, but overall effects are clearly positive. Second, to the extent that integration contributes to increased productivity and growth, increases in wage inequality need not lead to higher poverty rates. Third, increases in the returns to skills provide added incentives for students to stay in school, a key ingredient for future improvements in productivity, and an important vehicle for social mobility. It is important to keep in mind, however, that the effects on inequality may have different dimensions. In particular, while some regions may flourish with integration, others may be left behind.

Trade, then, clearly promises net benefits. But there is a catch, albeit with a remedy: the net benefits are distributed unequally, and inequality can be avoided only with the effective deployment of compensatory mechanisms. This has been a highly sensitive issue in Europe, where important compensatory mechanisms have been introduced through regional and cohesion funds. This problem has not yet been adequately addressed in the context of the regional integration initiatives in the Americas. Serious and persistent shortcomings in designing and financing compensatory policies have clearly been the Achilles' heel of globalization and the new regionalism.

AN AGENDA FOR THE FUTURE: SIMULTANEOUS ADVANCES ON MULTIPLE FRONTS

The launch of the new multilateral Doha Development Agenda in November 2001 put in place a critical missing piece in terms of building a successful regional integration process. The GATT/WTO is one of the most important international public goods created in the post-war era and a principal factor behind the remarkable growth of world trade. The non-discriminatory multilateral system constitutes a base, or floor, for preferential regional agreements. Moreover, as the multilateral system advances and policy barriers to trade fall, the pull of geography becomes stronger and so may the incentives to pursue deeper regional integration arrangements.

However, the failure of the 1999 ministerial meeting in Seattle to launch a new round of multilateral talks stalled the momentum that multilateralism achieved in the Uruguay Round, revealing some serious shortcomings in terms of transparency, interaction with civil society, and the capacity of developing country members to fully participate. While the failure high-

lighted some of the virtues of a regional approach to liberalization, it also introduced stress, as certain items on regional agendas are difficult if not impossible to complete without further liberalization at the multilateral level. Hence, a successful completion of the Doha Development Agenda clearly is an important goal for Latin America's trade agenda. To live up to its name, the round will have to succeed in achieving much-postponed access to markets in sectors in which Latin America has a comparative advantage, but for which high levels of protection have persisted over decades. This will require strong political will of all parties to fulfill the "development" promise of the agenda. It also will require active and effective negotiations by the countries of the region, which should benefit from increased trade-related technical assistance, in accordance with the commitments included in the Doha Declaration.

The second front for action in building a successful integration process is subregional integration itself. This process brings together like-minded countries in agreements that have trade at their initial core, but that aim at much more than a commercial relationship. It is an effort to work together to achieve strategic development goals in an ever more competitive and globalized economy, and to address neighborhood problems and opportunities that can be better addressed, or only addressed, through subregional cooperation. This level of action is critical right now, since some agreements have the ambitious goal of completing common markets by the middle of this decade, while at the same time an uncertain economic environment and macroeconomic instability have made advancing integration more difficult. In some cases, these problems have even eroded the collective political vision that is at the core of successful subregional initiatives.

Intersecting both of the above fronts for action are the emerging North-South integration initiatives, which offer important opportunities for development and have important synergies with the subregional and multilateral agendas. At the same time, these initiatives raise strategic issues that must be managed carefully by the subregions if their potential benefits are to be fully realized. Given that progress in North-South agreements (and particularly the FTAA) could have important consequences for subregional agreements in the Americas, the agenda that follows will begin by focusing on North-South initiatives.

North-South Integration Initiatives

Completing a Balanced FTAA

One of the most important immediate objectives of the regional integration strategy of the countries of Latin America is to complete the Free Trade Area of the Americas in a way that balances the interests of all parties. This is important for several reasons. First, guaranteed reciprocal access to the markets in the Americas matters greatly to all the countries in the region, which at present face barriers or insecure access to these markets. Particularly important is access to the U.S. market, although there are also substantial opportunities for increased trade among existing subregional groups that still trade little with each other. Second, the FTAA may contribute to locking in the structural reforms carried out by the countries in the region, some of which are being called into question in the current uncertain international and regional economic environment. Indeed, experience has shown that subregional initiatives among developing countries cannot always provide the same incentives for avoiding a reversal of the reforms as are found in agreements in which an industrialized country participates. Third, the FTAA may help consolidate political links at the hemispheric level, reducing the likelihood of potential conflicts and, perhaps, serving to strengthen and lock in U.S. cooperation with the countries of the region. In effect, increased trade and investment in the hemisphere, and their contribution to the competitiveness of U.S. firms in the global economy, increase that country's stakes in the prospects of Latin America.

Taken together, these three elements—improved market access, enhanced credibility of economic reforms, and an increased U.S. focus on the region—may add up to a big difference in the prospects for development in Latin America. While falling far short of the impact of the EU on Southern Europe and countries that are in line for accession, a comprehensive and balanced FTAA could nevertheless serve as an anchor for the Latin American economies, boosting their credibility at home as well as abroad in financial and investment markets.

Within the FTAA initiative, secure market access plays a central strategic role and is the main objective of Latin America. In fact, without a significant change in this dimension, the benefits of signing on to the FTAA would be less obvious and the cost of abandoning the agreement would not be as substantial, which means the lock-in effects of the reforms become weaker. Absent market integration and lock-in, the prospects for a sustained favorable evolution of U.S. hemispheric relationships could be reduced.

For Latin American countries, effective market access will depend on the dismantling of existing barriers in the industrialized markets of the North; the existence of, and respect for, rules that ensure a secure and predictable environment in the application of contingent protectionist measures; the establishment of an efficient procedure for settling disputes; and the existence of mechanisms to ensure balanced outcomes in the operation of an agreement with 34 heterogeneous countries, some of which have limited institutional capacities.

One of the most important and sensitive sectors in market access negotiations will be agriculture. Significant progress must be made in the FTAA negotiations, but a full response will probably be linked to success in the parallel Doha Development Agenda negotiations on agriculture, where developing countries are demanding multilateral action on agricultural tariffs, export subsidies and distortionary domestic support. Meanwhile, the gains for Latin America from more open markets in the North will have to be weighed against the concessions that must be made in any trade negotiation. In the context of the FTAA, it is critical that the Latin American countries effectively evaluate the impact of requests from the North in areas such as intellectual property, investment, government procurement, and trade in services, all of which are of particular interest to North America.

Clearly, the different players have different objectives when it comes to the FTAA. Indeed, this is what trade negotiations are all about and what creates the potential for a mutually beneficial agreement. But there are different ways to advance toward the completion of the FTAA. And the outcome of the negotiations may be different depending on the manner in which they are carried out.

On the one hand, there is the formal process

of negotiation, launched during the Miami Summit, in which all 34 nations are represented. On the other, there is the increasing tendency to pursue bilateral agreements parallel to the FTAA negotiations. Recent increased interest by the United States in initiating and concluding bilateral trade negotiations (with Chile, Central America and Uruguay, for example) has raised the possibility that the FTAA will emerge as an envelope of these different bilateral agreements.

It is possible that the bilateral approach can prod the process forward. While 34 countries are an easier vehicle for negotiation than the 140-plus WTO membership, it is still a cumbersome number. But an FTAA emerging implicitly from evolving hub-and-spoke bilateral agreements poses potential risks as well as benefits. A strong agenda-setting country in the FTAA is even stronger in a bilateral setting. So as the agenda setter pursues a bilateral approach parallel to its FTAA negotiations, there are challenges and responsibilities if the FTAA is its ultimate goal.

Under the most favorable scenario, the agenda-setting nation would approach bilateral negotiations with a balanced view of the longer-term political and economic interests of the hemisphere, as well as the real capacities and specific development needs of all its trading partners. In this case, its bilateral agreements could become an effective building block for an FTAA that enhances the welfare of all.

Alternatively, the hub-and-spoke approach could be geared primarily to achieving the country's narrow commercial interests through sheer leverage in the bilateral negotiations—or through inclusion in some of them of issues that may not entail important concessions for the bilateral counterpart—and then using them as precedents to forge similar FTAA agreements. In this way, the agenda setter would obtain an agreement that is closer to meeting its own goals, without having to make many concessions in return. Such an approach could stifle the formation of an FTAA— leaving a less efficient hub-and-spoke system in place—or even create a welfare decreasing one, which would be politically conflictive and probably not sustainable. Finally, while the formal 34-country negotiations and the hub-and-spoke roads are presented here as polar strategies, in reality they are parts of the same process of negotiation, in which actions on one dimension influence actions and the progress in the other.

The strategic use of bilateral and subregional agreements in the context of the FTAA negotiations is not unprecedented. An earlier proposal by Brazil for creating a South American Free Trade Area (SAFTA) fits perfectly within this strategy. Similarly, a number of recent bilateral agreements have included provisions that were relevant to the agreements in question, but could set precedents that will influence the FTAA negotiations as a whole. Examples are the export of NAFTA disciplines by Mexico into an array of bilateral agreements; Chile and Canada's abandoning of anti-dumping rules in their bilateral agreement, with the aim of setting an example for the FTAA; and the labor and environment provisions agreed to by Costa Rica and Canada, which emphasize technical cooperation rather than sanctions.

As should be obvious, the process of negotiating a comprehensive FTAA among 34 heterogeneous countries is an extremely difficult task. While the recent passage of trade promotion authority in the United States has removed a major obstacle to completing negotiations, the final outcome of the FTAA process is still a question mark, and the scope and depth of a resulting agreement is still an unknown.

EU-Latin America Initiatives

Just as the FTAA would bring benefits in terms of making subregional blocs more open and less trade diverting, free trade agreements with Europe could do the same. One of the reasons Mexico pursued an agreement with the EU, even though the great bulk of its trade was with the United States, was to minimize residual trade diversion, diversify to new export markets, and attract European FDI and know-how. The Chilean agreement with the EU, as well as the participation by Mexico, Chile and Peru in APEC, are based on similar grounds.

Hemispheric integration could be enhanced were the EU to finalize ongoing negotiations for an Association Agreement with Mercosur and initiate similar negotiations with the other subregions as soon as possible. The EU currently treats CARICOM countries as part of the African, Caribbean and Pacific Group of States (ACP). Several factors suggest that there would be substantial benefits from moving the agenda forward between the EU and Latin America:

• Many countries in the region trade as much with Europe as they do with the United States and Canada. Findings in this volume (see Appendix 2.1 in Chapter 2) suggest that the benefits of trade liberalization for several subregions vis-à-vis the EU would be of the same order of magnitude as would be gains from the FTAA.

• The EU offers a different model of North-South integration in which well-funded cooperation plays an integral role. Linking up with the EU also offers opportunities for the subregions to be exposed to and learn from the vast integration experience of the EU, which could be particularly valuable if subregional agreements become deeper integration projects. Moreover, these agreements can bring technologies and best practices to the region that may be different than those that can be acquired through the FTAA. Progress in the EU negotiations, by providing an alternative route to access markets in industrial countries, may enhance the bargaining capacity of Latin American countries and subregions as they engage in the FTAA negotiations. The FTAA, in turn, could enhance the region's bargaining power in its dealings with Europe.

• With the recent launching of the euro, the current priorities for the EU clearly are to deepen its own integration process and to expand. This may help explain why progress in negotiations with the Americas has advanced at a slower pace. With regards to expansion, it is important to note that the countries in line for EU accession generally do not compete directly with most Latin American countries, and their accession may actually afford more opportunities for trade with Europe.

Asia

Apart from advancing negotiations with the EU, it is also important for Latin America to continue to make progress in strengthening trade and investment links with Asia. These markets are relatively unexploited and may offer several of the same benefits as those associated with links with the EU. The recent more favorable attitude in Asia with respect to regional integration may make it possible for Latin American countries to engage more actively in bilateral agreements with this region.

Bilateral and Subregional Agreements

The FTAA will create a basis or benchmark for determining the relevance of existing as well as potential subregional and bilateral agreements. Those that exceed the FTAA in some significant dimension would have a reason to survive, subject to the additional benefits exceeding the costs of administration. If the FTAA ends up being a shallow agreement, bilateral and subregional agreements will play a larger role. In any event, the formal ambitions, at least, of subregional agreements in Latin America aim for customs unions and common markets, which by definition exceed the obligations of a free trade area. In this context, the logic of continued subregional commitments takes on various dimensions:

• Countries that have subregional agreements may benefit from negotiating as a bloc, both at the WTO level, in negotiations with other regions such as the EU, in FTAA negotiations, or even later during the development and implementation of future agreements. Moreover, this negotiating leverage could be used in other international forums that go beyond trade. Naturally, in order to offer concessions collectively, there has to be a strong commitment to act as a bloc in some dimension, such as tariffs. For this reason, countries in customs unions are probably better suited to negotiate as a bloc than are countries in free trade agreements. Similarly, blocs that will likely disappear following the formation of the FTAA may not offer a strong negotiating advantage to their member countries. Hence, agreements that aim to go beyond a free trade area may need to maintain momentum toward achieving their stated objectives if they are to be an effective vehicle for negotiating as a bloc.

• Even with a full-fledged FTAA, a subregion that has achieved a common market or beyond, with free movement of factors and other forms of economic cooperation, could combine national resources more effectively to compete within the FTAA, and in the global economy.

• If North-South agreements such as the FTAA or those with Europe and the WTO do not achieve as much progress as desired regarding market access, at least in the short term, and if it is still difficult to place some important goods in foreign markets, then subregional agreements would provide alternative accessible markets for the products in which countries have comparative advantage.

• The justification for forming subregional blocs has in part involved political objectives such as peace and democracy. While some have argued that regional trade agreements are not needed to work toward such objectives, interdependence through trade and investment flows that stem from collective commitments have been shown to be an endogenous force for cooperation, and hence can provide an effective platform for non-economic initiatives. Although the FTAA should contribute to strengthening the political relations in the region, given its hemispheric scope and the heterogeneity among the countries in terms of history, levels of development and geopolitics, the subregional agreements will probably maintain a comparative advantage in dealing with many political issues in "local neighborhoods."

• For similar "neighborhood" reasons, deeper subregional agreements may facilitate other beneficial forms of cooperation such as macro coordination, functional cooperation, integration of infrastructure, or the provision of regional public goods such as environmental or health projects. Moreover, this cooperation in turn may become a foundation for adopting similar cooperation initiatives at the hemispheric level.

• Coordination in different policy dimensions in turn may increase the credibility of such policies, making it easier for national authorities to withstand pressures from local interest groups. Deep subregional initiatives are a more likely vehicle than the FTAA to provide this type of policy coordination.

Those are the potential gains from subregional commitments. There are, however, some potential drawbacks as well. First, the coexistence of an FTAA with subregional and bilateral agreements will likely increase the complexity and reduce the transparency of hemispheric and world trading systems, i.e., the so-called "spaghetti bowl" effect. Second, although subregional agreements have been negotiated under the purview of the new regionalism in the sense that they have accompanied liberalization vis-à-vis third parties, there remain some pockets of excessively high protection or distortionary regulations that have proven difficult to reform (e.g., special automobile regimes in several subregional agreements). The umbrella of subregional mar-

kets may make it more difficult to advance liberalization of these sectors within the FTAA negotiations.

The bottom line is that, apart from pockets of persistently high protection, the potential benefits of subregional commitments appear to outweigh the possible drawbacks. The effects of the spaghetti bowl could be ameliorated by making rules across subregional integration agreements, and between these and the FTAA, more compatible. (Here the new WTO rules could help.) The problem does not seem to be too serious, as long as it is offset by other effects that are broadly conducive to competitiveness, growth and development.

The liveliest debate that has emerged regarding the merits of current subregional trade agreements is the concern about the extent of trade diversion. As mentioned earlier, empirical work suggests that, on balance, the new regionalism has created trade. Moreover, the FTAA will likely contribute to reduce the scope for trade diversion.

Indeed, the very creation of a WTO-consistent FTAA would automatically convert subregional agreements into more open blocs. By incorporating two world-class industrialized economies and a more open exchange between subregions, the FTAA would expose individual countries in the subregional agreements more to competition that mimics the whole range of comparative advantage in the world economy. In this environment, trade diversion problems should be reduced in most countries. Agreements with the EU would reinforce this effect.

In this context, pockets of high protection merit special attention and should be dealt with appropriately. Just as North America must be sensitive to the benefits of eliminating excessive protection in certain sectors, regional partners should use the FTAA negotiations and those with the EU to accelerate the dismantling of these protected pockets, even if liberalization of these sectors occurs only gradually.

Rethinking Subregional Integration Agreements: What Type? How Deep?

The FTAA represents a significant change in the integration landscape that will force countries to rethink the role of subregional integration agreements. Governments in the hemisphere have broadly accepted in their

FTAA negotiations that agreements that are less comprehensive than the FTAA will be absorbed by it. But would current subregional agreements, most of which consist of imperfect and incomplete customs unions, be worth keeping in their current form?

The answer is, probably not. The very fact that these customs unions are incomplete negates one of their principal advantages over free trade agreements—the elimination of rules of origin and other administrative burdens at the border. Moreover, the common practice by customs union members in the region of negotiating unilaterally with third parties erodes the potential advantages of negotiating as a bloc. In this context, the marginal advantages provided by current customs unions in the region may not be enough to offset the loss of sacrificing an independent trade policy. Subregional integration agreements looking to preserve a vehicle for group cooperation should complete the customs union, thus fully capturing its potential benefits, or consider falling back to a free trade agreement, provided that is a more comprehensive arrangement than the FTAA.

The benefits of completing the customs union would be considerably magnified if it were clearly an intermediate step towards an eventual common market. Moreover, regardless of the success and scope of the FTAA, subregions with common external tariffs should continue to reduce external tariffs, which can benefit all members, but especially smaller ones that are more prone to being affected by unwanted trade diversion. Subregions should also continue to pursue bilateral agreements with industrialized partners, and to gradually liberalize unilaterally on a most favored nation basis. Indeed, there is an immediate incentive for some smaller economies with higher levels of protection to take such steps. They could even consider leaving an agreement if larger members are reluctant to act on excessive levels of protection.

Consolidating Subregional Integration Agreements

For those agreements worth deepening, what is next on the agenda? What are the priorities? How can countries effectively consolidate agreements that they already have?

• Completion of the customs unions projects, which starts with full implementation of the common external tariff, should be a first priority. Exceptions to free trade within the agreement should be phased out, with removal of other non-tariff barriers to internal circulation of goods. Furthermore, within the context of a complete customs union project, once agreement has been reached on the implementation of the CET, bilateral deals with third parties by individual members of the union should be discouraged. Since the formation of customs unions will not be achieved overnight, modernizing and simplifying customs procedures would save valuable time in what was seen earlier to be a notoriously long delay at border crossings.

• Since movement of goods and people across borders drives de facto and de jure integration, success in deepening subregional integration (and FTAA and multilateral trade as well) will depend in no small part on the success in further developing regional infrastructure. Regional infrastructure projects have important externalities, so their undertaking requires coordinated action. In this regard, the IIRSA and PPP are historic cooperative ventures to coordinate the development of regional infrastructure on an inter-regional as well as intra-regional basis. The two processes are promising in terms of coordinating official positions, but to make projects happen, there will have to be more progress in encouraging active private sector participation.

• Viable deepening of subregional integration will require a stronger institutional framework than the subregions have today. One fundamental need is the development and use of transparent and modern dispute settlement mechanisms. The region sorely lacks effective dispute settlement mechanisms, but some assistance may come from the FTAA. Assuming a comprehensive and functional FTAA, it is likely that the center of gravity for dispute settlement for many regional trade-related issues would move to this arena, which would have, at least in the medium term, more credibility, more coverage in terms of precedent setting, and more enforcement capacity than subregional arrangements (as does the dispute settlement mechanism under the WTO). However, if there is progressive deepening in the subregions beyond FTAA commitments, there will be a corresponding urgency to make subregional dispute settlement mechanisms more robust and to use them more frequently.

Deepening integration creates many other

institutional demands as well, ranging from mechanisms for common customs collection and distribution (for customs unions), to agencies that can certify mutually recognized technical standards and other regulations, anti-trust policy and different forums for policy coordination. One institutional area of particular importance is member government support and oversight of a well trained and funded, career-oriented professional Technical Secretariat. The goal should be to strengthen a lean expert group so that it can systematically cultivate the respect of the national official and private sectors and thereby credibly monitor and help implement disciplines; technically support intra- and extra-regional negotiations; and even propose a future road map for new collective commitments and cooperation. The other part of the equation is to have competent national counterparts and high-level political leadership—particularly in the largest market partners—with a forward-looking vision of where regional integration should go and a strong commitment to fully and voluntarily comply with the regional commitments approved by the governments.

• One major obstacle to the smooth functioning of subregional integration agreements has been macroeconomic instability. Crises in the member countries and large exchange rate swings may stress the relationship among partners and erode political support for integration. Some form of macroeconomic coordination may be required to keep the impetus for integration at the subregional level alive. Macro coordination has its costs, however, as it entails the sacrifice of some of the government's discretion, for example, on fiscal or monetary policy. So what should countries do?

One alternative is to do nothing. But while this may not be an obstacle for further integration in agreements that are not particularly affected by these problems, in agreements where members are subject to substantial instability, this option may be tantamount to abandoning the subregional agreement and blending into the FTAA. At the other end of the policy spectrum is the creation of a monetary union, although most integration agreements in the region do not appear to be good candidates in terms of the criteria developed by the literature on optimal currency areas. A possible exception is the Central American Common Market, particularly if the currency is linked in some way to the U.S. dollar. More importantly, it is not clear at this point

how much member countries are prepared to deepen their agreements to the extent that it would make sense to put the complex and politically challenging issue of monetary union on the table. However, given the potentially endogenous nature of the optimal currency area criteria, and provided there is political will and leadership to advance toward deeper integration, the idea merits continued exploration.

A less ambitious intermediate option could be to try to limit exchange rate volatility, perhaps as a first step on the road toward a monetary union. The question is, what is the best way to accomplish this? There seems to be broad agreement that a system of exchange rate bands such as the European Monetary System would be unfeasible in a world of high capital mobility. A less demanding form of coordination would simply involve members of the agreement avoiding the coexistence of inconsistent regimes such as pegs and floating regimes. For example, were all members to adopt flexible regimes with similar inflation targets, this could contribute to reducing exchange rate volatility. Sharing information, increasing transparency and adopting common standards to allow easier comparison of data across countries also seem to be warranted. Beyond this, some suggest the need for coordinated targets à la Maastricht on inflation, fiscal deficits, current account deficits and credit to the public sector, an approach that some subregions have already very tentatively explored. Others are skeptical about such targets, and suggest a more institutional approach, such as strengthening budget institutions and making central banks independent. But why not consider doing both?

Beyond macro coordination, other measures that could help support a less volatile environment include transitory commercial compensation mechanisms in the face of abrupt swings in exchange rates, as well as regional financial monitoring units and regional funds to provide financial support in the event of substantial negative shocks or to set up incentive systems for compliance with regional targets. This is clearly an area where international financial institutions might be able to help.

International financial institutions also could assist by systematically adopting a regional perspective when supporting national programs that anticipate the effects of those programs on partner countries and on the regional commitments that the country has assumed. And, of course, moving towards a more socially efficient international financial architecture, while not directly related to integration, would certainly support the new regionalism.

Maximizing Benefits from Regional Integration Agreements

Foreign Direct Investment

While integration may bring more foreign direct investment, the benefits to the members of regional agreements may not be evenly distributed. In order to get the most out of the FDI that can potentially be attracted by such agreements, countries and subregions should strive to improve their institutions (particularly those involved with compliance with the rule of law), and reduce excessive regulation. Both of these dimensions have been shown to play a major role in attracting foreign investment. Countries should also upgrade the quality of education. While an educated labor force may not necessarily lead to more overall FDI (others may attract it on the basis of low wages, for example), it will affect the quality of FDI (in more advanced sectors, with more potential for technological spillovers) as well as the country's capacity to absorb these spillovers, and thus get the most out of the FDI that is attracted.

Policies such as performance requirements for foreign investment (for example, domestic content of inputs), which have been used in the past to try to increase the benefits from FDI, have proven to be ineffective, leading to loss of FDI inflows. They are even less likely to work in the context of regional integration, which expands the location opportunities for multinationals, and shifts the center of gravity from strategies to serve protected domestic markets to global production networks. In this context, national treatment of multinationals seems more than ever to be the way to go. Meanwhile, integration agreements must avoid costly incentive wars that can shift the distribution of benefits in favor of the firm to the detriment of the host countries. Although this is by no means an easy task, it is important to explore mechanisms to coordinate the incentive schemes to attract FDI.

Enhancing Productivity and Competitiveness

The evidence included in this volume based on the experiences of Mexico under NAFTA and Brazil under Mercosur suggests that trade and investment can be important catalysts for productivity gains. While the channels through which trade and FDI matter seem to be different in these two cases, one story that emerges is that their impact on productivity is greater when countries integrate with partners in the North. This does not mean that countries such as Brazil should abandon their subregional agreements; rather, it means that if the full range of potential benefits from integration in terms of productivity and growth is to be reaped, this strategy should be complemented by linking up with industrialized countries, be it through the FTAA, the Mercosur-EU Inter-regional Association Agreement, or further opening up at the multilateral level. These strategies need to be complemented with domestic policies to enhance productivity, including strengthening and modernizing credit and labor markets, upgrading institutions to generate an enabling environment for firms to operate in, upgrading the quality of education and the quality of infrastructure, and setting policies that allow firms to take advantage of information technologies.[1]

These competitiveness issues should also be addressed at the regional level. The European Union has addressed them both internally and externally by including cooperation in areas of competitiveness in its bilateral Inter-regional Association Agreements. This approach may be something to be emulated in the case of integration initiatives in the Americas, where there has been far less cooperation on issues of competitiveness. Opportunities for cooperation at the subregional level are many. For example, countries could cooperate on issues of technology and research and development, particularly when the appropriate technologies cannot easily be adapted from those used in industrial countries. An example would be the development of technologies for tropical agriculture, which are very different from those that are appropriate in temperate climates. Another dimension with potential

---

[1] See the 2001 edition of the *Economic and Social Progress Report* on competitiveness.

gains from cooperation is the marketing of products from the subregion in international markets, such as through the joint use of distribution channels. It may be difficult for individual countries to adequately carry out these and other activities, either because of their regional public good character, or the lack of adequate human resources at the individual country level.

And the Losers?

Given that theory and experience show that properly designed trade and integration initiatives can generate net benefits, but these benefits are not distributed equally, social policy prescriptions in this area must focus on how to protect the losers, and how to facilitate the adjustment process in the labor market. Policies that can be implemented to protect those who lose out in the integration process include the following:

• *Training and job search programs that can smooth the transition and help displaced workers become more productive sooner.* The availability of effective programs of this type in advance of further liberalization or integration initiatives may also help lower worker fears regarding integration, and may thus help consolidate political support for such policies. A recent example is the United States, where approval of trade promotion authority was accompanied by a number of initiatives to protect displaced workers.

• *Unemployment insurance and workfare programs.* Unemployment insurance programs should be carefully designed to avoid providing disincentives for beneficiaries to go back to work. In turn, workfare programs, in which participants receive a minimum wage in exchange for work, should be implemented in a transparent way in order to avoid politically motivated allocation.

• *Social safety nets.* While desirable tools, safety nets should not be targeted specifically to those directly hurt by the process of liberalization. They should be available to all those in poverty, regardless of its direct cause.

• *Improvements in education.* A labor force with a broad set of skills will be in a better position to take advantage of the opportunities afforded by globalization, and to weather the adjustments from changes in international prices and advances in technology. While it is tempting to protect highly vocal or

vulnerable groups, delaying the dismantling of protection creates new generations of potential workers with misaligned skills.

• *Measures to address regional inequality.* In addition to its effect on wage inequality, integration may also intensify regional inequality within a country. In Mexico, for example, border cities and towns along the main highways connected to the northern border were the main beneficiaries of NAFTA. Thus, developing the national transportation infrastructure may be key to ensuring that the benefits of integration are more evenly distributed geographically. Indeed, Mexico's participation in the PPP is designed in part to bring the benefits of integration more fully to the southern half of the country.

• *Public awareness that opening up by countries in the South must be matched by the dismantling of trade barriers in the North.* Liberalization in the agricultural sector, in particular, is critical to making free trade work for the poor. Poverty tends to be concentrated in rural areas throughout the region. Bound tariffs of the OECD countries for agricultural products are four times higher than those for industrialized goods. Meanwhile, trade-distorting subsidies are equivalent to $700 million a day, almost four times all official development assistance. Ongoing trade barriers, domestic support policies and subsidies for agriculture in the developed world keep the world price of commodities artificially low, which effectively blocks a path out of poverty for the approximately 20 percent of families in the region whose main livelihood comes from agriculture.

Regional Cooperation and Institutional Strengthening for Trade and Integration

Regional cooperation for institutional capacity-building in integration and trade is critical, but its delivery is still very much a work in progress.

Removing this bottleneck requires more effective coordination and less compartmentalization of action between donors and financial agencies that provide technical assistance, and between them and the ministries responsible for trade-related issues and related economic adjustments. Moreover, since trade agendas and adjustment problems greatly overlap between the major existing agreements and ongoing trade negotiations—on the FTAA and with the EU, Asia and the WTO—the benefits of any specific regional or subregional exercise in capacity-building spill over to other arenas in terms of promoting better agreements. Given these externalities, more centralized coordination in the delivery of financing and assistance might be advisable, perhaps organized around subregions where needs are generally relatively more homogeneous. One way to foster coordination would be for countries to develop (and be assisted where necessary) national action plans for their most pressing capacity-building needs in trade, integration and related economic adjustment. This exercise would lay out specifics of institutional capacity-building in terms of priorities, costs, optimal sequencing and timetables for action. It would also serve to better discipline the requests of countries for assistance and the offers of donors and financing agencies that supply it.

Development of national strategies would serve another purpose as well: it would mainstream trade and integration in national development agendas and in external financial institutions. All too often, the needs of ministries responsible for trying to harness the forces of trade and integration are at or near the end of the list in countries' pipelines for loans and grants in support of institutional capacity-building. Given that negotiations and implementation of these major trade agreements will regulate much of the interaction between the private sector and the world economy over the coming decades, much higher priority is

merited for strengthening these institutions. This requires effective coordination between those ministries that manage the process and those that regulate their access to external financing.

Multilateral Liberalization and the Doha Development Agenda

While not part of the focus of this study, the link between successful regionalism and a healthy multilateral system is fundamental. First, progress in Geneva on certain key negotiation topics such as agriculture and anti-dumping could condition advances in similar topics in the FTAA negotiations, as well as those taking place with the EU and Asia. Second, the Doha Agenda includes negotiations regarding regional rules, which regulate the link between regionalism and the multilateral system, and which have ample room for improvement. These negotiations should clarify issues such as restrictions on the formation and implementation of common external tariffs, preferential rules of origin in regional integration agreements, and mechanisms to encourage compliance with agreed-upon timetables in terms of commitments to such agreements. The bottom line is that success in the Doha Development Agenda is not only strategically critical for Latin America, but also a key to ensuring continued progress on a system of open regionalism, one that constitutes a building "bloc," not a stumbling "bloc," towards global free trade.

PART I

Dimensions of Regional Integration

Chapter 2

THE NEW REGIONALISM IN LATIN AMERICA

The dual forces of globalization and regionalization were very much at work during the 1990s. Globalization was in fact quite evident in the sharply increasing participation of international trade, finance and foreign direct investment flows in the world product, the strong presence of multinational corporations, and the increasing importance of immigration flows and worker remittances to their home countries (Table 2.1). Alongside this globalization process was increasing evidence of regionalization. While limitations on data make it more difficult to fully document regionalization, the picture emerges very clearly in trade. Regional patterns of international trade have been steadily growing. By the end of the 1990s, two-thirds of European merchandise trade was with European countries, while the comparable figures for the Asian-Pacific and Western Hemisphere were 40 percent and 50 percent, respectively (Table 2.2).

The centrifugal forces of globalization and the centripetal dynamics of regionalization may at first blush appear contradictory. However, they are increasingly interpreted as complementary forces of private market development (Oman, 1998). Indeed, the two processes are being driven by many of the same factors. Advances in the technology of transport, communications, information and other areas have rapidly extended the global reach of market activity, just as they did in the 19th century.

The process of globalization is in fact far from a new phenomenon. Economists have identified the early 19th century as the start of globalization, interrupted by the Great Depression but renewing itself in the post-war period. Then, as well as now, there was a sustained and marked increase in the international flows of goods, capital and people. Indeed, some flows such as labor migration were far superior than today, while it took much of the post-war period for capital and trade flows to exceed those recorded a century earlier (Williamson, 1997; Rodrik, 1997; and Crafts, 2000). At the same time, the post-war evolution of production technology has increased the relative demands for flexibility, timely supply, and decentralized responses to demand and tastes. This also creates economies of agglomeration that have encouraged regionalization of production, even for firms with a global strategy (Oman, 1998; Humphrey and Schmitz, 2000).

Policy also has been driving the dual forces of globalization and regionalization. Post-war unilateral liberalization and deregulation, as well as successive multilateral rounds in the General Agreement on Tariffs and Trade (GATT), have freed global trade and finance from the administrative restrictions of the inter-war period, while legal (and varying degrees of tolerance for illegal) cross-border movement of people has noticeably increased immigrant participation in many workforces.

Deliberate policy also has driven regionalization. An increasing number of countries are relying on formal regional integration to mediate the forces of globalization. During the 19th century, nation states mediated the global economy directly. However, the collective economic turmoil of the inter-war period induced countries to cooperate and lay the groundwork for the creation of the multilateral system that we

Table 2.1 | **Globalization Indicators, 1970–99**

Indicator	1970	1980	1990	1999
Trade (% of GDP)				
OECD	25.6	39.5	37.1	41.1
Africa	49.9	60.1	52.6	61.3
Asia	10.2	26.2	38.3	53.5
Latin America[1]	22.3	30.2	28.4	35.6
Capital flows				
Gross private capital flows (% of GDP, PPP)				
World	…	6.3	8.3	18.3
High-income OECD	…	7.1	11.8	28.2
Latin America	…	4.7	3.9	7.3
Gross foreign direct investment (% of GDP, PPP)				
World	…	1.0	2.2	4.6
High-income OECD	…	1.3	3.3	7.0
Latin America	…	0.6	0.4	3.0
Memorandum item				
Gross value of foreign capital stock (% of GDP)				
Developing countries[2]	10.9	…	…	21.7
Migrations and remittances				
Migration flows				
European Union immigration rate[3]	2.4	1.5	2.8	2.4
U.S. immigration rate[4]	…	2.1	3.1	3.6
U.S. population percentage Hispanic or Latino	…	6.4	9.0	12.5
Receipts of workers' remittances (balance of payments, % of GDP)				
Latin America	…	0.2	0.4	0.7

[1] Latin America corresponds to the Western Hemisphere definition of the IMF.
[2] The figure for 1970 refers to 1973; the figure for 1999 refers to 1998. See Maddison (2001).
[3] Net migration is estimated on the basis of the difference between population change and natural increase (corrected net migration). Annual rate is per 1,000 EU population. The figures for 1960 to 1980 refer to EU-10.
[4] The annual rate is per 1,000 U.S. population; 1980 refers to 1971–80; 1990 refers to 1981–90; 1999 refers to 1991–98.
Sources: IDB calculations based on World Bank (2001); U.S. Bureau of the Census; Eurostat; and IMF data.

know today, which is designed to promote an international environment conducive to more stability and to expand participation in the world economy (James, 2001). This was further complemented by a web of bilateral agreements between countries covering any number of issues. But as the forces of globalization have gathered force, there have been additional policy responses. These have included decentralization in administration by nation states (IDB, 1997), which has allowed local adaptation to the challenges of globalization, and formal regional integration initiatives.

Although regional integration initiatives have a long history in the world economy, there has been a remarkable expansion of this activity in recent years, especially since 1990. Between 1948 and 1979 some 54 regional integration initiatives were notified to the GATT, then another 15 during the 1980s. However,

during the 1990s there was a virtual explosion of new agreements that dwarfed past notifications (Figure 2.1). While there are various reasons for pursuing regional integration, many can be summarized as steppingstones to more effective participation in the multilateral trading system and a globalizing world economy.

REGIONAL INTEGRATION IN LATIN AMERICA

At the level of policy, the Latin American and Caribbean region has simultaneously pursued the global and regional paths. Sparked by the economic crisis of the 1980s, the region began to undertake ambitious structural reforms. These included unilateral policies to open up economies to the rest of the world

Table 2.2 | **Intra-regional Trade Shares, 1980–2000**

(Percentage of intra-regional trade/total trade)

Region	1980	1990	1999	2000
Asia Pacific Cooperation Forum (APEC)[1]	55.1	63.8	68.4	68.6
European Union and Eastern Europe[2]	57.5	65.6	66.1	64.2
European Union	57.2	64.5	62.0	60.0
Western Hemisphere	44.6	44.1	53.0	53.3
Asia Pacific[3]	33.4	32.9	38.9	40.6

Note: Intra-regional trade shares are simple averages.

[1] Includes Australia, Brunei, Canada, Chile, People's Republic of China, Hong Kong, Indonesia, Japan, Republic of Korea, Malaysia, Mexico, New Zealand, Papua New Guinea, Peru, Philippines, Russia, Singapore, Chinese Taipei, Thailand, United States and Vietnam.

[2] Includes the European Union plus Bulgaria, Czech Republic, Hungary, Poland, Romania and the Slovak Republic (Czechoslovakia replaces the Czech and Slovak republics prior to 1993).

[3] Includes Brunei, Singapore, Thailand, Malaysia, Indonesia, Philippines, Cambodia, Laos, Myanmar, Vietnam, China, Japan, Korea, Australia and New Zealand.

Source: IDB calculations based on IMF (2001).

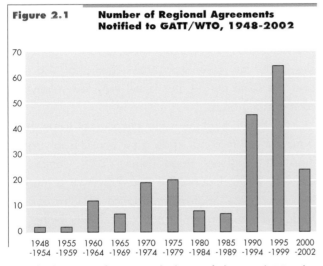

Figure 2.1 **Number of Regional Agreements Notified to GATT/WTO, 1948-2002**

Note: The data consist of agreements that have notified to GATT/WTO under Article XXIV and under the Enabling Clause. Some agreements included are no longer in force. Accessions to existing agreements are counted in their own right. The data are organized by year of entry into force of the agreement.
Source: WTO Secretariat.

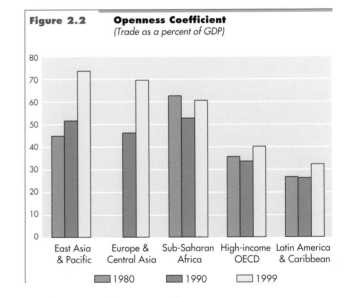

Figure 2.2 **Openness Coefficient**
(Trade as a percent of GDP)

Note: The openess coefficient is a simple average.
Source: World Bank (2001).

and deregulate them in order to provide more space for private sector activity. As an illustration, average tariffs in the region declined from over 40 percent in the mid-1980s to about 12 percent in the mid-1990s. This was combined with participation in the multilateral Uruguay Round and assumption of its very comprehensive disciplines. The region complemented this global opening with a web of new regional integration initiatives—nearly 30 since 1990, ranging from free trade areas to customs unions with ambitions of becoming a common market. Any number of other agree-

ments are in different stages of negotiation (Table 2.3).

These trade policies are reflected in trade performance. The global opening of the region's economies contributed to average annual growth of extra-regional trade exceeding the expansion of world trade (10.8 percent vs. 6.6 percent) in the 1990s,[1] with growth of imports notably faster than that of exports

---

[1] Without Mexico, Latin America's extra-regional trade was 7.8 percent.

Table 2.3 | Latin American Integration Agreements

	Date of signature
Intra-regional Free Trade/ Customs Union Agreements	
Central American Common Market (CACM)	1960[1]
Andean Community (AC)	1969[1]
Caribbean Community (CARICOM)	1973[1]
Southern Cone Common Market (Mercosur)	1991
Chile-Venezuela	1993
Colombia-Chile	1994
Costa Rica-Mexico	1994
Group of Three (G-3)	1994
Bolivia-Mexico	1994
Chile-Mercosur	1996
Bolivia-Mercosur	1996
Mexico-Nicaragua	1997
CACM-Dominican Republic	1998[2]
Chile-Peru	1998
Chile-CACM	1999
Chile-Mexico	1999
Mexico-Northern Triangle of Central America	2000
CARICOM-Dominican Republic	2000
Costa Rica-Trinidad and Tobago	2002[2]
El Salvador-Panama	2002[2]
North-South Agreements	
Mexico: NAFTA	1992
Chile-Canada	1996
Mexico-European Union	1999
Mexico-EFTA	2000
Mexico-Israel	2000
Costa Rica-Canada	2001[2]
Chile-European Union	2002

Negotiations in Progress

Intra-regional Free Trade Agreements
Mercosur-AC
Costa Rica-Panama
Mexico-Panama
Mexico-Peru
Mexico-Ecuador
Mexico-Trinidad and Tobago

North-South Agreements
Free Trade Area of the Americas (FTAA)
Mercosur-European Union
Chile-EFTA
Chile-United States
CARICOM-European Union (post-Cotonou reciprocal arrangements)
Central America-4-Canada
CACM-United States
Uruguay-United States
Mexico-Japan
Chile-South Korea

Others
Brazil-China
Brazil-Russia

[1] Relaunched in the 1990s.
[2] Awaiting ratification.

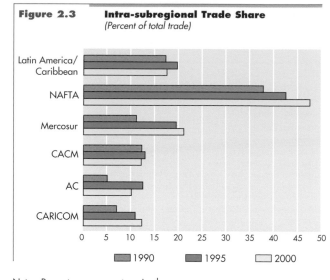

Figure 2.3 | Intra-subregional Trade Share
(Percent of total trade)

Legend: 1990, 1995, 2000

Notes: Percentage represents a simple average.
Source: IDB calculations based on IMF (2001).

(12 percent vs. 9.7 percent) (IDB, 2000). Figure 2.2 shows that the region's openness coefficient also rose over the same period, but is still very low relative to other trading areas.

Pointing up the regionalization of trade, Latin American subregional trade grew considerably faster than extra-regional trade (Figure 2.3). Comparing 1990 to 2000, Figures 2.4 and 2.5 show a marked increase in the relative importance of intraregional trade, with subregional trade agreements being the primary vehicle for the countries that are members of them. Box 2.1 summarizes the main characteristics of the subregional integration agreements and Box 2.2 provides a more detailed review of the Caribbean Community (CARICOM) as an illustration of the deep integration objectives that characterize all the Latin American initiatives.

Incorporating the North American market into the picture shows that its importance for Latin America also was on the rise in the 1990s. On the whole, then, the relative importance of the Western Hemisphere in the region's trade increased, largely at the expense of the European Union (EU).[2] Hence, the 1990s exhibit a clear pattern of intensifying regionalization of Latin American trade. Meanwhile, Brazil, Chile and a few

[2] For a more detailed analysis, see IDB (2002).

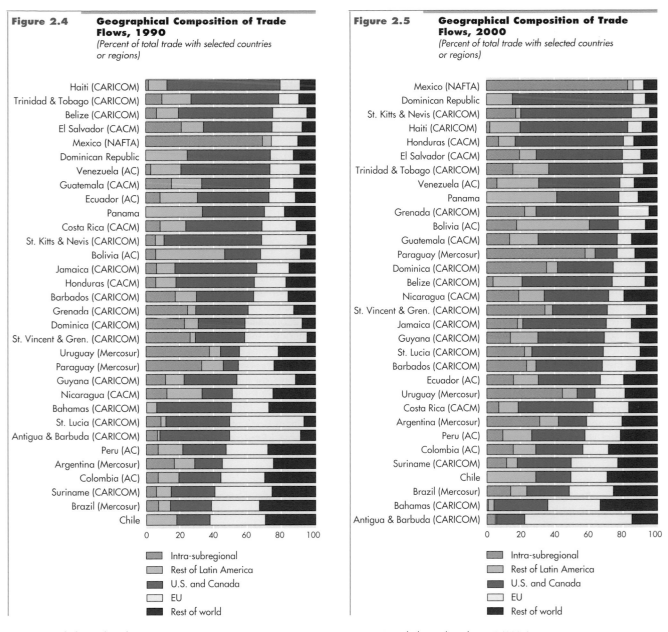

Figure 2.4   Geographical Composition of Trade Flows, 1990
(Percent of total trade with selected countries or regions)

Source: IDB calculations based on IMF (2001).

Figure 2.5   Geographical Composition of Trade Flows, 2000
(Percent of total trade with selected countries or regions)

Source: IDB calculations based on IMF (2001).

CARICOM countries display a pattern of a more global character.

Many factors have driven the regionalization of Latin America. They include the unilateral opening of economies, which exposed borders and allowed for the natural pull of geography and common culture and tastes to take hold. But policy-induced regionalization, or regionalism, has also played a role through the aforementioned creation of regional integration agreements that have provided for, among other things, pref-

erential elimination of tariffs among partners and more secure market access than that which is offered by the rest of the world.

Regionalization has gone beyond trade. While data are extremely limited and values relatively low compared to extraregional flows, there are indications of increased intra-Latin America investment flows during the 1990s (Garay and Vera, 1998). Meanwhile, NAFTA has been a magnet for U.S. foreign direct investment (FDI). Mexico experienced a marked

Box 2.2   The CARICOM Single Market and Economy: Current Status and Pending Issues

Members: Antigua and Barbuda, the Bahamas, Barbados, Belize, Dominica, Grenada, Guyana, Haiti, Jamaica, Montserrat, St. Kitts and Nevis, St. Lucia, St. Vincent and the Grenadines, Suriname, and Trinidad and Tobago.

In 1989, the members of the Caribbean Community (CARICOM) agreed to create a CARICOM Single Market and Economy (CSME) that entailed the removal of obstacles to trade in goods and services; the free movement of skilled persons; the end of restrictions on capital movements; a common external tariff (CET) and common trade policy; and greater coordination in other areas of economic policy. Nine modifying protocols to the CARICOM's founding treaty aim to facilitate completion of the CSME. These cover its Institutional Framework (Protocol I); Establishment, Provision of Services and Movement of Capital (II); Industrial Policy (III); Trade Policy (IV); Agricultural Policy (V); Transport Policy (VI), Disadvantaged Countries, Regions and Sectors (VII); Competition Policy (VIII); and Dispute Settlement (IX). Four of the protocols have entered into force (I, II, IV and VII) and three (III, V and VI) are being applied provisionally by most members. Most countries have signed Protocols VIII and IX, but only one has applied them provisionally.

The process of institutional change mandated under Protocol I has been completed and CARICOM's new political and policy-making bodies have been operational since 1997. Intra-regional trade in goods is virtually free: all tariffs and most unauthorized quantitative restrictions have been removed. Trade is affected by some revenue replacement taxes and by authorized exemptions from the free trade regime. Protocol VIII permits anti-dumping actions and the CARICOM Secretariat is drafting model legislation for those countries that lack a modern anti-dumping law. Export subsidies, now prohibited, must be removed before 2003. Efforts have been made to harmonize national customs laws, but member states have yet to implement the corresponding legislation. CARICOM has instituted a regime governing common standards for trade in goods, and is establishing a Caribbean Regional Organization for Standards and Quality (CROSQ).

The CET is fully implemented in 10 of 15 countries, with several national exceptions. Additionally, maintenance of a common tariff on third country imports is affected by the right of member states to negotiate bilateral trade agreements with third countries. Protocol IV lessens the flexibility for bilateral initiatives by obliging members that negotiate such accords to seek the approval of the Council for Trade and Economic Development when tariffs are being negotiated. CARICOM nationals engaged in industrial, commercial and professional non-wage activities are accorded the right of establishment anywhere in the CSME. Member states are to remove all obstacles in this area by 2005. The same deadline applies to the full liberalization of intra-regional services trade. In linking intra- and extra-regional policies, Protocols II and IV have extended CARICOM's capacity to devise and apply joint policies on trade in goods and services. Members have created a joint mechanism for external trade negotiations, the Regional Negotiating Machinery (RNM).

As regards the free movement of capital, Protocol II foresees the removal of restrictions on banking, insurance and other financial services, and on capital and current transactions, as well as greater coordination of foreign exchange policies. Some progress has been made on the cross-listing and cross-border trading of securities on stock exchanges in the region; on reducing or abolishing exchange controls; and on upgrading stock exchanges to facilitate trading and settlement. The free movement of people is limited to certain professional categories. The need for university graduates, media professionals, artists, musicians and athletes to obtain work permits is to be eliminated by 2003. Member states have agreed to establish a CSME accreditation system with harmonized standards for certification, mutual recognition of qualifications, and a regional accreditation body. An agreement on the transfer of social security benefits entered into force in 1997, but not all countries have enacted the corresponding legislation. A CARICOM identity card is to be issued by 2003 for all intra-regional travel.

Member countries have sought to harmonize regulatory frameworks. Efforts are also being made to enhance coordination on fiscal, industrial, agricultural and transport policies. Success will depend partly on CARICOM's ability to mobilize the necessary technical and financial resources. Financing is also needed to establish a fund to assist the less developed countries and to effect other institutional changes such as the creation of the Caribbean Court of Justice (CCJ), a competition commission (to ensure adherence to business rules), and the various legal bodies envisaged under the new dispute settlement mechanism.

THE NEW VERSUS THE OLD REGIONALISM

The contemporary wave of regionalism has been coined the "new regionalism" (Ethier, 1998; ECLAC, 1994).[3] However, regionalism itself is not new for Latin America. In fact, some of the first initiatives after many countries gained independence involved proposals for political union. There also are a number of historical attempts at economic integration. Indeed, this latter type of regionalism was quite widespread in the early post-war period, with the formation of ambitious initiatives such as the Latin American Free Trade Association (South America plus Mexico), which evolved into ALADI, the Central American Common Market, the Andean Group (a common market project that evolved into the Andean Community) and the Caribbean Free Trade Association (later CARICOM, also a deep integration project).

What is new about the current wave of regionalism is the objectives, modalities and outcomes. This can be seen by contrasting the stylized facts of the pattern.

The Old Regionalism

Latin America led the way with import-substitution industrialization (ISI) development strategies that dominated early post-war development policy and theory. This approach had its seeds at the start of the 20th century in some variations of the then dominant liberal economic policy, but gained full expression in the Great Depression when private markets and international trade and finance collapsed and governments throughout the world dramatically raised protectionist barriers. In the face of these developments, Latin American countries also raised their barriers and governments undertook a much more direct role in the economy in order to stimulate investment and growth during these difficult years.

The post-war arguments for an ISI strategy developed out of some prevailing assumptions, many of which had profound roots in the experience of the Great Depression. These included pessimism about the secular trends in the external terms of trade for commodity exporters; skepticism about the entrepreneurial vocation of the private sector; faith in the effectiveness of public enterprise and state planning; fear of dependence on foreign firms and their extraction of exploitative

rents; and marginal interest in the GATT and the multilateral trading system (only eight Latin American countries were members during the 1950s, and that number increased only to 11 by the end of the 1960s).

On the basis of these assumptions, development strategies promoted infant industries behind high levels of external protection, deployed state economic planning with a leading role for public enterprises in strategic sectors, and demanded regulation of FDI.

While the world economy began to rebuild itself in the early post-war period with gradual processes of liberalization and recovering flows of international trade and finance, Latin America's growth performance began to flag, initially for the smaller economies and later for the others. But the development model, perhaps victim of its own success, was not fundamentally questioned.[4] Rather, the prevailing diagnosis of the time was that the small domestic markets had exhausted possibilities for efficient ISI and there was a need for a larger market environment in order to achieve the efficiencies of economies of scale, especially in heavy industries that were at the core of this strategic approach.

In the development debate, regional integration emerged as one of the potential strategic tools for strengthening ISI. Oversimplifying, the approach aimed to eliminate trade and investment barriers among partner countries, maintain or even raise protection against third parties, extend planning and state intervention to a regional level, regulate foreign direct investment, and support all of this with a collective institutional architecture in which the emerging European integration project was a clear point of reference.

The results of these early regional economic integration initiatives were generally limited in terms of sustained regional tariff liberalization and trade and investment flows, with Central America being something of an exception for a while. By the mid-1970s, the processes showed very clear signs of fatigue. Some of the key obstacles included:

---

[3] It was ECLAC that first documented the new approach to regionalism under the logo of "open regionalism."

[4] As Diaz-Alejandro (1985) has pointed out, while New York was enduring the Great Depression, the mills were humming in São Paulo.

• *The tendency for national protectionism.* The opening up of a regional market was handicapped by the national protectionism inherent in the model. Hence, regional liberalization was generally carried out by a laborious "positive lists" approach, often with results of limited scope. In effect, the strategic tool of regional integration was undermined by the very model that it was designed to rescue.

• *Tension between the state and the private sector.* On the one hand, this reflected extensive state intervention in market decisions, and on the other, the protectionist habits of the private sector. The tension was further aggravated by the top-heavy regional institutions that some of the agreements engendered.

• *Macroeconomic instability.* The ISI model was inherently unbalanced and prone to aggravate macroeconomic instabilities, as it placed heavy demands on capital and intermediate goods imports without a corresponding generation of exports. This was aggravated by unstable commodity prices and financial flows.

• *Distribution of benefits.* Uneven trade balances among partners created serious political tensions in the agreements.

• *Infrastructure.* Sparse regional infrastructure was a limiting factor for growth of regional trade.

• *Authoritarian governments.* The period was dominated by authoritarian governments that stimulated national rivalries, border conflicts and restrictions on the flow of goods, people and development of regional infrastructure.

• *U.S. skepticism.* The U.S. government was not comfortable during this period with regional approaches, as its focus was exclusively on the multilateral system.

The New Regionalism

The onset of the debt crisis in the early 1980s was a deathblow for the flagging ISI approach to development and the already faltering integration schemes that were introduced to support it. Once again, crisis was the handmaiden of a major shift in Latin America's development paradigm. The region's economic collapse of the 1980s was localized as the world economy continued to expand and world markets remained open. Moreover, by then, there were clear demonstra-

tion effects in the OECD countries and in Asia of the growth potential from opening markets and exports to the world economy. Under the pressure of a prolonged economic collapse and a shifting policy consensus, the region embarked on another historic venture involving the major structural economic reforms mentioned earlier.

The defining difference between the new regionalism of the 1990s and earlier post-war experiences was the policy environment. In effect, the new regionalism was inserted into a framework of policy reform that promotes open and competitive private market-based economies in a modern democratic institutional setting. Indeed, the new regionalism was an extension of that very structural reform process that got underway in the mid-1980s (Ethier, 1998; Devlin and Estevadeordal, 2001).

Perhaps the most dramatic change in character was the gradual shift during the 1990s from the traditional intra-regional focus for integration ("South-South") to growing interest in inter-regional ("North-South") agreements that commercially link industrialized countries in reciprocal free trade, often in conjunction with ambitious functional cooperation programs (Table 2.3). This would have been politically inconceivable before the new policy framework that emerged in Latin America. The new regionalism is generally viewed as having the following objectives:

• *Strengthening structural economic reforms.* The overarching motive of the new regionalism is to create a strategic policy tool to reinforce the structural economic reform process in a period of highly competitive globalization. Countries now value greater participation in the world economy as a way to stimulate investment and growth. Regional integration is viewed as an additional policy tool to complement and strengthen national reform processes. The clearest link to the structural reform process is enhancement of commitments to trade liberalization, which has been a central feature of many developing countries' development strategies. As will be analyzed in detail in Chapter 3, regional economic integration has become the final tier of a mutually reinforcing three-tier process that also includes unilateral and multilateral openness. Regional trade liberalization has overcome many of the credibility problems of the old regionalism by working in tandem with unilateral and multilateral openness, and

Table 2.4 | **Manufacturing Exports, 1980–2000**

(As a percent of intra- and extra-regional total trade)

Market	1980	1986	1992	1998	2000
AC					
Intra-regional	29.5	47.5	45.5	56.0	46.5
Extra-regional	3.6	6.9	11.3	12.8	10.1
CACM					
Intra-regional	74.3	72.5	63.7	59.2	54.7
Extra-regional	5.7	10.7	17.1	36.5	38.9
Mercosur					
Intra-regional	40.7	33.7	49.3	55.8	55.7
Extra-regional	28.1	35.4	38.2	35.1	39.7
Mexico (NAFTA)					
Intra-regional	9.2	52.8	74.7	85.1	84.5
Extra-regional	16.7	24.2	43.9	67.2	61.4
Latin America[1]					
Intra-regional	46.3	50.7	57.9	60.8	55.9
Extra-regional	10.5	26.2	38.9	54.0	56.1

Note: Figures are simple averages.
[1] Includes Argentina, Bolivia, Brazil, Chile, Colombia, Costa Rica, Ecuador, El Salvador, Guatemala, Honduras, Mexico, Nicaragua, Panama, Paraguay, Peru, Uruguay and Venezuela.

it has also helped to further lower average levels of protection and improve competitiveness. Moreover, regional openness as a policy tool benefits from some nontraditional political economy considerations: the compensatory dimension of reciprocity, the ability to lock-in the reform through legally binding rule-based commitments, and the possibility of signaling liberalization commitments to the private sector, especially when it is not feasible to pursue further unilateral or multilateral openness (Fernández, 1997). Meanwhile, regional trade agreements, especially those with deep objectives—including second-generation free trade areas that go beyond traditional market access in goods—encourage the structural modernization of institutions directly through the disciplines they introduce, and indirectly through the increased demands brought about through regional competition.

• *Economic transformation.* While liberalization and increased participation in the world economy are viewed as instrumental to modernizing the region, countries have serious vulnerabilities because of a narrow export base and insufficient competitiveness of much of the private sector's export supply. The reciprocal openness, guarantees of market access, prefer-

ences and other aspects of a regional scheme can provide new opportunities for export experience and diversification and thereby over time serve as a strategic stepping stone to compete more effectively in a global economy. As can be seen in Table 2.4, interregional trade has a considerably greater presence of higher value-added manufactures than does extraregional trade, which is more heavily laden with commodities. Moreover, this participation has tended to increase in the context of principal trade agreements. Regional markets also serve as an outlet for an important array of products in which Latin America has a comparative advantage—such as textiles, dairy goods, meat, and food processing—but faces persistently high levels of international protection.

Thus, while the new regionalism should aim to create trade, its underlying primary objective is to build on longer term strategic considerations arising from the need to overcome imperfect and incomplete markets at home and abroad that put developing countries at a serious disadvantage in the world marketplace. In effect, dynamic transformation effects are sought through the support of preferential access to a secure, enlarged market and the more specific information

Box 2.3 Why Intra-Regional Intra-Industry Trade Matters

Intra-industry trade is two-way trade in similar products. It is a widely observed phenomenon apparently at odds with the standard traditional theoretical models that explain international trade with differences in factor endowments. Building on the pioneering work of Lancaster (1979) and Krugman (1981) a "new" strand of theoretical trade literature provides a rationale for this phenomenon based on the role of economies of scale and product differentiation. The seminal index proposed by Grubel and Lloyd (1975), when computed at a sufficiently disaggregated level, can be used to illustrate the transformation of trade patterns. Table 1 presents the evolution of the Grubel and Lloyd index of intra-industry trade observed in intra- and extra-regional trade flows of Latin American countries or subregions.[1]

The index shows the dramatic impact of regional integration in the promotion of intra-industry trade. In fact, with the exception of the Dominican Republic, whose intra-industry trade relations with the United States are particularly intense even in the absence of a regional trading agreement, the index was higher in intra- than in extra-regional trade in 1997 in all countries and subregions. Through NAFTA, Mexico achieved the highest measure of regional intra-industry trade. Its levels today are comparable to those of developed economies. Mercosur and the Andean Communi-

Table 1 Grubel and Lloyd Index, 1980–97

Market	1980	1985	1990	1995	1997
AC					
Intra-regional	7.2	7.0	11.3	28.7	30.2
Extra-regional	2.8	3.9	7.6	8.4	6.7
CARICOM					
Intra-regional	17.5	11.5	23.0	18.4	14.2
Extra-regional	9.4	16.7	15.4	8.3	6.0
CACM					
Intra-regional	31.0	36.7	25.7	33.9	33.3
Extra-regional	2.9	3.8	7.2	6.8	17.0
Mercosur					
Intra-regional	17.0	21.1	36.7	47.9	51.2
Extra-regional	10.7	15.7	18.8	15.5	15.1
Mexico					
Intra-regional	14.4	50.2	34.4	56.8	60.0
Extra-regional	6.4	8.8	14.6	16.5	15.3
Chile					
Intra-regional	4.4	6.3	6.3	12.2	15.7
Extra-regional	2.1	2.1	3.5	3.2	3.3
Dominican Republic					
Intra-regional	0.3	1.1	0.8	1.9	2.3
Extra-regional	2.0	17.3	37.3	37.5	38.5
Panama					
Intra-regional	4.2	8.6	4.7	5.0	5.5
Extra-regional	0.2	0.4	0.7	0.2	0.3

Source: IDB calculations based on Feenstra (2000).

ty also feature an important and increasing degree of two-way intra-regional trade. In these groups, the expansion of regional intra-industry trade clearly accelerated in the last decade parallel to the implementation of new regional integration commitments.

At the microeconomic level, the surge of regional intra-industry trade provides preliminary evidence of the qualitative structural transformation fostered by regional integration. In fact, as intra-industry trade typically arises in trade of differentiated industrial products, it is not only a sign of a progressive maturing of the product composition of trade, but also of an expanding matrix of quality and of an emerging functional fragmentation of productive processes among regional partners.

At the macroeconomic level, the development of regional intra-industry trade alters the structure of interdependence through trade and promotes an increasing correlation of macroeconomic cycles. In fact, when national economies of an integrated regional market specialize in intra-industry trade, demand and productivity shocks affect partners in the same way. This, in turn, augments the correlation of macroeconomic cycles and points to macroeconomic policy coordination as an optimal policy choice.

Another interesting feature is that intra-regional specialization along the lines of intra-industry trade assuages the political economy resistance to trade liberalization, since such trade entails smaller labor market adjustment costs than inter-industry trade. Moreover, the mobility of labor across firms and occupations might be greater within industries than between industries, rel-

ative wages might be more flexible within industries, and other factors of production might also be more mobile within industries. In this light, intra-industry trade could be one of the factors helping to explain why the new regionalism of the 1990s has been relatively better received than globalization by Latin American societies as a tool of economic and institutional transformation

It is too early to precisely track the determinants of the intra-industry trade pattern of Latin American economies. Nevertheless, in the coming years, regional policymakers will probably want to nurture the development of intra-industry trade through the implementation of WTO-consistent sectoral policies.

---

[1] For each country, the trade-weighted intra-industry trade index is calculated for each single partner i and sector j according the following formula:

$$IIT = \sum_{i=1}^{m} \left(\frac{X_i + M_i}{\sum X_i + \sum M_{i=1}} \right) \sum_{i}^{n} \left(\frac{X_i + M_i}{\sum X_i + \sum M_i} \right) \left(1 - \frac{|X_i - M_i|}{X_i + M_i} \right)$$

where X_{ij} and M_{ij}, respectively, represent exports to and imports from country i in product j. Calculations were performed using data aggregated at the four-digit level of the SITC (Rev. 2). Regional figures are weighted averages of the national indexes, using the relative share of each country in the total intra- and extra-regional trade of the selected region as weight. Intra-regional trade refers to trade occurring with regional partners; extra-regional trade refers to trade with the rest of the world.

flows, defined market competition and identifiable export opportunities that come from an institutionally organized regional platform. Over time, these advantages vis-à-vis the rest of the world are expected to serve as a catalyst for export diversification, investment, greater specialization via economies of scale and product differentiation, and inter-industry trade (see Box 2.3), all of which increase productivity, competitiveness, employment and growth. In the process, regional integration can also contribute to improving home markets in such areas as labor, finance and technology (Devlin and Ffrench-Davis, 1999).[5]

• *Attracting foreign direct investment.* There is

worldwide competition between developing countries to attract FDI because of its potential to improve export networks, technological and know-how spillovers, and institutional modernization. By creating a larger liberalized rules-based market with locational advantages, a regional agreement can distinguish member countries and help them compete for and attract FDI (Blöm-

---

[5] There is some evidence that regional agreements such as NAFTA are associated with productivity gains. Meanwhile, some sectoral case studies supported by IDB/INTAL (1999) show mixed results regarding the productive transformation effects of regional integration, and are suggestive of both how those effects take place and how flawed policies can undermine them.

Box 2.4   An Emerging Opportunity for the FTAA: Hemispheric Petroleum Cooperation and Trade

The hemispheric energy imbalance presents a signifi-cant opportunity to deepen trade relations and conti-nental integration all along the energy vector. This means not only the trade of primary energy, but also the trade of capital, technology, goods and services to pro-duce energy-intensive goods from Latin America's large endowment of energy sources.

On the one hand, the United States has a grow-ing energy deficit, currently importing 60 percent of the petroleum it consumes: 11 million barrels daily (MBD) with a consumption level of 19 MBD. The energy gap has tripled over the past 15 years, from 3.5 MBD in 1985 to nearly 11 MBD in 2001, as consumption levels have gone up with increased economic activity, and pro-duction levels have fallen as North American reserves have been depleted. If the trends of the past 15 years continue, U.S. imports could grow by approximately 9 MBD, or nearly double, over the next twenty years.

Both the magnitude and composition of imports have considerably changed in the past 15 years. At present, 50 percent of U.S. petroleum imports come from sources outside the hemisphere, while 30 percent are from NAFTA trading partners (Mexico and

Canada), and 20 percent from the Andean Community, particularly Venezuela. In the late 1980s, extra-hemi-spheric sources provided less than 30 percent of U.S. oil imports. Imports from outside the continent have quintu-pled in 15 years. This growing dependency presents concerns for the United States in terms of the security of supply. If net exports from the rest of the hemisphere to the United States do not increase in the future and the growth tendencies of U.S. imports continue, the country could reach an oil import dependence of up to 75 per-cent on extra-hemispheric sources, entailing greater security risks in terms of supply (see Figure 1).

The Latin American countries, on the other hand, are net exporters of energy and have the reserves needed to cover the United States' current and future hydrocarbon import needs. Over the past 15 years, Latin American net petroleum exports have doubled from 2 MBD to 4 MBD. If production and consumption trends remain the same, Latin America's net exports could grow by 2 MBD or 50 percent over the next twen-ty years.

However, even if we assume that all net exports from Latin American countries will go to the Unit-

Figure 1   Production, Consumption and Imports of Petroleum
(In millions of barrels per day)

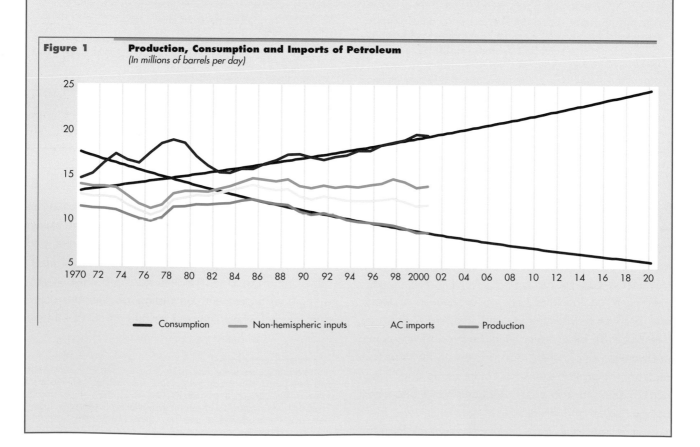

— Consumption   — Non-hemispheric inputs   AC imports   — Production

ed States, their share of total U.S. oil imports would still drop from the current level of 32 percent to 27 percent by 2020. If, on the other hand, Latin American countries want their exports to rise to 50 percent of U.S. imports by 2020, exports to the United States would need to grow by 6 MBD instead of 2 MBD. This would mean practically doubling current production over the next 20 years.

There appear to be two possible scenarios for Latin American petroleum production. In the first, which we call "tendential," production and consumption levels follow the same trajectory as during the past 15 years. Consumption grows by 4 MBD, production by 6 MBD, and thus exports by 2 MBD. In the second scenario of accelerated growth, production increases by 10 MBD, and as a result, exports grow by 6 MBD.

Both scenarios would require respective investments of either $120 billion or $200 billion just to increase production. And if the costs of maintaining the increase in production were added to these investments, total expenditures in the petroleum sector for both scenarios would hit between $143 billion and $233 billion, respectively. Finally, both directly and indirectly, the impact on the regional GDP is estimated at between $200 billion and $320 billion. These numbers represent 10 percent and 17 percent of the current aggregate value of the Latin American economies in one year. This impact would be significant—greater than the impact of any other individual industrial activity in the region.

strom and Kokko, 1997). Moreover, FDI tends to cluster, so initial success can lead to more success (Ethier, 1998). However, the strategic response of FDI to regional agreements is very complex. The 1990s coincided with a boom in flows of FDI to Latin America. There is evidence that some of this was the result of development of regional agreements such as NAFTA, but in general other domestic market-based factors appear to have been more important (Amann and Vodusek, 2001; IDB/INTAL, 1999).

• *Geopolitics.* A group of like-minded countries can use a regional agreement to establish a safety net for fragile democracies, promote disarmament and peace among neighbors, and enhance bargaining power in international fora. These motives were in part behind the decisions of Mercosur, the Andean Community and CARICOM to negotiate trade agreements in blocs. The partners of Mercosur and the Andean Community have collaborated to overcome threats to democracy in member countries and to help resolve border conflicts (Devlin and Estevadeordal, 2001).

• *Functional regional cooperation.* For several reasons, reciprocal preferential trade agreements are a common point of departure or core strategic compo-

nent in the launch of formal regional integration initiatives (Devlin, Estevadeordal and Krivonos, 2002). First, trade usually attracts support from the relatively well-organized and financed private business communities. Second, unlike many other economic arrangements, the mutual benefits of trade agreements and their distribution can be reasonably assessed ex ante by participants and monitored and enforced ex post, as they usually contain very precise legal clauses. In addition, the institutions for negotiating cross-border agreements and administering them are already in place through trade-related ministries and established negotiating fora and practice. Third, trade agreements accommodate nationalist sentiments, as they can be designed in ways that initially involve little concession of national sovereignty, as do free trade areas. Fourth, these trade agreements are subject to certain multilateral rules and procedures in the WTO. Finally, a critical mass of regional trade among partners acts as a "hanger" on which other areas of regional cooperation can be draped. (Box 2.4).

Indeed, growing and mutually beneficial economic interdependence among partners typically induces demands for additional regional economic

Table 2.5 | Regional Cooperation Programs in APEC

Trade-related cooperation
Deregulation, dispute mediation, implementation of WTO obligations, customs procedures, standards and conformance, intellectual property rights, competition policy, government procurement and rules of origin

Non-trade cooperation
Economic
Macroeconomic policy, financial stability, structural reforms, economic infrastructure, business facilitation, financial systems, free movement of investments, mobility of businesspeople, capital markets, energy, tourism, fisheries, transportation, telecommunications, small- and medium-sized enterprises, agriculture, rural infrastructure, food production and biotechnology

Political
Political dialogue through ministerial meetings

Social and cultural
Public safety, social development and gender integration

Environment
Environmental protection and marine resource conservation

Human resources, science and technology
Industrial science and technology, human resources development, knowledge and skills development, information and communications technology, and electronic commerce

Other
Emergency preparedness

Source: Devlin, Estevadeordal and Krivonos (2002).

cooperation to exploit more fully the advantages of a maturing regional market. Moreover, demands for noneconomic and even political cooperation arise from the social externalities generated by closer economic ties. Thus, the centripetal forces of trade among partners can be an effective handmaiden of deeper formal integration, whether planned or not. There is the contemporary example of Western Europe, where growing interdependence through trade has served to drive forward a political agenda of certain partners for deep integration and broad-based cooperation. In effect, the opening of the regional market in Europe became functional to widening the scope of cooperation, or in the words of Garcia Herrero and Glöckler (2000), to "integration by stealth."

Regional cooperation between two or more countries also can take place without pretensions of regional integration as such (Balassa, 1961). This more "functional" regional cooperation involves an adjustment of policies and activities between countries to achieve outcomes that the parties prefer to the status quo, and is possible in practically any field of public policy. While functional regional cooperation can and

does emerge independently of formal integration, it also can constitute a parallel track to such a formal process, or over time contribute to the emergence of that process.

As the regionalization of trade has progressed in the 1990s, there has been growing interest in functional regional cooperation among members of different integration agreements in economic, social and political areas that address externalities arising from increasing interdependencies or dependencies in regional, hemispheric and interregional markets. Development of regional infrastructure has become a focal point of functional cooperation in Latin America, as reflected in the South American Initiatives for Regional Infrastructure Integration (IIRSA), which involve 12 countries, and the Puebla-Panama Plan (PPP), which involves eight countries. Support for business, control of natural disasters, environmental protection and regional security are some of the other principal emerging areas of regional cooperation in Latin America.

There are also several ambitious cooperation initiatives that accompany North-South free trade ini-

Table 2.6	Santiago Summit – Areas of Action

• *Education*

• *Preserving and strengthening democracy, justice and human rights*
  Democracy and human rights
  Education for democracy
  Civil society
  Migrant workers
  Strengthening municipal and regional administration
  Corruption
  Financing electoral campaigns
  Prevention and control of illicit consumption of and trade in
    drugs and psychotropic substances and other related crimes
  Terrorism
  Building confidence and security among states
  Strengthening of justice systems and judiciaries
  Modernizing the state in labor matters

• *Free Trade in the Americas*
  Free Trade Area of the Americas (FTAA)
  Strengthening, modernizing and integrating financial markets
  Science and technology
  Regional energy cooperation
  Hemispheric infrastructure
      - General infrastructure
      - Transportation
      - Telecommunications

• *Eradication of Poverty and Discrimination*
  Fostering the development of micro and SMEs
  Property registration
  Health technologies
  Women
  Basic rights of workers
  Indigenous populations
  Hunger and malnutrition
  Sustainable development
  Cooperation

Source: Summit Declarations and Plans of Action.

Table 2.7	Typical Areas of Cooperation in EU-Latin America Inter-regional Integration Agreements

• *Political dialogue*
Peace and stability
Confidence and security building measures
Protection of human rights, democracy and rule of law
Sustainable development
Action on drug traffic, arms traffic, organized crime and terrorism

• *Economic cooperation*
Industrial cooperation
Technical regulations and conformity assessment
Services
Investment promotion
Macroeconomic policy
Scientific and technological cooperation
Energy cooperation
Transport
Telecommunications
Agriculture
Fisheries
Customs procedures
Statistics
Environment
Consumer protection
Data protection

• *Financial and technical cooperation*
Public administration modernization
Inter-institutional cooperation
Cooperation on regional integration

• *Social and cultural cooperation*
Social cooperation
Education and training
Social dialogue
Drugs and organized crime
Culture

Source: Devlin (2001).

tiatives. (See Tables 2.5 through 2.7) The 34 democracies of the Western Hemisphere in 1994 launched a number of cooperative initiatives along with the eventual creation of a Free Trade Area of the Americas (FTAA). Meanwhile, the free trade initiatives of the EU are also accompanied by a battery of economic cooperation and political dialogue programs. Extensive cooperative programs are integral to the APEC free trade process as well.

Functional cooperation is inherently challenging. The difficulty of negotiating non-trade issues is related to their very nature: whereas preferential trade arrangements, the typical starting point for formal eco-

nomic integration, are concerned with removing distorting policies, cooperation in other economic areas as well as in social and political fields often requires *introducing* additional policies, which can be more difficult. Moreover, non-trade areas often have less installed institutional cross-border capacities than does trade, and hence need more intensive mobilization of collective financial, logistical and technical support. Finally, many areas of functional cooperation are not easily subject to quantifiable targets, effective monitoring and evaluation of results. These complexities become especially daunting when functional cooperation is inter-regional and involves a large number of heterogeneous countries, as in the case of the hemispheric summit process (Devlin, Estevadeordal and Krivonos, 2002).

Potential Costs of the New Regionalism

Regional integration agreements are an integral part of the structural reform process, but like any other structural change, they require adjustments and bear potential costs for the participating countries. Countries should design agreements that minimize unnecessary costs where possible. Some of the typical costs for countries associated with regional integration agreements are:

• *Trade diversion.* Preferences in regional trade agreements (coupled with rules of origin in free trade areas) can potentially divert trade away from more efficient locations in non-member countries. Some trade diversion is inevitable in preferential arrangements, which has costs for domestic consumers and non-members. This must be weighed against trade creation and the potential for the trade diversion to evolve into cost-reducing and welfare-enhancing transformation effects that promote future growth and import capacity (Corden, 1972; Ffrench-Davis, 1980).

The trade creation vs. trade diversion debate goes back to the days of Jacob Viner (1950) (Box 2.5). He pointed out the risks of trade diversion during the era of the old regionalism, when protection against third parties was very high and even rising (Devlin and Estevadeordal, 2001). That risk again has emerged as a source of concern in the contemporary debate over the new regionalism (Bhagwati and Panagariya, 1996). However, recent empirical evidence points largely to the trade creating effects of the three-tier liberalization process, of which regional integration is a part.

• *Vulnerability of regional goods.* A regional agreement can create trade but at the same time support the circulation of goods in the regional market for which there is little demand in the rest of the world. The lack of an external market may be due to the idiosyncratic nature of certain goods based on local culture and tastes, to rigid intra-firm export and marketing networks, or to a lack of international competitiveness of the goods (due, for example, to low productivity or an overvalued exchange rate), which is accommodated by preferences and rules of origin.

If regional trade is created or diverted much faster than the dynamic forces leading to international competitiveness, growing trade and interdependence with a partner country may lead to a member or members becoming excessively vulnerable to recession or exchange rate depreciation in the regional market. This is because in the face of a recessive regional market or depreciation by a major partner, exports cannot be easily redirected to alternative third markets. As noted by Bevilaqua and Talvi (1999), this problem has occurred in Mercosur, where Argentina, Paraguay and Uruguay are very dependent on the regional market for their exports. It may also be a factor in some sectors in Mexico, where through NAFTA there is a high level of integration with the production and marketing networks of the U.S. economy (Dussel Peters, Paliza and Loria Diaz, 2002).

This type of vulnerability can occur in any integration arrangement where regional trade expands rapidly under an umbrella of external protection for industrial sectors that is significantly higher than the rest of the world, where rules of origin are restrictive, or where simultaneous exchange rate appreciation among partners could drive sales to the regional market (Devlin and Ffrench-Davis, 1999). Such vulnerability points to the need to progressively reduce external protection and the restrictiveness of rules of origin as commercial interdependence deepens among partners of a regional agreement, and to guard against premature or abrupt currency appreciation with the rest of the world.

• *Redistributive effects from lost tariff revenue.* When there are serious asymmetries in the average external tariff levels between partners of an economic integration agreement, the loss of tariff revenue in the high tariff country can have a serious redistributive impact on the partners (Panagariya, 1996). In effect, part of what would have been realized as tariff revenue on imports by the high tariff country from the lower tariff partner prior to the agreement is transferred to the lower tariff country's producers as tariffs are eliminated in the regional agreement. This is because the low tariff country's exporters refer to the partner's significantly higher third party tariff when establishing their pricing. The problem is aggravated by trade diversion.

Box 2.5   Trade Creation versus Trade Diversion

Although regional integration agreements are seldom implemented exclusively on the basis of economic rationales (Fernández and Portes, 1998), their welfare effects have been the main focus of an extensive and growing body of literature surveyed both for academic and policy-oriented purposes.[1] The analysis is very complex, as preferential trade liberalization engenders second-best equilibria for which analysts need comprehensive analytical frameworks and sophisticated empirical techniques.

The early seminal contribution of Viner (1950) to the theory of customs unions set the stage for the debate highlighting the static *trade creation and trade diversion* effects of regional integration agreements on single industries. As a result of preferential trade liberalization, trade creation is the substitution of a lower-cost source of supply from a member country for a higher-cost domestic source of supply, while trade diversion is the substitution of a higher-cost source of supply from a member country for a lower-cost source of supply from a third country. Under certain conditions, regional integration agreements can result in welfare-enhancing outcomes for member and nonmember countries (Kemp and Wan, 1976), while trade creation and diversion effects may materialize even prior to entry into force of the agreement, as traders and investors anticipate signing of an accord (Freund and McLaren, 1999). The assessment of the net effect therefore needs a careful analysis of the market structure and costs in which integration policy intervenes, a full account of its dynamic effects in the longer run, and an explicit account of the institutional forms of regional integration agreements (Pomfret, 1997).

Applied research also provides a progressively better understanding of the magnitude of the effects of regional integration. In particular, in the case of Latin America, the new regionalism of the 1990s stimulated an emerging empirical literature that has progressively mitigated early concerns about the harmful effects of regional integration on the welfare of members and nonmembers. A complete survey of the empirical literature on the region would extend beyond the scope of this study, but a few of the significant contributions focusing on the trade creation/diversion impact of the region's major agreements are reviewed below.

Early comprehensive assessments of NAFTA such as Hufbauer and Schott (1993) converge around the conclusion that the extraordinary expansion of intra-regional trade flows did not take place at the expense of the rest of the world. Analyzing the geographical evolution and the composition of trade flows at the sectoral level, Krueger (1999) notes that the implementation of preferential trade policy has been more trade-creating than trade-diverting, given the already high intra-region-

al share among the members of the agreement and the parallel increase of trade flows with the rest of the world. Krueger also stresses the role of the evolution of the real exchange rate in explaining the expansion of intra-regional trade flows. The analysis found that the entry into force of the regional integration agreement did not significantly alter the trade pattern, a conclusion also suggested by Soloaga and Winters (1999).

Mercosur has received less empirical attention, but it nevertheless has generated a very lively debate. In an early study, Yeats (1997) concluded that the regional orientation of exports grew faster in products where member countries do not have comparative advantages, and accordingly concluded that there was significant trade diversion. This conclusion has been challenged by Nogues (1996), who stressed the actual existence of intra-regional comparative advantages among Mercosur members in certain sectors. Meanwhile, Devlin (1997) noted that an analysis of the trade pattern distortions should be focused on imports, which suggests that the regional bias has been mitigated by the unilateral liberalization that paralleled implementation of the agreement. Nagarajan (1998) comes up with a similar empirical conclusion, hence pointing to the fact that trade creation probably outweighed trade diversion. In addition, Giordano (2001) shows that the reorientation of regional trade flows crucially hinged on the divergent path of the intra- and extra-regional real effective exchange rates. These conclusions are supported by Soloaga and Winters (1999), who, using a gravity model, assert that the significant trend in members' trade presumably reflects unilateral trade liberalization and suggests that trade performance was dominated by currency overvaluation rather than trade policy as such. Meanwhile, Echavarría (1998), examining intra-regional trade flows in the Andean Community, points to the trade-creating effects of the agreement.

Finally, computable general equilibrium studies of regional integration that incorporate the findings of the new growth theory have invariably found that trade creation greatly dominates trade diversion (Robinson and Thierfelder, 1999). In the case of NAFTA, this is confirmed by Francois and Shiells (1994) who conclude that all members stand to gain, particularly Mexico, which could increase welfare between 1 and 5 percent. In the same vein, analyzing Mercosur, Flôres (1997) showed that Argentina, Brazil and Uruguay might increase GDP by 1.8 percent, 1.1 percent and 2.3 percent, respectively.

---

[1] For academic purposes, see Baldwin and Venables (1995), Winters (1996) and Panagariya (2000). For policy-oriented purposes, see OECD (1995), WTO (1995) and World Bank (2000).

Panagariya (1996) indicates that this effect was significant for Mexico when it joined NAFTA, since the United States and Canada had much lower third party tariffs. It was clearly a price Mexico was willing to pay as part of the trade-off in pursuing the benefits of economically integrating with North America. To offset this cost, Mexico has been lowering average levels of protection by signing free trade agreements with most Latin American countries and the European Union, while pursing such an agreement with Japan.

- *Asymmetric development impact.* In the absence of corrective mechanisms, the development benefits of regional integration are often asymmetrically distributed among partner countries or regions within them (Puga and Venables, 1997). European integration has been very sensitive to this problem, reflected in the creation of a comprehensive battery of collective institutional mechanisms to address potential imbalances (Pastor, 2001).

Severe imbalances in trade and adjustments historically have been a major source of tension for Latin American regional initiatives and in some cases have even led to their demise (Salgado, 1979). In the old regionalism, there were extensive provisions for special and differential treatment for less developed countries to address some of these problems. However, the new regionalism has tended to give much less attention to special treatment, typically restricting it to somewhat longer liberalization schedules for the lesser developed partner (Devlin and Estevadeordal, 2001).

Asymmetric liberalization may facilitate the phase-in of regional liberalization, but there are many other sources of imbalances and tension among partners when regional trade reaches significant proportions. As economies become more interdependent in the course of developing regional agreements, lack of coordination of macroeconomic policy and exchange rate regimes can be an especially corrosive factor in regional commitments. Indeed, parallel to Latin America's successful phase-in of regional free trade has been a growing and largely unaddressed need to better coordinate macro and exchange rate policies among partners.

Regional integration also can have clear asymmetric effects within a partner country. This has occurred in Mexico, where the pull of NAFTA has been

heavily concentrated in the northern states, aggravating a North-South development divide in that country (Perry, 2001). The Puebla-Panama Plan launched in 2001 was inspired in part by the Mexican government's desire to provide compensatory forces of development for its southern states.

- *Spaghetti bowl.* A growing number of economic integration agreements with different liberalization schedules, preferences, rules of origin and other norms and disciplines creates a virtual "spaghetti bowl" of regulatory systems for trade. This reduces transparency and raises administrative costs (Wonnacott and Wonnacott, 1995). As will be seen in Chapter 3, the "spaghetti bowl" in the Americas is large and growing. An additional inefficiency is when hub-and-spoke arrangements emerge in which a hub country has free trade agreements with a number of partners that do not have similar agreements with each other. This encourages trade and investment diversion (Wonnacott, 1996). With their multiple agreements, Mexico and Chile have become trade hubs in the Americas. The United States could become a major trade hub as well if it continues to pursue bilateral reciprocal agreements.

- *Investment diversion.* While enlarged regional markets and preferences can attract foreign direct investment, they potentially could divert FDI from more efficient locations (Winters, 1998). In the Vinerian perspective, the location of FDI can be motivated by trade diversion arising from high tariffs and nontariff barriers (including rules of origin) in order to capture the discriminatory static effects of regional integration (Kindleberger, 1966). Even efficient location of FDI can have perceived costs for certain countries. For example, tariff-jumping FDI may relocate to a more efficient location in a partner country when regional trade and investment is liberalized.

- *Other costs.* It has been argued that integration agreements can create a "gang effect" that leaves outside countries with little option but to join for fear of trade and investment diversion (Winters, 2000). This clearly is a dynamic that countries face in the wave of the new regionalism. Uruguay and Paraguay probably could not have easily stood by as passive observers to integration between Brazil and Argentina. Mexico's joining of NAFTA contributed to the demand in Central America for free trade agreements with the

United States and Canada. Of course, the coercive effects of regional integration should be evaluated in terms of the contribution the agreements give to structural reform versus alternative paths to achieving this, and in this context the pressure for joining an initiative could be a benefit and not a cost.

Meanwhile, the formation of large regional blocs can create market power and shift the terms of trade with the rest of the world, a benefit for the region but a cost for others (Stein, 1994; Winters, 1998). In a world of perfect competition, this would represent a welfare loss; however, in the real world in which countries operate, one could not conclude that a priori. In any event, Schiff and Chang (2000) have estimated these effects in the case of the formation of Mercosur.

Evaluating the Balance of Benefits and Costs

Finally, it must be remembered that regional integration is not an end in itself but an instrument to achieve an objective. Hence, not all regional integration initiatives make economic sense, and even those that do can go awry if the policy framework is inadequate. Hence, evaluating the benefits of initiatives, and weighing those benefits against the costs, is the only way to determine whether an agreement makes sense for the participating countries and the rest of the world. One key question regarding an agreement is its economic relevancy. There has been a proliferation of nearly 30 integration initiatives already in the region and several more are being negotiated. But have they generated trade? Figure 2.6 shows that most of the agreements are associated with a significant amount of increased trade.[6] The possibility of new markets for trade is only one consideration of the economic value of new agreements. A much more through empirical analysis of effects is required. Unfortunately, empirical evaluation is inherently difficult due to extremely serious gaps in data availability, the complex causality of dynamic productive transformation effects (where one expects the big effects to lie), and the methodological difficulties in generating plausible conclusions from broad counterfactual analysis (Devlin and Ffrench-Davis, 1999).

Since the new regionalism is about much more than trade as such, the attention of analysts must go beyond the "static" trade creation-diversion examination (which has had its empirical problems as well; see

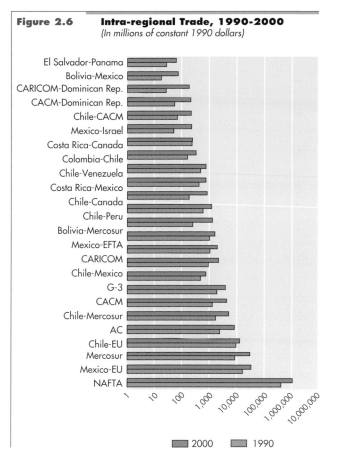

Figure 2.6   Intra-regional Trade, 1990-2000
(In millions of constant 1990 dollars)

El Salvador-Panama
Bolivia-Mexico
CARICOM-Dominican Rep.
CACM-Dominican Rep.
Chile-CACM
Mexico-Israel
Costa Rica-Canada
Colombia-Chile
Chile-Venezuela
Costa Rica-Mexico
Chile-Canada
Chile-Peru
Bolivia-Mercosur
Mexico-EFTA
CARICOM
Chile-Mexico
G-3
CACM
Chile-Mercosur
AC
Chile-EU
Mercosur
Mexico-EU
NAFTA

1   10   100   1,000   10,000   100,000   1,000,000   10,000,000

■ 2000   ■ 1990

Source: IDB calculations based on IMF (2001).

Winters, 2000) to focus more on the difficult-to-evaluate world of dynamic sectoral and economic productivity and growth effects (or lack of them), and on the contribution of regionalism to the political economy of structural reform. Moreover, political objectives also must be assessed, since these weigh heavily in many initiatives, particularly in agreements aimed at a common market or community. This type of comprehensive evaluation has largely escaped the debate to date.

North-South Agreements and the FTAA

The growing interest in Latin America for regional agreements with industrialized countries is in some ways the best expression of the new regionalism. Such agreements link countries in the process of structural

---

[6] Of course, more analysis is needed to determine the causality between the agreement and trade.

reform with countries that have already achieved a high degree of liberalization. Hence the burden of liberalization in the regional agreement weighs asymmetrically on the reforming country. Moreover, the agreements tend to have a comprehensive second-generation scope of disciplines, so the implications for structural change are large for the developing country partner.

Why do countries subject themselves to an asymmetrical liberalization process? Basically because many expect that when a regional agreement is anchored by a credible industrialized country, the benefits for structural reform outlined earlier will be magnified at an acceptable cost.

One of the primary goals of the developing country partner is market access. Even though the industrialized partners typically have low average most favored nation (MFN) tariffs and extensive non-reciprocal preferences for the region, there are tariff peaks, quotas and other non-tariff barriers and distortions that inhibit trade in many goods for which Latin America has a clear international comparative advantage. Agricultural products are a notorious example of this problem. Moreover, some analysts have pointed out that North-South agreements are less prone to trade diversion than South-South agreements because of the more general standard of international competitiveness in the industrialized area and the already relatively high participation of trade with these markets (Venables, 2001).[7] In any event, simulations of a Computable General Equilibrium model suggest that North-South market access agreements such as the FTAA, or those with the EU, would have significant impacts on export and GDP growth, assuming that trade barriers in the partner countries are eliminated comprehensively and include agriculture (see Appendix 2.1).

Perhaps even more important for the developing country partner is the desire to stabilize market access through a comprehensive set of rules and dispute settlement mechanisms with the industrialized partner. This is because market access can be interrupted by unilateral measures such as anti-dumping action, safeguards, withdrawal of non-reciprocal preferences, and tariff increases within WTO bound rates. Regional agreements are an opportunity to reciprocally confine the use of these types of threats to market access. Another major motivation is to anchor

economies by a regional agreement with a credible industrialized country; this would be expected to significantly lower the country's risk premium and attract investment flows (Ethier, 1998; Fernández-Arias and Spiegel, 1998). Finally, lock-in effects for reforms of subregional agreements have a checkered history. While they have been better in the era of new regionalism, they still are far from perfect (Devlin and Estevadeordal, 2001). In contrast, lock-in is expected to be stronger in North-South agreements, since industrialized countries tend to have considerable economic power and a battery of national institutional arrangements that vigorously enforce and monitor compliance of agreed rights and obligations (Devlin, Estevadeordal and Garay, 2000).

Meanwhile, the motivation of industrialized areas for integration agreements includes eliminating tariff barriers, since average tariffs in the region are three to five times higher than those in the Northern markets. But the major focus is on promoting commitments beyond WTO levels (and setting precedents to expand this frontier even further) on new trade-related areas such as services, investment, intellectual property, and government procurement. Another objective is to promote national policy agendas that are not widely agreed upon in multilateral fora, such as trade and labor standards, transparency, and issues related to consultation with civil society.[8] Another important goal is geopolitical market positioning in an age of globalization.

The North-South agreements are challenging indeed for the region. The implications for opening markets are substantial in view of the relatively higher levels of protection in the region. Also, Latin America has not yet advanced substantially in many of the new trade issues. For example, liberalization of financial services often has not moved much beyond protocols

---

[7] However, this is not true for all of the important sectors (e.g., textiles), and hence serious trade diversion can be a risk (Panagariya, 1996).

[8] This dynamic can be seen in the behavior of the United States and the European Union. U.S. interest in a free trade area with Canada and its extension to NAFTA (breaching that country's singular traditional focus on multilateralism) was spurred by creation of a single market in Europe and an effort to use the NAFTA agenda to drive home U.S. negotiating objectives in a lagging Uruguay Round. Meanwhile, the EU's recent interest in pursuing reciprocal free trade with Latin America is probably partially related to advances in the FTAA (IDB, 2002).

Figure 2.7   Structure of the FTAA Negotiations

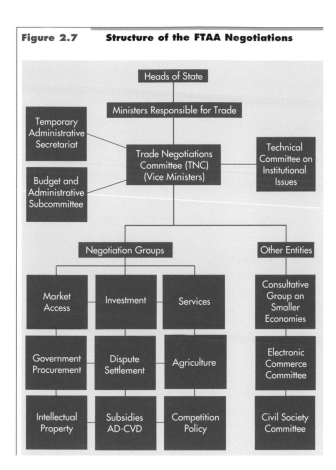

ica but also between the subregions that do relatively little trade with each other.[9] The process was launched at the December 1994 Miami Summit, but only with great difficulty, as trade did not appear on the program until just a few months before the event due to some initial ambivalence in North America (Hayes, 1996). Pressure from Latin America was decisive in putting trade at the center of the summit agenda.[10]

The FTAA initiative bears all the characteristics of a modern second-generation trade agenda. A comprehensive preparatory process began in June 1995 and ended with the beginning of formal negotiations in September 1998 involving nine areas (Figure 2.7). The goal is a balanced and comprehensive WTO-consistent agreement by January 2005 that will be determined by consensus and be a single undertaking. The agreement must take into account the needs, economic conditions and opportunities of the smaller economies of the region, which confront special vulnerabilities (Box 2.6). The FTAA can coexist with bilateral and subregional agreements to the extent that the rights and obligations under these agreements are not covered or go beyond the rights and obligations of the FTAA (FTAA Declaration of San José, 1998). Hence a comprehensive FTAA could potentially absorb some of the hemisphere's free trade areas or even subregional agreements if because of problems they do not advance beyond (or slip back into) de facto simple free trade zones.

The process has proceeded steadily since 1995 (Table 2.8), with disciplined organization and strong commitments on the part of governments in terms of participation, time and expense. For example, negotiations in 2000 involved 184 meeting days with more than 3,000 participants, generating more than 2,000 negotiating documents. A bracketed draft text of the negotiated FTAA agreement was publicly released in 2001. Meanwhile, in May 2002 the delegations agreed on the methods and modalities for product and sectoral specific liberalization, which sets the stage for the final round of negotiations involving offers and

or statements of intentions. Moreover, there is an asymmetric capacity between the industrialized country and the region to negotiate sustainable agreements and implement them. And, of course, many adjustments will be needed to make up for lost fiscal revenue from tariff elimination, ensuring stable financial systems and macroeconomic environments in the face of capital inflows set off by the agreements, and establishing a policy framework that addresses the impact of trade on poverty and equity. A challenging agenda, but one that many Latin American countries are willing to take on in order to capture the potential trade and political economy benefits from fortifying links with their major markets.

The FTAA is clearly the region's biggest North-South initiative, involving all democratic Latin American countries and North America. It would be the world's largest free trade area: 34 countries with 800 million people and a $10 trillion regional economy. It promises not only to liberalize trade with North Amer-

---

[9] For instance, less than 5 percent of Andean and Mercosur trade is between the two blocs (IDB, 2000).

[10] The decision was by consensus of 34 countries.

Box 2.6   Challenges Facing Small Countries

The onset of globalization and the ongoing process of multilateral trade liberalization have sparked an international debate on the unique circumstances of small countries in the world economy, particularly their vulnerability to adverse external shocks and natural hazards. The debate has spurred proposals that small economies should enjoy longer transition periods to comply with commitments; fewer and less onerous international obligations; assistance with trade adjustment and risk management; and greater security and predictability in market access.

Such proposals stem from characteristics these countries share based on their smallness and remoteness. Relative to larger regional neighbors, they tend to have more specialized and less diversified economies, often with exports concentrated in few commodities. They have diseconomies of scale and investment; are unusually open to external economic developments in the areas of trade, capital flows and technology; are heavily dependent on foreign capital flows; and have high international transport costs. An extensive and growing economic literature highlights these common features and examines a number of common problems related to them.

Income Volatility

Small countries often have higher rates of growth than larger neighbors, but their growth rates fluctuate more widely. They tend to rely heavily on external trade in goods and services, and to be open to foreign investment, as means of overcoming the inherent scale limitations of small domestic markets and resource bases. Since the share of trade in such countries' GDP is often especially large, and since their exports are generally concentrated in both products and markets, they experience much greater variations in their terms of trade and their growth rates. Small states' standard deviation of annual real per capita growth might be some 25 percent higher than in large countries (Commonwealth Secretariat/World Bank Task Force on Small States, 2000). It has been argued that the disadvantages of volatility are offset by the advantages of trade openness (Easterly and Kraay, 1999). Greater market access, however, does not automatically entail greater market entry: the balance of benefits and risks depends on whether more openness in small countries is matched by more secure market penetration in their trading partners.

External Shocks and Access to Capital

Product concentration and export specialization in a small number of key commodities, part of an effort to achieve economies of scale in small countries, can boost productivity and competitiveness in global markets. The limited diversification, however, makes these countries vulnerable to shocks and market disruptions such as commodity price fluctuations, market access difficulties, natural disasters, and product blight, as well as to the strong bargaining power of multinational firms. The banana dispute between the United States and the European Union over the preferential treatment of Caribbean bananas in the European market illustrated the fragility of small states that are reliant on preferential arrangements, as well as their susceptibility to disruptions in market access. Limited diversification also heightens economic risk, which in turn affects the capacity of smaller economies to access international financial markets. Moreover, they are perceived as riskier than large countries. In effect, they are discriminated against: when the quality of their policies and human capital is comparable to that of bigger countries, they are still judged to be a greater investment risk, face higher risk premia, and typically pay higher interest rate spreads. Additionally, intense competition to attract investment prompts the need for ever greater (and fiscally pernicious) incentives and the commitment of increasing resources to investment promotion (Commonwealth Secretariat/World Bank Task Force on Small States, 2001).

Trade Liberalization and Revenue Loss

Many small states have benefited from preferential market access and relatively high levels of official development assistance from OECD countries. Members of the African, Caribbean and Pacific (ACP) group of states have enjoyed a special relationship with the EU in both of these areas. As preferential access to traditional markets is eroded by trade liberalization, small states face a dual problem. On the one hand, they must adapt to the loss of preferences in the markets of their main trading partners. On the other, they are obliged to lower or eliminate their own trade barriers. Since they have a small domestic tax base, however, many small countries have depended on tariff income as a substantial source of government revenue. Such earnings will necessarily decline as tariffs are reduced and must be replaced by sizeable adjustments of tax structures to bring in new sources of revenue.

Limited Institutional Capacity

Smaller economies have low staffing levels in their public administrations. Personnel tend to be overextended and responsible for multiple tasks, while specialists are often not retained. Limited financing contributes to high staff turnover and precludes frequent training, which in turn hinders the accumulation of management skills and constrains innovation (ECLAC, 2000). One outcome is a curbed capacity to engage effectively in the negotiations that underpin trade and integration initiatives.

Business Adjustments and Private Costs

Greater competition from import liberalization leads to the local concentration of small firms in sectors where they have a competitive advantage. The specialization and resource reallocation required for that purpose can have significant adjustment costs, the burden of which often falls on workers in firms and industries that face the immediate prospect of redundancies, and on poor households for which unemployment is highly problematic. The social benefits of reform can offset the social costs over the longer term, but the *private* costs of adjust-

ment are inequitably distributed, and resistance to them can thwart trade liberalization efforts (Gonzales, 2000). Additionally, the higher transport costs prompted by distance and limited trade volumes, as well as fragmented production bases, conspire to frustrate the greater productivity necessary for international competitiveness. This is especially the case in island and archipelago states, where the problem is not simply one of distance: in some cases there is a small number of transport providers holding a monopoly on service provision.

Natural Disasters

Many small countries, notably in Central America and the developing island states of the Caribbean, are unusually exposed to natural hazards. Caribbean countries in the hurricane belt annually face the prospect of devastation and share with other countries of the Americas a natural exposure to volcanic activity, earthquakes, mudslides and floods. Since the economies, land area and populations of these countries are small, natural disasters can adversely affect a large proportion of economic activity and export capacity.

requests for achieving defined liberalization schedules by December 2004.

As pointed out by Blanco and Zabludovsky (2002), while the negotiations have advanced steadily to date, this last stage will be critical and extremely difficult. Although the 34 countries of the FTAA represent a more compact negotiating vehicle for obtaining consensus than the 140-plus WTO membership, agreement among countries as heterogeneous in terms of levels of development (from some of the poorest to the richest in the world) and geopolitical perspectives as those in the FTAA will demand creative formulas that provide for both balance and substantial liberalization. Examining trade patterns, Blanco and Zabuldovsky observe that the most aggressive targets of many countries' FTAA trade agendas are often the most politically sensitive defensive sectors of others, and vice-versa. Then there are complex technical issues such as what types of rules of origin are need-

ed to ensure full participation in FTAA trade opportunities, minimize trade and investment diversion, and provide for a manageable administrative burden. How to treat the smaller economies will be a delicate political issue. Bridging these and other tradeoffs will not only tax the technical skills of negotiators, but also require renewed political leadership to overcome the region's recent economic difficulties and increasing signs of protectionist pressures in the hemisphere.

Meanwhile, sustainable agreements require effective negotiation and implementation as well as policies to foster socially efficient adjustment. On all these accounts, the institutional capacity of many Latin American countries leaves much to be desired. Agreement on a cost efficient and effective FTAA institutional architecture also may prove difficult given fiscal restraints on all member countries and the diverse traditions in the hemisphere, ranging form purely intergovernmental arrangements to more comprehensive

Table 2.8 | Chronology of the FTAA Process

Date	Event	Action
Pre-negotiation period		
December 1994	First Summit of the Americas (Miami)	Launches the FTAA process.
January 1995	OAS Special Committee on Trade	Establishes initial work plan and timetable.
June 1995	Denver Ministerial Meeting	Seven working groups established; IDB-OAS-ECLAC Tripartite Committee charged with providing technical support.
March 1996	Cartagena Ministerial Meeting	Four additional working groups established.
May 1997	Belo Horizonte Ministerial Meeting	Working groups mandated to complete all work by next Ministerial Meeting; one additional working group established.
March 1998	San José Ministerial Meeting	Launch of negotiations recommended; agreements reached on structure, calendar, leadership and location of negotiations. Nine negotiating groups, two committees and one consultative group established.
April 1998	Second Summit of the Americas (Santiago)	Heads of state launch negotiations.
Negotiation period		
June 1998	Buenos Aires Trade Negotiations Committee meeting	Vice Ministers set forth comprehensive work program for each group and committee.
September 1998		FTAA Administrative Secretary established in Miami.
September 1998		Commencement of negotiating group and committee meetings.
November 1999	Toronto Ministerial Meeting	Annotated outlines of eventual FTAA chapters reviewed; package of business facilitation measures approved; negotiating groups mandated to produce bracketed text of eventual chapters.
January 2000		Implementation of business facilitation measures begins, thereby fulfilling mandate to make "concrete progress" by 2000.
March 2001		Transfer of Administrative Secretariat to Panama City.
April 2001	Buenos Aires Ministerial Meeting	Review of bracketed text, issuance of new instructions.
April 2001	Third Summit of the Americas (Quebec City)	Public release of the FTAA bracketed text in four languages.
May 2002		Launch of product-sector specific negotiations.
October 2002	Ecuador Ministerial Meeting	
November 2002		Commencement of Brazil/United States Co-Presidency.
March 2003		Transfer of Administrative Secretariat to Mexico City.
December 2004		Conclusion of negotiations.
December 2005		Entry into force of the FTAA agreement.

EU-like institutions. Finally, progress in certain important areas of the FTAA negotiations—e.g., agricultural domestic support—may be intrinsically linked to advances in the WTO's complex Doha Development Agenda, also scheduled to finish in 2005.

While completing the FTAA will be a technical and political challenge of major proportion, it is important to note that the process is already leaving a positive legacy for the development of Latin America (Iglesias, 1999). Some of the positive externalities emerging from the launch of the process in 1995 are quite impressive. For instance, after nearly eight years of regular FTAA meetings, there is a certain familiarity and esprit de corps among the delegations that has allowed them to use FTAA fora to resolve bilateral trade problems and launch new initiatives. The process also has enhanced transparency by generating a wealth of hemispheric comparative data on national trade and regulatory norms that heretofore were unavailable or very difficult to obtain. Countries have also used the FTAA negotiations as a learning laboratory for WTO disciplines and new pioneering second-generation trade issues (e.g., competition policy and e-commerce) as well as for exploiting opportunities to hone negotiating skills through the extensive participation and leadership that the process has encouraged even for the smallest countries of the hemisphere. The FTAA process also has approved and implemented customs procedure measures to facilitate business and has fostered an emerging hemispheric business community that meets regularly around the FTAA trade ministerial.

THE NEW REGIONALISM AND THE MULTILATERAL SYSTEM

One of the major points of contention about the new regionalism has been its relationship with the multilateral system. The GATT and the WTO that succeeded it are based on multilateral principles. Ruggie (1992) has conceptualized multilateralism with the defining characteristics of indivisibility (allegiance to a system as a whole), generalized rules of conduct, and diffuse reciprocity. As Winters (2000) has pointed out, the multilateral trading system shares these characteristics: "It is indivisible in that it permits an extremely dense and far

reaching network of trade links and of intergovernmental contacts and is viewed as having an existence separate from all individual trade links between participants, and in that its separate existence is seen as valuable. The trading system's most obvious generalized norm is non-discrimination (MFN), which immediately and automatically extends bilateral agreements to all members. Reciprocity is diffuse in that governments do accept individual actions that appear not to be in their immediate interests, but it is generally accepted that, overall, every country has to gain."

Regional integration includes trade liberalization among a group of like-minded countries usually defined by some geographical boundaries. The preferential nature of regionalism makes it exceptional with respect to the MFN principle underlying the GATT/WTO, and it is in fact treated as an exception with legal rules that attempt to circumscribe the practice (Article XXIV of the GATT reinforced by its Understanding of the Uruguay Round agreements and Article V of the GATS).[11]

Along with the formalization of the Uruguay Round's more stringent rules governing world trade in the 1990s, attention increasingly shifted toward the systemic effects of regional integration on the multilateral trading system. Concerns were raised about the discriminatory behavior of the new regionalism, which runs counter to the non-discriminatory principles of the multilateral trading system and is perceived by some as having the potential to discourage participation in the system, whose goal is the advance of worldwide trade liberalization. Thus, studies have emerged that address whether the proliferation of the multilateral trading system is in fact beneficial or detrimental to the strengthening of worldwide trade liberalization (Krugman, 1981; Summers, 1991). The concepts of either *building* or *stumbling* blocs (Bhagwati, 1991) have gained as much prominence as those of trade creation and diversion in the discussion of regional integration.

Although it is theoretically plausible that the dynamic interaction between regionalism and multilateralism could lead to the weakening of the latter (Bhag-

---

[11] The other formal exception for integration in developing countries is the Enabling Clause.

APPENDIX 2.1
EVALUATING HEMISPHERIC FREE TRADE AGREEMENTS: A COMPUTABLE GENERAL EQUILIBRIUM APPROACH[1]

A crucial element for policymaking is to accurately assess and compare the impact of a country's different trade liberalization options. Among the various methodologies available to policymakers, computable general equilibrium (CGE) models have been widely used in trade policy evaluation and for other policies. Being necessarily a simplified representation of the whole economy, they capture both the aggregate and sectoral impact of policy changes on the economy under study as well as the partners. This is its distinguishing feature vis-à-vis other types of economic models.

The model enables us to evaluate the impact by comparing the economies' initial situation (benchmark equilibrium computed from the country's or countries' real data) with the new numeric equilibrium resulting from the adoption of the policy change under study. Although the adjustment time is not specifically mentioned, it is assumed to be long enough for the markets to readjust and thus achieve the new equilibrium. The addendum to this note contains a more detailed description of the model as well as its main advantages and disadvantages.

CGE simulations were used to evaluate and compare the differentiated effect of alternative trade agreements involving Latin America, including the FTAA and free trade agreements between the Mercosur and Andean Community countries with their two major partners (the European Union and the United States). All the agreements considered are either being negotiated or have been announced. Since part of the recent discussion on the new regionalism has been concentrated on the relative advantages of North-South versus South-South agreements (Venables, 2001), the results will also provide some insight on this issue.

The CGE model used is a multi-country and multi-sector comparative static model that incorporates trade-linked externalities and economies of scale in the manufacturing industries. The policy variables in this exercise are the elimination of tariff protection (including ad valorem as well as specific, mixed tariffs and

tariff-rate quotas),[2] export subsidies, and producer support estimates (for the NAFTA countries and the EU). One should note that market access is only one part of the potential net benefits of a free trade agreement, and hence simulations are a very conservative estimate of effects.

Appendix Figures 2.1a and b compare the impact of the three agreements for Mercosur and the Andean countries. They show the percentage increase in exports that a free trade agreement with the EU, the United States and the FTAA would have on the economies. For simplicity, we aggregate the 15 sectors into three broader groups: primary goods, light manufactures and heavy manufactures. Although the high degree of aggregation makes for an imprecise definition of these groups, they are relatively correlated with the relative use of factors: primary industries are land-oriented, light manufactures are labor-oriented and heavy manufactures are, in general, capital-oriented.

In terms of scenarios, the highest impact on export growth for Mercosur would be the free trade agreement with the EU (12 percent increase), followed by the FTAA (8 percent increase). For the Andean Community, the FTAA would bring an increase in exports of 6 percent, while an agreement with the EU would increase exports by 3 percent. Although there are many reasons behind these results, they are very much affected by the initial trade links between countries engaged in an agreement (for example, as a destination market, the EU weighs heavier for Mercosur than for the Andean Community), and by the initial trade protection faced by countries. In any event, both the EU and the FTAA are important enough markets that pursuing free trade agreements should not be interpreted as an either/or proposition.

The analysis by sectors shows that in all scenarios light manufactures are the faster growing sector, although the relative impact is bigger under a free trade agreement with the EU than in the other two scenarios considered. As expected, light manufactures is

---

[1] Results presented in this appendix come from Monteagudo and Watanuki (2002).

[2] Although most tariffs are ad valorem, non-ad valorem tariffs are frequent for agriculture products, especially in the most developed countries.

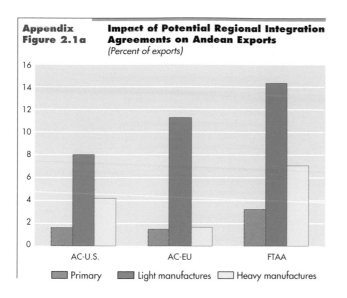

Appendix Figure 2.1a — **Impact of Potential Regional Integration Agreements on Andean Exports**
(Percent of exports)

Primary Light manufactures Heavy manufactures

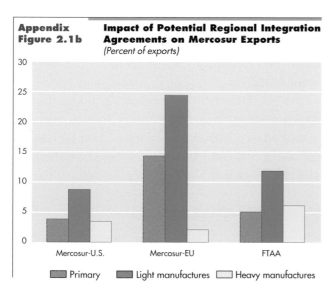

Appendix Figure 2.1b — **Impact of Potential Regional Integration Agreements on Mercosur Exports**
(Percent of exports)

Primary Light manufactures Heavy manufactures

led by agriculture-related products (meat and processed food) that are among the sectors facing the highest protection in both the U.S. and EU markets. This result confirms the subregion's comparative advantage in terms of an agreement with more developed countries. As expected, the FTAA reflects the same pattern of growth across macro-sectors as does the agreement with the United States: specialization in light manufactures, followed by heavy manufactures and then primary goods, reflecting in part that the primary sectors are relatively less protected in the Western Hemisphere compared with the EU market. In most cases, the increased heavy manufacturing exports in Mercosur and the Andean countries are resource-based manufactures.

Appendix Figure 2.2 presents the impact of the FTAA by macro-sector. Total export growth ranges from 4 percent to 9 percent across Latin America, except for Mexico (2 percent) because of NAFTA. By sectors, all of the region's countries considered (except Venezuela) specialize relatively more in light manufactures exports (mainly textiles in the Central American and Caribbean group, processed food and other light manufactures in the Mercosur countries, and a more mixed combination for the Andean countries). The heavy manufacturing sector follows as the second fastest growing sector, made up mostly of new exports of automobile and machinery equipment from Brazil and more natural resource-based heavy manufactures such as petroleum in Venezuela and Argentina (also

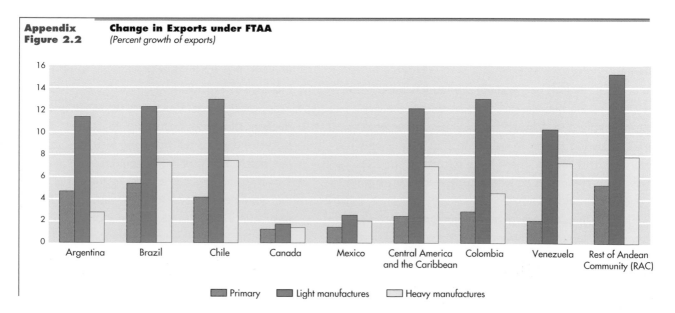

Appendix Figure 2.2 — **Change in Exports under FTAA**
(Percent growth of exports)

Primary Light manufactures Heavy manufactures

chemicals in this case), and iron and steel in the group formed by Bolivia, Ecuador and Peru (RAC).

Finally, an interesting result is to see what difference the presence of Latin American countries makes in the FTAA. Appendix Figure 2.3 shows first that more than 40 percent of the new exports will go to the regional market for all countries, except for Central America (as a result of its high dependence on the U.S. market). The colored cells show the cases where the share of Latin American countries in increased exports is more than 50 percent. Another result worth mentioning is that for primary goods exports, the regional market absorbs more than 50 percent of new exports; these percentages rise to 69 percent for light manufactures and to 72 percent for heavy manufactures. To the extent that specializing in manufactures is an attractive strategic consideration, this is an important result to bear in mind when addressing the importance of the intra-Latin American market in the FTAA negotiations.

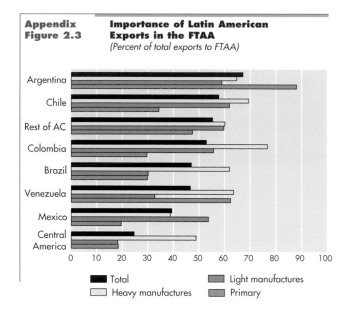

Appendix Figure 2.3

Importance of Latin American Exports in the FTAA
(Percent of total exports to FTAA)

■ Total
▨ Light manufactures
□ Heavy manufactures
▨ Primary

METHODOLOGICAL ADDENDUM TO APPENDIX 2.1: THE USE OF COMPUTABLE GENERAL EQUILIBRIUM MODELS IN THE EVALUATION OF TRADE LIBERALIZATION POLICIES

Basic Features of CGE Models

CGE models are based on the general equilibrium theory in which equilibrium prices and quantities are determined *simultaneously*. CGE models are nevertheless a simplified representation of the economy and only identify key economic actors or agents (such as households or consumers, firms or producers, and government).

CGE models are *equilibrium* models because they describe the behavior of the economy as the outcome of supply and demand for each product in each market, allowing prices to adjust so that supply and demand exactly match. There is no excess demand or supply, and all markets simultaneously clear, i.e., supply equals demand.

CGE models are *general* equilibrium models because they capture all the sectors in an economy and all the economic agents involved. This is the most striking advantage of CGE models compared with partial equilibrium models. Consequently, CGE models can

specifically examine the efficient use of resource allocation and the equity with which such resources are redistributed.

CGE models are *computable* models in that they provide a unique equilibrium solution and are quantified in a numerical way rather than by analytical means. This provides a precise measurement of the economic impact of a given policy.

What the CGE Captures

The CGE model captures the main effects of a trade liberalization predicted by standard theory of international trade:

- *Trade effects:* Tariff elimination causes an increase in imports and improved efficiency in the medium term due to the fact that the elimination of the tariff distortions will lead to an increase in exports.
- *Production effects:* Producers (firms) adjust production structures according to a new set of prices and factor returns along with their respective production possibility frontiers.
- *Government revenue effects:* In the short term, the government loses total revenues due to the reduction in tariff revenue; if not offset by alternative revenues, this decrease may lead to a decline in public spending.
- *Welfare effects:* Real household income is affected by a change in real wages and the price of

other factors (capital and land), as well as that of goods and services. All these factors presumably will increase welfare.

Main Advantages

Noteworthy among the advantages of using CGE models for economic policy analysis are that they:

- Allow policymakers to assess the specific impact of the various policy options under consideration by controlling the effects of other policy instruments.
- Take into account the complex interdependent connections that exist in real economies, or interactions among the sectors, households and with trade partners, which is different from partial equilibrium analysis.
- Explicitly model the entire economy.
- Examine the impact on resource allocation, equity and income distribution.
- Measure changes in welfare.
- Simulate policy alternatives.
- Provide numerical results so that alternatives can be compared and the available policy options easily ranked.

Main Disadvantages

CGE models do of course have disadvantages, although they share some of them with other methods of economic policy evaluation such as input-output, linear programming, optimal control and macroeconometric models. Some of the disadvantages concern model construction. CGE models are complex to con-

struct because of the large amount of data they use (national accounts, input-output tables, trade flows, balance of payments, etc.). Much fine-tuning and adjustment of the data is needed in order to construct a compatible and consistent benchmark database.

Other disadvantages are related to the implementation of the model. CGE models are highly dependent on the benchmark data (i.e., on the economic conditions in the base year), and they are very sensitive to certain parameter estimations or assumptions (such as elasticities).

Lastly, the results of CGE models must be carefully interpreted because they do not consider any other economic policy action or shocks during the period of adjustment of the economy to the new equilibrium, and because they do not reflect non-economic effects (such as institutional impacts). Finally, most CGE models deal with the real side of the economy, excluding monetary or financial variables and dynamic effects of capital accumulation.

Characteristics of the CGE Model Used

The model comprises 12 countries or regions. Each of these 12 economies includes 15 sectors grouped into three main macrosectors: the primary sector, light and heavy manufactures, and services. Among the main features of the model is that it includes positive externalities linked to trade flows, reflecting the idea that trade liberalization leads to increased productivity. To some extent, this feature offsets the static nature of the model (since it does not reflect capital accumulation from one period to the next). The benchmark year for this model is 1997.

REFERENCES

Amann, E., and Z. Vodusek. 2001. Overview: Trends and Main Findings. In Ziga Vodusek (ed.), *Foreign Direct Investment in Latin America*. Washington, DC: Inter-American Development Bank.

Balassa, B. 1961. *The Theory of Economic Integration.* Irwin, Inc.

Baldwin, R., and A. Venables. 1995. Regional Economic Integration. In G. Grossman and K. Rogoff (eds.), *Handbook of International Economics,* vol. 3. Amsterdam: Elsevier

Bhagwati, J. 1991. *The World Trading System at Risk.* Princeton, NJ: Princeton University Press.

Bhagwati, J., and A. Panagariya. 1996. Preferential Trading Areas and Multilateralism: Strangers, Friends or Foes. In J. Bhagwati, and A. Panagariya, *The Economics of Preferential Trade Agreements.* Washington, DC: American Enterprise Institute.

Bevilaqua, A., and E. Talvi. 1999. *Macroeconomic Interdependence in MERCOSUR.* Montevideo: Catholic University of Rio de Janeiro and CERES.

Blanco, H., and J. Zabludovsky. 2002. Alcances y límites de la negociación del ALCA y escenarios de su interacción con las negociaciones multilaterales. Integration and Regional Programs Department, Inter-American Development Bank, Washington, DC.

Blömstrom, M., and A. Kokko. 1997. Regional Integration and Foreign Direct Investment. World Bank International Trade Division, Washington, DC.

Commonwealth Secretariat/World Bank Task Force on Small States. 2000. Small States: Meeting Challenges in the Global Economy. March.

———. 2001. Lowering the Threshold: Changing Private Investors' Perceptions by Reducing their Cost and Risk Assessment in Least Developed, Small and Vulnerable Economies. August.

Corden, W. 1972. Economies of Scale and Customs Union Theory. *Journal of Political Economy* 80.

Crafts, Nicholas. 2000. Globalization and Growth in the Twentieth Century. In International Monetary Fund, *World Economic Outlook. Supporting Studies.* Washington, DC: IMF.

Devlin, R. 1997. En defensa del MERCOSUR. *Archivos del Presente* no. 7.

———. 2001. The Free Trade of the Americas and Mercosur European Union Free Trade Process: Can They Learn Something from Each Other? In P. Giordano, A Valladão and M. F. Durand (eds.), *Towards an Agreement between Europe and Mercosur.* Paris: University of Political Science.

Devlin, R., and A. Estevadeordal. 2001. What's New in the New Regionalism in the Americas. In V. Bulmer-Thomas (ed.), *Regional Integration in Latin America and the Caribbean.* London: The Institute of Latin American Studies (ILAS).

Devlin, R., and R. Ffrench-Davis. 1999. Towards an Evaluation of Regional Integration in Latin America in the 1990s. *The World Economy* 22(2) March.

Devlin, R., A. Estevadeordal, and L. J. Garay. 2000. Some Economic and Strategic Issues in the Face of the Emerging FTAA. In Jorge Domínguez, *The Future of Inter-American Relations.* New York: Routledge.

Devlin, R., A. Estevadeordal and E. Krivonos. 2002. *The Trade and Cooperation Nexus: How Does the Mercosur-EU Process Measure Up?* Paris: University of Sciences-Po.

Diaz-Alejandro, Carlos. 1985. The Early 1980s in Latin America: 1930s One More Time. Paper presented at the Expert Meeting on Crisis and Development in Latin America and the Caribbean, ECLAC, Santiago, April 29-May 3.

Dussel Peters, E., L. M. G. Paliza, and E. Loria Diaz. 2002. Vision macroeconomica de los impactos de la integración regional en la inversión inter e intrarregionales. El caso de la inversión extranjera directa en México. RedINT, Inter-American Development Bank.

Easterly, W., and A. Kraay. 1999. Small States, Small Problems. Paper presented to the Small States Conference, St. Lucia, February 17-19.

Echavarría, J. J. 1998. Trade Flows in the Andean Countries: Unilateral Liberalization on Regional Preferences. In World Bank, *Trade: Towards Open Regionalism*. Washington, DC: World Bank.

Economic Commission on Latin America and the Caribbean (ECLAC). 1994. Open Regionalism in Latin America and the Caribbean. ECLAC, Santiago.

_____. 1998. Foreign Direct Investment in Latin America and the Caribbean. ECLAC, Santiago.

_____. 2000. The Vulnerability of Small Island Developing States of the Caribbean. ECLAC, Santiago. March.

Estevadeordal, A. 1999. *Negotiating Preferential Market Access: The Case of NAFTA*. INTAL-ITD Working Paper no. 3, Inter-American Development Bank Integration and Regional Programs Department, Washington, DC.

Ethier, W. 1998. The New Regionalism. *The Economic Journal* 108(449) July.

Feenstra, R. 2000. World Trade Flows, 1980-1997 with Production and Tariff Data. University of California, Davis. Mimeo.

Fernández, M. 1997. Returns to Regionalism: An Evaluation of Non-Traditional Gains from RTAs. World Bank, International Trade Division, Washington, DC and New York University.

Fernández-Arias, E., and A. Spiegel. 1998. North-South Customs Unions and International Capital Mobility. *Journal of International Economics* no. 46.

Fernández, R., and J. Portes. 1998. Returns to Regionalism. An Evaluation of Nontraditional Gains from Regional Trade Agreements. *World Bank Economic Review* no. 2.

Ffrench-Davis, R. 1980. Distorsiones del mercado y teoría de las uniones aduaneras. *Integración Latinoamericana* 5, INTAL.

Flôres, R. 1997. The Gains from Mercosur: A General Equilibrium, Imperfect Competition Evaluation. *Journal of Policy Modeling* no. 19.

Francois, J., and C. Shiells. 1994. *Modeling Trade Policy Applied General Equilibrium Assessments of North American Free Trade*. Cambridge, UK: Cambridge University Press.

Frankel, J., and S. Wei. 1996. Regionalization of World Trade and Currencies: Economics and Politics. In J. Frankel (ed.), *The Regionalization of the World Economy*. Chicago: Chicago University Press.

Free Trade Area of the Americas (FTAA). 1998. Declaration of San José. San José, Costa Rica, March.

Freund, C., and J. McLaren. 1999. On the Dynamics of Trade Diversion: Evidence from Four Trade Blocs. Federal Reserve Board. Mimeo.

Garay, L. J., and A. Vera. 1998. Naturaleza y evolución reciente de la inversión intraregional. In *Inversión extranjera directa en América Latina*. Madrid: Inter-American Development Bank and Institute of European-Latin-American Relations.

García Herrero, A., and G. Glöckler. 2000. *Options for Latin America in a Globalized World*. Frankfurt: European Central Bank.

Giordano, P. 2001. The Political Economy of Regional Integration in Mercosur. PhD dissertation, Institut d'Etudes Politiques de Paris.

Gonzales, A. 2000. Policy Implications of Smallness as a Factor in the Lomé, FTAA and WTO Negotiations. Consultancy report, Inter-American Development Bank, September.

Grubel, H., and P. Lloyd. 1975. *Intra-industry Trade, the Theory and Measurement of International Trade in Differentiated Products*. London: McMillan

Hayes, M. 1996. *Building the Hemispheric Community: Lessons from the Summit of the Americas Process*. Washington, DC: Inter-American Dialogue.

Hufbauer, G., and J. Schott. 1993. *NAFTA: An Assessment*. Washington, DC: Institute for International Economics.

Humphrey, J., and H. Schmitz. 2000. *Governance and Upgrading: Linking Industrial Cluster and Global Value Chain Research.* Institute of Development Studies Working Paper no. 120. November.

IDB/INTAL. 1999. Impacto sectorial de la integración en el MERCOSUR. INTAL, Buenos Aires.

Iglesias, E. 1999. Statement at the Fifth Meeting of FTAA Ministers Responsible for Trade, Toronto, November 1-4.

Inter-American Development Bank (IDB). 1997. *Economic and Social Progress Report.* Washington, DC: IDB.

———. 2000. Periodic Note. Integration and Trade in the Americas, Integration and Regional Programs Department. December.

———. 2002. Periodic Note. Integration and Trade in the Americas, Integration and Regional Programs Department. May.

International Monetary Fund. 2001. *Direction of Trade Statistics.* Washington, DC: IMF.

James, H. 2001. *The End of Globalization.* Cambridge: Harvard University Press.

Kemp, M., and H. Wan. 1976. An Elementary Proposition Concerning the Formation of Customs Unions. *Journal of International Economics* 6.

Khrishna, P. 1998. Regionalism and Multilateralism: A Political Economy Approach. *Quarterly Journal of Economics* 113.

Kindleberger, C. 1966. European Integration and the International Corporations. *Columbia Journal of Business* 12.

Krueger, A. 1999. *Trade Creation and Trade Diversion under NAFTA.* NBER Working Paper no. 7429.

Krugman, Paul. 1981. Intra-industry Specialization and the Gains From Trade. *Journal of Political Economy* no. 89.

Lancaster, Kevin. 1979. Intra-industry Trade under Perfect Monopolistic Competition. *Journal of International Economics* 10(2).

Levy, P. 1997. A Political Economy Analysis of Free Trade Agreements. *American Economic Review* 87(4) September.

López-Cordova, Ernesto J. 2001. *NAFTA and the Mercosur Economy: Analytical Issues and Lessons for the FTAA.* INTAL-ITD-STA Occasional Paper no. 9, Integration and Regional Programs Department, Inter-American Development Bank.

Maddison, A. 2001. *The World Economy: A Millennial Perspective.* Paris: Development Centre of the Organization for Economic Cooperation and Development.

Monteagudo, Josefina, and Masakazu Watanuki. 2002. FTAA in Perspective: North-South and South-South Agreements in the Western Hemisphere. Inter-American Development Bank, Washington, DC. Mimeo.

Multilateral Investment Fund (MIF). 2001. Remittances to Latin America and the Caribbean: Cooperative Statistics. MIF, Washington, DC. May.

Nagarajan, N. 1998. La evidencia sobre el desvío de comercio en el MERCOSUR. *Integración y Comercio* no. 2.

Nogues, Julio. 1996. Does Mercosur's Trade Performance Raise Concerns about the Effects of Regional Trade Arrangements? No. Mimeo.

Oman, C. 1998. The Policy Challenges of Globalization and Regularization. In Ian Joost Teunissen (ed.), *Regional Integration and Multilateral Cooperation in the Global Economy.* The Hague: FONDAD.

Organization for Economic Cooperation and Development (OECD). 1995. *Regional Integration and the Multilateral Trading Systems. Synergies and Divergences.* Paris: OECD.

Panagariya, A. 1996. The Free Trade Area of the Americas: Good for Latin America? *The World Economy* 19.

———. 2000. Preferential Trade Liberalization: The Traditional Theory and New Developments. *Journal of Economic Literature* no. 38.

Pastor, R. 2001. *Toward a North American Community: Lessons from the Old World for the New.* Washington, DC: Institute for International Economics.

Perry, G. 2001. *Mercosur Competitiveness: Are the Rankings Informative?* Washington, DC: World Bank.

Pomfret, R. 1997. *The Economics of Regional Trading Arrangements.* Oxford: Oxford University Press.

Puga, D., and A. Venables. 1997. *Trading Arrangements and Industrial Development.* Washington, DC: World Bank International Trade Division.

Robinson, S., and K. Thierfelder. 1999. *Trade Liberalization and Regional Integration. The Search for Large Numbers.* International Food Policy Research Institute Discussion Paper no. 34.

Rodrik, Dani. 1997. *Has Globalization Gone Too Far?* Washington, DC: Institute for International Economics.

Ruggie, J. 1992. Multilateralism: The Anatomy of an Institution. *International Organization* 45(3) Summer.

Salgado, G. 1979. El mercado regional latinoamericano: El proyecto y la realidad. *Revista de la CEPAL* no. 7 (April).

Schiff, M., and Won Chang. 2000. *Market Presence, Consistency, Stability and the Terms of Trade Effect of Regional Integration.* Washington, DC: World Bank and U.S. Treasury Department.

Serra, J., et al. 1997. *Reflections on Regionalism.* Washington, DC: Carnegie Endowment for International Peace.

Soloaga, I., and A. Winters. 1999. *Regionalism in the Nineties: What Effect on Trade?* World Bank Policy Research Working Paper no. 2156.

Stein, E. 1994. The Welfare Implications of Asymmetric Trading Blocs. Ph.D. thesis, University of California, Berkeley.

Summers, L. 1991. Regionalism and the World Trading System. In Federal Reserve Bank of Kansas City, *Policy Implications of Trade and Currency Zones.* Kansas City, MO.

Venables, A. 2001. Regionalism and Economic Development. Inter-American Development Bank Integration and Regional Programs Department, Washington, DC.

Viner, J. 1950. *The Customs Union Issue.* Washington, DC: Carnegie Endowment for International Peace.

Williamson, Jeffrey. 1997. Globalization and Inequality: Past and Present. *Research Observer* 12(2) August.

Winters, L. A. 1996. *Regionalism versus Multilateralism.* World Bank Policy Research Papers no. 1687.

____. 1998. Assessing Regional Integration. In World Bank, *Trade: Towards Open Regionalism.* Washington, DC: World Bank.

____. 2000. Regionalism and Multilateralism in the Twenty First Century. Inter-American Development Bank Integration and Regional Programs Department, Washington, DC.

Wonnacott, R. 1996. Trade and Investment in a Hub-and-Spoke System versus a Free Trade Area. *World Economy* 19.

Wonnacott, P., and R. Wonnacott. 1995. Liberalization in the Western Hemisphere: New Challenges in the Design of a Free Trade Agreement. *North American Journal of Economics and Finance* no. 6.

World Bank. 2000. *Trade Blocs.* Oxford University Press, Oxford.

____. 2001. *World Development Indicators.* Washington, DC: World Bank.

World Trade Organization. 1995. *Regionalism and the World Trading System.* Geneva: World Trade Organization.

Yeats, A. 1997. *Does Mercosur's Trade Performance Raise Concerns about the Effects of Regional Trade Arrangements.* World Bank Policy Research Working Paper no. 1729.

Yi, S. 1996. Endogenous Formation of Customs Unions under Imperfect Competition: Open Regionalism Is Good. *Journal of International Economics.*

Chapter 3

MARKET ACCESS

Trade liberalization through regional integration initiatives occupies a prominent chapter in any economic history of Latin America and the Caribbean in the 20th century, when external events played a key role in determining the development path for most countries in the region. When future economic historians look back at the region's turning point during the century, they will likely pay special attention to the role of the external trade policies of most countries in the region (and their most important partners) during the 1990s.

Among all the structural reforms implemented in the region in recent times, trade liberalization, particularly regarding market access, stands out as the most consistent policy. Although the extent of liberalization has varied from country to country and sector to sector, the period has clearly been the most open in the region since the period before the Great Depression of the 1930s.

Despite these historic changes, however, the agenda on hemispheric trade integration is far from completed. This chapter examines the region's complex web of unilateral, multilateral and preferential (bilateral or regional) trade liberalization efforts. These simultaneous policy endeavors have defined a new paradigm in the way that trade and integration policies have been designed and implemented throughout the region. This new paradigm was first labeled "open regionalism" by the Economic Commission on Latin America and the Caribbean, and most recently, in similar but more theoretical fashion, analyzed by Ethier (1998) and Devlin and Estevadeordal (2001) under the name of "new regionalism."

This chapter first provides an overview of Latin America's recent trade policy paradigm, quantifying the importance and the degree of trade liberalization and trade integration achieved on several fronts and with respect to various measures affecting trade. Next, the chapter focuses on agricultural trade integration, emphasizing the importance of looking beyond the region to understand the major market access constraints for agriculture. The final section evaluates the complexity of the regional trading system in the face of the challenge to negotiate further trade liberalization under the most ambitious trade negotiation effort ever in the hemisphere, the Free Trade Area of the Americas (FTAA).

UNDERSTANDING THE COMPLEX WEB OF TRADE LIBERALIZATION

Starting in the mid- to late-1980s, most of the developing world began moving toward substantial market-oriented economic reforms, which included, almost without exception, unilateral trade liberalization policies (IDB, 1996). This happened in the context of multilateral efforts in Geneva to liberalize trade in goods and services around the world, which culminated in the Uruguay Round Agreements of 1994 and the creation of the World Trade Organization in 1995. Moreover, a growing interest in regionalism was taking hold around the world, especially in Latin America, by way of traditional regional initiatives or newly crafted preferential trade agreements.

Figure 3.2   The Spaghetti Bowl: Trade Agreements Signed and Under Negotiation in the Americas

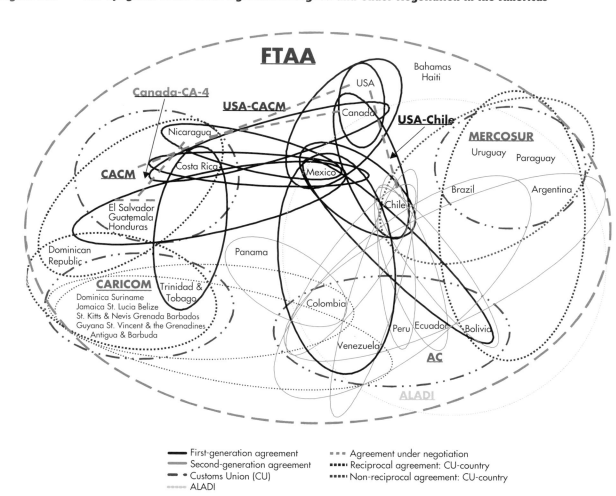

nomic advantages of free trade achieved at the multilateral level are well understood, it is sometimes difficult to evaluate net gains in a negotiating forum of more than a hundred countries with very different strategic interests acting as a constraint to new commitments. Regional and bilateral agreements offer certain advantages in this respect. These agreements are based on reciprocity principles involving a smaller group of countries. This can provide a better environment to reach consensus on the complex range of issues in modern trade agendas, better evaluate the potential gains from this bargaining exercise, and gain private sector understanding and support for the liberalization process. Ethier (1998) has pointed out that regional integration can spur multilateral liberalization by facilitating coordination. In sum, the wave of new

regionalism in the Americas—including the deepening of existing agreements and the ongoing FTAA negotiations—should be seen as complementing unilateral reforms and multilateral efforts.[1]

Preferential Tariff Liberalization

Market access negotiations under the "old" regionalism (Chapter 2) used to be carried out by means of a fixed preferential tariff under the most favored nation (MFN) tariffs and, in many cases, were only for a selected group of products or sectors. Unilateral and

---

[1] See Devlin and Ffrench-Davis (1999) and Devlin and Estevadeordal (2001).

Table 3.1 | Provisions in Selected Trade Agreements in the Americas

	NAFTA	Ecuador-Chile	G-3	Chile-Mercosur	Mexico-Nicaragua	Canada-Chile	Mexico-North Triangle	Bolivia-Mercosur	CARICOM-Dominican Rep.	Chile-Central America
Tariff elimination	√	√	√	√	√	√	√	√	√	√
HS-based rules of origin	√		√		√	√	√		√	√
ALADI-based rules of origin		√		√				√		
Special rules-auto sector	√	√	√	√		√				
Agriculture-separate chap.	√		√		√		√		√	
SPS measures	√	√	√	√	√		√	√	√	√
Technical barriers to trade	√	√	√		√		√		√	√
Investment	√	√	√	√	√	√	√		√	√
Investor-state dispute settlement	√	√		√	√	√				
Services	√	BE	√	√	√	√	√	BE	√	√
Temporary entry of business persons	√	√		√	√	√			√	√
Government procurement	√	BE	√		√				BE	√
Intellectual property	√		√	√	√		√		√	
Anti-dumping/countervail	√	√		√	√	√[1]	√	√	√	√
Competition policy						√				√
Dispute settlement	√	√	√	√	√	√	√	√	√	√
Labor/Environment	SA					SA				
Special and differential treatment		√		√				√	√	

Notes: SA = side agreement; BE = best endeavor to define in the future: the parties shall explicitly seek to develop disciplines in these areas in the future; HS = harmonization system.
[1] The parties agreed to a reciprocal exemption from the application of anti-dumping.

multilateral tariff reductions had the effect of progressively eroding the margins of preference initially agreed upon. In order to maintain those margins constant over time, countries had to renegotiate the agreements on a continuous basis. Alternatively, some agreements were negotiated by means of preferential tariff reductions as a percentage of current MFN applied rates, in this way keeping the margins of preference constant over time. Today, most new regionalism FTAs have followed the NAFTA model,[2] moving towards tariff elimination programs that are relatively quick, automatic and nearly universal. The tariff elimination mechanism follows pre-specified timetables ranging from immediate elimination up to generally a 10-year phase-out, with longer transitional periods for those products regarded as "sensitive." The negotiations usually start with an agreement on a base rate or

base level from which phase-out schedules will be applied. These rates can also be subject to negotiations with the aim of beginning the phase-out schedules from lower rates.

Figure 3.3 shows the evolution of MFN tariffs vis-à-vis the preferential rates from 1985 to 1997. The figure compares the average MFN rate for 11 Latin American countries with the average preferential rate that each country applies to all partners in this group under different bilateral or regional trade agreements. It shows in a particularly striking way the simultaneous lowering of external and internal barriers as one of the key features of new regionalism minimizing the proba-

---

[2] The internal tariff elimination mechanism in Mercosur also followed an automatic linear program.

Box 3.1   A Primer on the Gravity Model

The gravity model provides a useful framework for assessing the impact of policy variables on the behavior of bilateral flows between countries, such as trade, foreign direct investment (FDI) or migration flows. The gravity model was first applied to the analysis of international trade flows by Tinbergen (1962), Poyhonen (1963) and Linnemann (1966). Its name is derived from its passing similarity to Newtonian physics, in that large economic entities such as countries or cities are said to exert pulling power on people (migration models) or their goods (trade models) or capital (FDI models). The simplest form of the gravity model for international trade assumes that the volume of trade between any two trading partners is an increasing function of their national incomes and populations, and a decreasing function of the distance between them. It is also common to use the so-called dummy variables to capture geographical

effects (such as signaling whether the two countries share a border, or if a country has access to the sea), cultural and historical similarities (such as if two countries share a language or were linked by past colonial ties), regional integration (such as belonging to a free trade agreement or sharing a common currency), as well as other macroeconomic policy variables (such as bilateral exchange rate volatility). Although widely used because of its empirical success, the gravity model had lacked rigorous theoretical underpinnings, and was long criticized for being an ad hoc model. However, Anderson (1979), Bergstrand (1985), and Helpman and Krugman (1985) have derived gravity equations from trade models based on product differentiation and increasing returns to scale. Evenett and Keller (2002) provide a good overview of this debate.

whether those agreements are good or bad for world welfare from a theoretical perspective. However, the empirical evidence is still relatively limited, and we know very little about the magnitude and significance of changes in trade barriers on a preferential basis and the resulting changes in bilateral trade volumes. Most of the recent literature has explored the effects of preferential trade agreements on trade volumes using a gravity model with the inclusion of dummy variables for trade agreements (see Box 3.1).[5] In general, the effects of a free trade agreement on intra-area trade are quite large. Frankel (1997) has found that the formation of the EC raised trade among European countries by about 65 percent, and Mercosur and the Andean Pact promoted trade by a factor of about two-and-a-half among their partners. Estevadeordal and Robertson (2002) have examined the effects of preferential agreements on the volume of bilateral trade employing a gravity equation by precisely measuring preferential tariffs.[6] They analyze the role of preferential and MFN tariffs on the volume of trade, based on a specification advocated by Anderson and van Wincoop (2000) with data from several Latin American countries and its major industrialized partners, the United States, Canada, Europe and Japan.

One of the key advantages of this gravity approach is that it directly compares the contributions of "policy" frictions, such as tariffs, with "geographical" frictions due mainly to transportation costs.[7] A consistent result of the gravity equation literature is that transportation costs, as proxied by distance to markets, have a large and significant effect on trade volumes. If distance dwarfs the effects of trade barriers, then countries that are relatively far from larger markets may not experience large benefits from integration agreements. Estevadeordal and Robertson (2002), however, find that tariff elasticities (the percent change in trade vol-

---

[5] See Frankel (1997). There is also considerable literature based on general equilibrium models that estimates the impact on trade of liberalization, including scenarios of regional trade agreements not reviewed here.

[6] Linnemann and Verbruggen (1991) have explicitly studied the impact of tariffs on bilateral trade patterns using a gravity model framework. However, Estevadeordal and Robertson (2002) is the first study that explicitly incorporates preferential tariff rates in a gravity model.

[7] It is important to understand the magnitude of the impact of removing those frictions on trade, since some studies also find a positive relationship between trade and growth (Frankel and Romer, 1999). However, the argument that trade liberalization leads to growth has been disputed by others (Rodríguez and Rodrik, 1999).

umes induced by a 1 percent change in tariffs) are almost equivalent in magnitude to the effects of distance. This suggests that while countries cannot change their location, they can change trade policy in a way to increase the benefits of trade. For example, Chile, which suffers a geographical disadvantage in terms of distance from most industrialized markets, experienced a large increase in bilateral trade after signing a bilateral FTA with Mexico. A similar result is expected from Chile's recent agreement with Canada and one currently being negotiated with the United States. Therefore, FTAs are a speedy way to look for new trade opportunities with distance partners, as in the case of the agreements with the European Union or other Northern partners.

Rules of Origin

Rules of origin are an important but often forgotten aspect in analysis of market access in FTAs. Under an FTA, each country maintains its own external tariffs vis-à-vis the outside world.[8] To the extent that these barriers differ, there is always the incentive to import a good through the country with the lowest barriers. Rules of origin are required to prevent such trade deflection. They specify the conditions that goods must meet in order to be deemed as "originating" and hence be eligible for preferential tariff treatment. The growth of international trade in goods that are not manufactured in a single country has made the issue of the rules for determining the "origin" of traded goods one of the most important and complex areas of preferential market access negotiations.

While the simpler rules rely on a single uniform criterion across all products, such as in ALADI-type agreements, the more complex agreements such as NAFTA[9] use a general rule plus additional specific rules negotiated at the product level, combining in different ways three methods to establish "substantial transformation." Those methods can be defined in terms of a "tariff shift" approach, a "value-added" criterion, or a "technical test."[10] Immediate precedents of the NAFTA model, with a lower degree of specificity, are the rules of origin contained in the FTA between the United States and Canada. The rules negotiated under the G-3 agreement, the Mexican bilateral agreements with Costa Rica and Bolivia, and the recent Chilean

bilateral agreement with Mexico and Canada are also close to the NAFTA model. Meanwhile, rules introduced under Mercosur and its bilateral agreements with Chile and Bolivia, as well as the Central America Common Market, can be considered intermediate models between the two extreme cases.[11]

Although rules of origin are well known to trade lawyers and customs specialists (Vermulst and Bourgeois, 1994), they have only recently caught the attention of economists. While the impact of political and economic interests in shaping rules of origin is well known, there have been few attempts to estimate those effects. Economic analysis has been relatively limited both in terms of formal modeling as well as empirical testing. It has been argued that the way in which rules of origin are defined and applied within modern preferential agreements plays an important role in determining the degree of protection they confer and the level of trade distortion effects that they produce (Hoekman, 1993). One of the most convincing treatments of the potential "hidden" protectionism of rules of origin has been by Krishna and Krueger (1995), who argued that, provided that margins of preference are large and rules are restrictive, they can induce a switch in the sourcing of low-cost nonregional to high-cost regional

---

[8] This is a key difference with a customs union, where the members maintain common external tariffs vis-à-vis the rest of the world.

[9] NAFTA arguably contains the most sophisticated origin regime yet devised. These highly disaggregated and heterogeneous rules run for many pages and make liberal use of the different types of origin methodologies. Understandably, the negotiating history of NAFTA is replete with battles over the content of specific rules of origin, for the difference between a favorable and unfavorable rule can easily run in the millions of dollars annually for some firms.

[10] The "tariff shift" criterion requires that after transformation of one or several imported inputs in the exporting (originating) country, the processed product exported falls under a different heading of the tariff nomenclature than that under which the imported inputs were classified. The "value-added" criterion prescribes the minimum percentage of value that must be added in the exporting country or the maximum percentage of value accounted by imports in order to be qualified as originating. Finally, the "technical test" is based on manufacturing or processing operations that are required to confer originating status.

[11] While the method for conferring origin to a product constitutes the central element of an origin regime in a free trade agreement, there are other important provisions that are not analyzed in this chapter. These include the cumulative provisions that establish the conditions under which imports from certain sources may be counted as domestically supplied in the preference-receiving exporting country. Other provisions related to origin consideration include whether or not there are duty drawback rules.

Appendix 3.2
Agriculture Trade Policy Reform
in the Americas[1]

Agricultural trade barriers and producer subsidies distort global agriculture, a sector where Latin America and the Caribbean have a salient comparative advantage and strong export competitiveness. Trade barriers lower demand for products from trade partners; domestic support creates an excess supply of agricultural products, and export subsidies lead to lower prices. The current negotiations on market access and agriculture in the FTAA process will offer promising opportunities and potential gains for countries in the region.

To evaluate the potential trade effects of agricultural reform, a multi-region, multi-sector, comparative static CGE model was used. The analysis focuses on three pillars of agricultural policies distorting world prices and restricting trade flows: market access (trade barriers), domestic support, and export subsidies. The model simulates to examine the individual and complementary effects of these policy variables in the Western Hemisphere. It also assesses the impact of the liberalization of agriculture between Mercosur and the European Union under negotiation.

In the Western Hemisphere, the elimination of all tariffs (including tariff equivalents) increases Latin America's exports by 14 percent. However, the impact significantly differs by sector. Due mainly to high protection across the hemisphere, dairy and beverage/tobacco exports grow fastest at 25 percent and 22 percent, respectively, followed by sugar and oilseeds (23 percent and 19 percent, respectively). The removal of domestic support has few positive effects on Latin America's exports except for oilseeds (2.7 percent), and eliminating export subsidies alone does not appear to enhance exports.

For Mercosur, the patterns of trade gains from the Mercosur-EU liberalization are sharply distinguished from those of the hemispheric agricultural reform process. The elimination of tariffs between the two blocs increases Mercosur's exports by 37 percent. Among the agricultural exports from Mercosur, bovine

---

[1] Based on Monteagudo and Watanuki (2002).

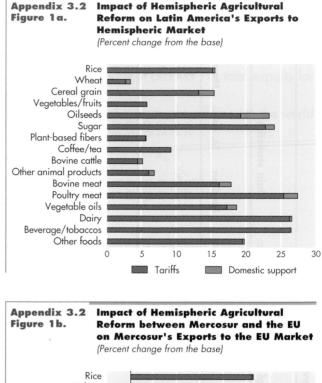

Appendix 3.2 Figure 1a. **Impact of Hemispheric Agricultural Reform on Latin America's Exports to Hemispheric Market**
(Percent change from the base)

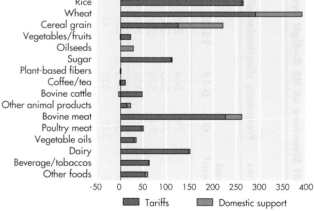

Appendix 3.2 Figure 1b. **Impact of Hemispheric Agricultural Reform between Mercosur and the EU on Mercosur's Exports to the EU Market**
(Percent change from the base)

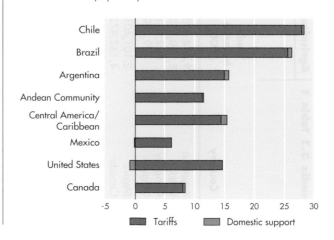

Appendix 3.2 Figure 1c. **Impact of Agricultural Reform on Exports in the Western Hemisphere**
(In percent)

meat dramatically jumps by almost 230 percent, due largely to the EU's highest initial protection (55 percent ad valorem equivalent). Mercosur also increases exports of other foods and poultry meat by more than 10 percent. The EU's removal of domestic support increases the bloc's exports by 2.7 percent. Exports of bovine meat jump by 36 percent and oilseeds by 27 percent. The abolishment of the EU's export subsidies in a variety of agricultural commodities again does not boost exports. However, due to strong complementary effects among policy variables, the implementation of all agricultural reforms chiefly in the European Union raises Mercosur's exports by 55 percent from the baseline.

In sum, Latin America will greatly benefit from agricultural reform in the Western Hemisphere and beyond. The elimination of high protection for agricultural commodities in the form of tariffs is the primary factor contributing to the potential trade gains. Compared with the hemispheric agricultural reform, the liberalization process with the European Union also generates sizable positive effects (on Mercosur). The simulation therefore suggests that the simultaneous integration process would likely create strong cross-fertilization effects for countries in Latin America.

Krishna, K., and A. O. Krueger. 1995. Implementing Free Trade Areas, Rules of Origin and Hidden Protection. In A. Deardorff, J. Levinsohn, and R. Stern (eds.), *New Directions in Trade Theory Safeguard.* Ann Arbor: University of Michigan Press.

Linnemann, H. 1966. *An Econometric Study of International Trade Flows.* Amsterdam: North-Holland.

Linnemann, H., and H. Verbruggen. 1991. GSTP Tariff Reduction and Its Effects on South-South Trade in Manufactures. *World Development* 19(5) May.

Monteagudo, J., and M. Watanuki. 2002. Evaluation of the Potential Effects of Agricultural Reform in Regional Negotiations. FTAA and Mercosur-EU Agreement. Inter-American Development Bank, Washington, DC. Mimeo.

Olarreaga, M., and I. Soloaga. 1997. Endogenous Tariff Formation: The Case of Mercosur. World Bank Development Research Group.

Organisation for Economic Co-operation and Development (OECD). 2001. *Agricultural Policies in OECD Countries: Monitoring and Evaluation 2001.* Paris: OECD, Agriculture and Food Division.

Panagariya, A. 1992. Input Tariffs and Duty Drawback in the Design of Tariff Reforms. *Journal of International Economics* 32.

Poyhonen, P. 1963. A Tentative Model for the Volume of Trade Between Countries. Weltwirtschaftliches Archive, vol. 90.

Rodríguez, F., and D. Rodrik. 1999. *Trade Policy and Economic Growth: A Skeptic's Guide to the Cross-National Evidence.* NBER Working Paper no. 7081, April.

Sandrey, R. 2000. *The Relative Tariff Ratio Index.* New Zealand Trade Consortium Working Paper no. 7.

Serra, J. et al. 1996. *Reflections on Regionalism.* Washington, DC: Carnegie Endowment for Peace.

Skully, D. 2001a. Economics of Tariff-Rate Quota Administration. Economic Research Service/USDA.

———. 2001b. Economics of Price Bands and Price Band Efficiency. SP/SAC-OMC/Di 17. March.

Tinbergen, J. 1962. Shaping the World Economy-Suggestions for an International Economic Policy. The Twentieth Century Fund.

Tsigas, M., and M. Ingco. 2001. Market Access Liberalization for Food and Agricultural Products. A General Equilibrium Assessment of Tariff-Rate Quotas. U.S. International Trade Commission.

UNCTAD. 2001. Improving Market Access for Least Developed Countries. UNCTAD/DITC/TNCD/4, United Nations.

Vermulst, E., and J. Bourgeois (eds.). 1994. *Rules of Origin in International Trade. A Comparative Study.* Ann Arbor: University of Michigan Press.

Wollrath, T. 1998. RTAs and Agriculture Trade: A Retrospective Assessment. In M. Burfisher and E. Jones, *Regional Trade Agreements and U.S. Agriculture.* Washington, DC: Economic Research Service, Market and Trade Economic Division, U.S. Department of Agriculture.

World Trade Organization (WTO). 2001 Market Access: Unfinished Business. Economic Research and Analysis Division.

Chapter 4

REGIONAL INSTITUTIONS AND DISPUTE SETTLEMENT MECHANISMS

Over the last couple of decades, there has been a growing awareness in academic and policymaking circles regarding the importance of institutions for economic development. Institutions constitute the rules of the game in a society or, more precisely, the restrictions designed by members of a society to influence human interaction. Any transformation affecting these rules may clearly have a direct impact on behavioral patterns (North, 1990).

As new cross-country institutional databases have become available, a growing body of empirical work has been confirming the important role played by the quality of institutions in a wide variety of dimensions of economic performance, such as the depth of financial markets, success in attracting foreign direct investment (FDI) or keeping inflation under control, and, most importantly, the growth performance of nations.

While institutions have an impact on economic development, important economic reforms, such as the creation of a regional integration agreement, may in turn affect the development of national institutions. They do so by establishing new rules and expectations as to how various policy options should be selected and implemented; by opening up new opportunities as well as establishing restrictions in the design and application of economic and trade policy; by generating new stakeholders while disenfranchising previous ones; and by laying the groundwork for a new philosophy in development policy. Accordingly, Rodrik (1999, 2000) has pointed out that assessing the ultimate effectiveness of economic and trade policy reforms should be based not only on their immediate impact on economic variables, but also in terms of their contribution to the development of a high-quality institutional environment in a given country.

The move toward trade liberalization in the countries of Latin America under the framework of the World Trade Organization (WTO), as well as the formation of regional trade agreements, has tested the adequacy of the prevailing institutions, both at the national and regional level, and in various instances led to their strengthening and reform.

Just as national institutions are key determinants of national economic performance, regional integration agreements also require their own well-functioning institutions in order to be effective. The effectiveness of regional integration agreements, in terms of their impact on trade and investment flows, is closely related to the capacity of the countries involved to enforce the obligations stipulated in such agreements. This chapter describes the key institutional factors involved in integration experiences in the region. In particular, it looks at the development of dispute settlement procedures, discusses the extent to which they have been used, and demonstrates the vital policy role that these mechanisms play in the process of economic integration.

INSTITUTIONAL ASPECTS OF THE REGIONAL INTEGRATION PROCESS

Observance of the rule of law plays a vital role in sustaining and increasing trade and investment flows between countries participating in an integration scheme. To that end, private players consider an effective, transparent regulatory and legal framework, as well as the establishment of institutional mechanisms and structures to regulate the interaction between the different players involved, to be a necessary precondition for the integration process.

The structures of institutional organization that accompany the coordination and implementation of trade integration must be considered as part of this process. In other words, how will the necessary communication and decision-making links, as well as the mechanisms to settle disputes arising between countries, be established?

Examination of regional integration finds two model institutional structures regarding the vertical dimension: minimalist and maximalist (Mattli, 2001).[1] These models explain the extent to which decision-making and authority shift from the national levels to the regional or global ones (Box 4.1).

Intergovernmental Institutional Model

Under the intergovernmental or minimalist institutional model, the countries, protective of their national sovereignty, retain power and initiative for decision and action. The process is therefore based fundamentally on interaction between governments. Under this scheme, the institutions are agents to which the governments grant few powers. As a result, the institutions lack sufficient authority and cannot effectively move the integration process forward any more quickly than dictated by the wishes of the countries, according to their interests and priorities. Under this minimalist institutional model, the larger countries exercise de facto veto power over the rules of the process, which tend as a result to converge toward the lowest common denominator reflecting the interests of those countries. Some experts believe that this model also entails the problem of supervision and how to avoid noncompliance with agreements.

Supranational Institutional Model

At the other extreme is the supranational, or maximalist institutional model, under which the policy players are persuaded to transfer their activities and expecta-

tions to a new, broader central authority in which the institutions have some jurisdiction over the member countries. In contrast with the minimum institutional model, the governments give broad powers to the supranational institutions so that they are not merely specialized technical agents serving the countries, but play a strategic role in the integration process, with a clear mandate for its promotion. The capacity and autonomy of supranational institutions to play this strategic role depend, however, on the rules established and the discretion of the mandate that they are given.

Regional Experience

Based upon the objectives of the agreements involved, regional economic integration processes in the Western Hemisphere have been developed on the basis of both the intergovernmental institution model as well as on supranational institutional structures.

The North American Free Trade Agreement (NAFTA) is clearly the best example of a minimalist institutional integration model. From the beginning of the negotiations, the participating countries made two fundamental decisions on the architecture of the treaty: that it would be strictly a free trade agreement and that the governing mechanisms and institutions would be limited to a minimum. The deliberate decision to establish a minimalist institutional arrangement is explained by the hesitance of the U.S. executive branch and Congress to establish new institutions.[2] This preference was welcomed by the governments of Canada and Mexico, as the negotiators from all three countries shared two concerns about the institutional structure of the treaty—its repercussions on national sovereignty and its costs—and these concerns prevailed in the design and architecture of NAFTA.

The special concern of the United States, the largest partner, about sovereignty was also reflected in the dispute settlement mechanisms provided in the treaty. Washington's position, for example, was that

---

[1] According to Mattli, horizontal integration refers to the mechanisms of communication and integration between the public sector, the private sector, and civil society in general.

[2] Weintraub (1994, p. 28).

Box 4.1 Institutional Organization in Regional Integration Arrangements: Decision-making and Executive Bodies

Supranational or Maximalist Model

The supranational or maximalist model generally involves subregional organizations with international legal status and powers transcending those of the member countries. These organizations typically include certain permanent decision-making and executive bodies.

A *policy steering body* comprised of presidents or ministers of the member country governments and vested with legislative powers is generally the highest authority in the process. It exercises maximum political representation for the group, formulates policy on integration, and is responsible for making decisions to ensure that the objectives of the process are met.

The policy steering body is generally complemented by an *executive body* that ensures compliance with and execution of arrangements and programs adopted by the member countries, generally in direct coordination with the jurisdictional authority. These bodies typically have the capacity to make proposals to the competent legislative authorities.

In addition, there is generally a *jurisdictional body* that is responsible for enforcement and uniform interpretation of the agreement. It hears disputes in which member countries may be involved, and its decisions are binding. In most cases, the jurisdictional body also presides over disputes that involve subregional institutions, firms and individuals.

Many arrangements based on the maximalist model also include a *parliamentary body* as well as bodies representing other sectors of society. The parliamentary body, comprised of representatives from member country legislatures, generally plays a consultative and deliberative role and has few if any legislative pow-

ers. Other bodies generally include representatives from economic and social sectors, including the private sector.

Inter-Governmental or Minimalist Model

The minimalist model rests exclusively on inter-governmental decision-making and coordination authority and as such has no supranational institutions with independent legal status. The decision-making and executive bodies under this type of arrangement generally include an *administrative commission for the agreement* that is responsible for enforcement and proper application of obligations. Comprised of ministers of trade and integration, it serves as a consultative body, with responsibility for settling disputes between countries related to the application and interpretation of the agreement. The commission has limited powers to propose and agree on new regulatory texts.

Another component of this model is the *technical committees, working parties and expert groups*. These entities are responsible for technical monitoring of the implementation of specific obligations stipulated in the agreement, for proposing ad hoc recommendations to the administrative commission on various topics, and for conducting technical studies.

Finally, the *dispute settlement bodies* serve as mechanisms for resolving differences between the parties through settlement proceedings conducted by an impartial outside authority (panel), based on standards and principles previously approved and established in the agreement.

each country's national legislation should apply in the treatment of laws against unfair trade practices. In other words, the agreement substantially constitutes an instrument to ensure transparent application of national regulations. This is also the spirit of the parallel agreements on labor and environment. The situation is different, however, in the case of the mechanism for settling disputes between countries, which is analyzed below.

The NAFTA negotiation for all three countries involved a key foreign policy initiative. As a result, no complex institutional structures were required to hold the governments' interest in the process. Because of the importance that it represented to all three countries, NAFTA also helped improve the technical and decision-making capacity of the three signatory countries by introducing important institutional changes in all

ments: they must be expeditious, effective and inexpensive.

They must be expeditious in that they must have the capacity to determine quickly whether or not a given measure is compatible with the obligations under the trade treaty. If a given measure has been contested, it is likely that in practice the measure represents a substantial source of economic damage to a given economic sector. Hence the need for issuing a resolution on the legality of this measure as quickly as possible in order to avoid lengthy interruptions and distortions to free and normal trade flows. An expeditious settlement process becomes a particularly pressing objective when the controversy involves relatively small, highly vulnerable enterprises in the export markets, as is normally the case when one of the parties to the dispute is a small economy.[12]

Despite the vital importance for a dispute settlement mechanism to operate expeditiously, this goal is in fact often difficult to achieve in practice. First, the country affected by the contested practices will be required to dedicate some time to amicable consultations with the government that imposed the measures, in order to explore the possibility of reaching a settlement. Second, depending on the obligation in question and the contested measure, settlement of the conflict may require establishing numerous facts and complex scientific or technical records, inherently requiring the participation of experts in the process. This process tends to be time-consuming.[13]

It is also vitally important that dispute settlement mechanisms be effective. Such mechanisms should serve as the last resort to induce the party that violated an obligation to comply with the settlement. The effectiveness of the systems should also be such that the penalty or threat thereof must be sufficiently credible to serve as a clear deterrent against violating the obligations involved. The effectiveness of these mechanisms is vital to executing the intrinsic function of the system—what good is a settlement if it is not observed? Further, effectiveness is basic to the credibility of the system and the economic integration process as a whole. Despite the importance of effective mechanisms, however, there are many cases in the Western Hemisphere when resolutions are ignored by the party involved, seriously undermining the credibility of the integration process.

Another fundamental feature of dispute settlement mechanisms, particularly in the context of developing countries, is to be usable at a low cost. The cost of resorting to dispute settlement proceedings should be substantially lower than the cost of tolerating the disputed measure. Further, if another function of the legal dispute settlement system is to try to smooth the immense asymmetries derived from economic or political differences between the countries, then the weakest countries are those that most need such settlement mechanisms to defend their interests.

Countries having greater economic weight, in fact, are in a better position to defend their interests with alternative methods to legal settlement. The facts, however, indicate an ironic reality. In many regional integration arrangements in the Western Hemisphere, and at the multilateral level in the World Trade Organization, the relatively more developed countries are the ones that most frequently use dispute settlement mechanisms. This suggests not only the need to assess the incidence of the costs of such proceedings on their use by relatively less-developed countries, but also the need to strengthen the institutions by establishing technical teams in the competent agencies to enable countries to make effective use of the dispute settlement mechanisms theoretically available to defend their trade interests.

EVOLUTION AND USE OF DISPUTE SETTLEMENT MECHANISMS

Experience in the settlement of trade disputes at the regional and multilateral levels can be analyzed from

---

[12] For an enterprise whose total income is generated by foreign sales, being prevented from placing products on its traditional export market as a result of a problem under a trade agreement is tantamount to undergoing financial suffocation. This vulnerability increases in the case of small economies for which the exporting enterprises tend to have export markets highly concentrated in one or several countries. This underscores the need for dispute settlement mechanisms to include precautionary measures and remedies to avoid irreparable damage. In this connection, however, there is much scope for improvement in international legal doctrine and negotiating practices at the regional and multilateral levels.

[13] In light of the WTO, there are also delays attributable to the requirement to conduct the proceeding in more than one language. One of the challenges of the WTO's dispute settlement mechanism has been the need to translate the lengthy reports from panels into the organization's three official languages.

two standpoints. First, it is important to observe the actual features of dispute settlement mechanisms under different integration arrangements in order to identify predominant patterns in the legal evolution of this type of regulation. The second standpoint focuses not on the evolution of dispute settlement procedures, but on their use in different subregional integration schemes as well as in the WTO.

Evolution: "Legalization" and Regulatory Migration

Although experience with regional integration in Latin America dates to the 1960s, the topic of negotiation and the use of dispute settlement processes conceived as adjudication instruments did not begin to take effect until almost 30 years later with the rise of what has been called the "new regionalism" of the 1990s.

Until the early 1990s, interpretation of or compliance with the obligations established under economic integration agreements tended to be viewed as problems that could or should be resolved by the parties themselves. As a result, settling trade disputes in these treaties was originally designed primarily as processes of political consultation between the interested parties rather than settlement processes. This can be seen in the many bilateral agreements of partial scope negotiated between the 1960s and 1980s in the framework of the Latin American Integration Association (LAIA).[14] By contrast, in customs unions established during the 1960s and 1970s, the formal existence of supranational courts either proved ineffective or did not become effective until the 1990s.[15]

The negotiation of legally oriented dispute settlement mechanisms beginning in the 1990s reflects the events in the multilateral arena during that period. The "legalization" of the dispute settlement system was one of the main results of the Uruguay Round that culminated in the establishment of the new institutional structure of the multilateral trade system. With the entry into force of the Dispute Settlement Understanding (DSU) in 1995, the legal orientation of dispute settlement mechanisms of the multilateral trade system was consolidated with the development of two fundamental characteristics: the possibility that a resolution by a panel could be binding, even without the unsuccessful party's consent; and the establishment of the Appellate

Body responsible exclusively for examining potential legal errors in resolutions by panels.

The fact that the resurgence of the regional economic integration process in the Western Hemisphere began during the early 1990s, when the Uruguay Round was still pending completion, largely explains the influence of the latter on the architecture of the integration schemes that began to be negotiated during that period.

This "regulatory migration" resulted in part from the interest of the United States in reflecting at the regional level the same trade agenda that was proposed in the multilateral arena. It is therefore no accident that NAFTA negotiations comprised practically the same content as the Uruguay Round, including what were known at the time as new issues, which until then had been excluded from regional trade agreements. Once NAFTA was negotiated, it became a model free trade agreement that was reproduced throughout Latin America—first by Mexico and later by Chile and the countries of Central America.

The influence of the WTO in determining the characteristics of the dispute settlement procedures included in the hemisphere's subregional economic integration agreements has been an ongoing process. Lessons learned from the application of the WTO's Dispute Settlement Understanding were reflected in the dispute settlement instruments negotiated recently among countries in the hemisphere. Moreover, preferential agreements negotiated in the region provided solutions to problems that arose in application of that understanding.[16]

---

[14] Resolution 114 of the LAIA provides for consultation by the parties or intervention by the Committee of Representatives as mechanisms to settle disputes regarding obligations under the 1980 Montevideo Treaty.

[15] See footnote 7 regarding the Central American Court of Justice. In the case of the Andean Community, the court was not established as a legal body until 1979. The Cochabamba Protocol, which has been in effect since 1999 and now governs the functioning and competence of that court, was not signed by the AC members until 1996.

[16] For example, recently negotiated dispute settlement instruments such as the Mercosur Olivos Protocol, the CACM Dispute Settlement Treaty, and the chapter on dispute settlement in the free trade agreement between Canada and Costa Rica explicitly prohibited one of the parties in a dispute from determining unilaterally whether the other party had effectively complied with the recommendations of the panels, thereby eliminating any doubt in connection with the application of Article 21.5 of the Dispute Settlement Understanding disputed in the context of the WTO.

Table 4.2 | **Number of Trade Disputes between Western Hemisphere Countries**

	1995	1996	1997	1998	1999	2000	2001
Referrals to the WTO	3	5	9	2	7	14	13
Subregional disputes:[1]	8	7	4	17	19	26	15
NAFTA	7	3	1	5	0	1	0
AC	1	3	3	10	14	23	7
Mercosur	0	1	0	1	5	2	8
CACM	0	0	0	1	0	0	0

[1] Conflicts formally submitted to dispute settlement mechanisms.

dispute settlement mechanisms. In such cases, the governments of the parties do not hold the monopoly on activating the dispute settlement mechanism, which multiplies the risk that petitions not sponsored by any government are filed, which could lead to problems in system compliance and effectiveness.

From a time standpoint, Table 4.2 shows a trend that merits discussion owing to its important implications. While in both the Andean Community and Mercosur, the number of disputes grew substantially beginning in 1998, in the case of NAFTA, the number of requests for consultation were concentrated during 1995-98, and began to decline substantially in 1999. In the Andean Community, the number of disputes submitted for consideration by the Andean Court of Justice tripled in 1998 compared with the preceding year—a trend that continued in 1999, intensified in 2000, and declined abruptly in 2001. In the case of Mercosur, the number of disputes brought before the dispute settlement mechanism began to increase in 1998, and increased further in 1999 and 2001.

In the cases of Mercosur and the Andean Community, the increased use of the dispute settlement mechanism would seem to be associated with pressures derived from financial and political crises that affected virtually all member countries during that period.[19] This trend would also seem evident in the case of NAFTA. The highest number of requests for consultation were registered from 1995—which marked the beginning of the Mexican financial crisis and the devaluation of the peso—until 1998. Of the 16 dispute settlement cases filed during that period, more than

half were initiated by Mexico, and all were against the United States, suggesting Mexico's reaction to the restrictive trade measures implemented by its main trading partner.

The increased used of trade dispute settlement systems in times of crisis—at least in some trading blocs—suggests two concepts vital to understanding the context and function of these mechanisms. An initial conclusion seems to be that governments are more likely to apply protectionist measures in times of crisis (see Chapter 7). A second conclusion, perhaps less evident and more important than the first, is that increased use of dispute settlement mechanisms in times of crisis would appear to highlight the important function of these mechanisms as a protective shield for the gradual process of economic liberalization and as a counterweight against protectionist pressures that tend to gain negotiating power against governments whose political capital is eroded by the crisis.[20]

Lessons from the WTO

The credibility of the WTO Dispute Settlement Understanding is reflected in the increasing use that countries in the hemisphere have made of this mechanism, in

---

[19] Brazil was forced to devalue the real and most members of the Andean Community recorded serious economic imbalances.

[20] See Echandi and Robert (forthcoming), for a more specific analysis of particular trends in the use of mechanisms to solve trade disputes under certain specific integration agreements and the WTO.

proportions that even exceed the relative share of their reciprocal trade flows in world trade. Approximately 25 percent of the total dispute settlement cases filed under the WTO were between countries in the Western Hemisphere.[21]

Many of these cases involved countries of the region that were not members of any integration scheme or free trade agreement amongst themselves, and therefore had no alternative dispute settlement mechanism under such preferential agreements. As a result, recourse to the WTO was the only option. It is interesting to note, however, the substantial number of conflicts that have arisen in the framework of the WTO Dispute Settlement Understanding between countries in the region that are both members of a preferential agreement for trade or integration. This is true of Canada, the United States and Mexico, as well as some of the conflicts that have occurred between Mercosur countries and between the latter countries and others with which they have some preferential association agreement, such as Chile.[22]

The substantial number of cases between countries in the region that are not members of preferential trade or integration schemes or agreements evidences the importance that an ultimate dispute settlement scheme would have within the context of the Free Trade Area of the Americas (FTAA).

There is another hypothesis as to why countries that have alternative mechanisms at their disposal under preferential arrangements are increasingly turning to the WTO Dispute Settlement Understanding. Clearly, even if a preferential arrangement exists, the challenged measure may involve a violation of obligations under multilateral agreements rather than those stipulated in the framework of preferential arrangements. In this case, recourse to the multilateral mechanism is the only option.

It would seem, however, that other variables also explain the frequent use of the multilateral mechanism to resolve conflicts between members of a bilateral or subregional agreement. In some cases, there may be the perception that the multilateral mechanism might be more effective considering the sensitivity of the issue or conflict in question, and that the subsequent politicization of the controversy in the framework of preferential regional or bilateral relations might make the conflict difficult to resolve. In addition, recourse to the multilateral system enables alliances to be developed with other countries having similar interests, thus helping intensify the pressure to eliminate or amend the questioned measure. For example, in many conflicts that have arisen in the WTO between countries of the region, other countries of the Western Hemisphere, besides the defendant or complainant, have appeared as interested third parties. Last, use of the multilateral mechanism provides incentives to promote the creation of jurisprudence, which is found to be quite important, particularly when addressing very sensitive issues that also have more global implications and scope.

The satisfactory record of compliance in the WTO shows the effectiveness of the multilateral mechanism and lends it great credibility, which is quite important for countries in the region, particularly when dealing with economies of different sizes and having substantial asymmetries in terms of political and economic power.

Trends in the use of the Dispute Settlement Understanding by Western Hemisphere countries also indicate the importance of existing interrelations between the multilateral trade system and regional and bilateral agreements. This is particularly important in the context of the negotiations in progress in connection with the WTO as well as the FTAA.

These dynamics will create vital synergies between both processes of negotiation, with important implications in the area of dispute settlement. The synergies will probably promote a greater "regulatory migration" between both agreements, as was true for the NAFTA and the WTO agreements negotiated during the Uruguay Round.[23]

The foregoing presents major challenges for countries of the region, which, with their aim to create

---

[21] More than half the cases are related to the application of unfair trade practices and safeguard measures. In addition, in a number of cases, disputes were related to patent protection and compliance with obligations under the agreements on agriculture, agricultural goods, and textiles and clothing.

[22] See Echandi and Robert (forthcoming).

[23] In many free trade agreements in effect in the Western Hemisphere, the trend has been to refer to WTO regulations to govern certain aspects of bilateral trade (such as technical barriers to trade and sanitary and phytosanitary measures), and the provisions of the WTO regulation have been incorporated into the free trade agreements.

Table 5.1 | Current Foreign Bank Ownership in Selected Developed and Emerging Markets, 2001

Region	Total assets (US$ billions)	Number of banks	Foreign control[1] (%)
Developed countries			
New Zealand	83.9	16	99.20
Luxembourg	493.0	118	92.71
Finland	254.0	11	63.48
United States	10,800.0	744	10.3
Japan	8,720.0	211	0.02
Sweden	557.0	28	0.42
Emerging markets			
Europe			
Czech Republic	50.3	21	92.99
Hungary	28.2	29	68.84
Poland	85.4	39	63.58
Turkey	156.0	45	6.68
Uzbekistan	4.7	8	0.93
Yugoslavia	26.8	13	0.00
Latin America			
Mexico	156.0	38	76.53
Argentina	166.0	97	54.50
Peru	20.1	17	53.75
Chile	77.1	28	43.71
Venezuela	31.6	70	42.28
Brazil	397.0	138	30.61
Colombia	31.4	39	21.35
Asia			
Malaysia	180.0	51	16.76
Korea	496.0	27	8.73
Thailand	155.0	23	6.37
Indonesia	87.4	67	4.92
India	273.0	75	0.80
China	1,090.0	37	0.21

[1] Ratio of assets of banks where foreigners own more than 50 percent of total equity to total assets.
Source: IDB estimates based on data from Fitch IBCA's Bankscope database.

i) the lack of the political cohesion necessary to carry through on protocols and develop the parallel legislative programs that need to accompany financial integration; ii) the heterogeneity of domestic regulatory institutions and the persistence of fiscal imbalances; iii) the lack of recognition of foreign regulations, constraining the "home country control" principle; iv) the frequent acquiescence to interest group pressures; and v) the threat implied by currency misalignments. Clearly, achieving European levels of financial integration in Latin America does not seem viable at least in the short run. However there are particular groups that have vested interests in achieving at least some more basic forms of financial integration, such as by harmonizing regulations and institutional arrangements for information sharing across countries, as discussed above. Examples of these groups are foreign banks or corporations that have business in or with several countries of the region, and that would benefit directly from financial integration.

The lack of capital in the region has led to a strong North-South de facto integration as opposed to a South-South integration pattern. Even formal efforts to integrate into external markets have focused on gaining access to financial markets in the North. For this reason, the remainder of this chapter will focus on de facto integration, particularly the internationalization of the banking and stock market sectors, discussing in each case its evolution, as well as the benefits and costs associated with it.

FOREIGN BANK PENETRATION IN DOMESTIC FINANCIAL SYSTEMS

Foreign direct investment (FDI) worldwide was notably dynamic during the 1990s. FDI in emerging markets grew from $19.3 billion to $142.6 billion during the decade. FDI in financial services was also of note, particularly that originating in OECD countries, which accounted for nearly 23 percent of total FDI from OECD countries in 1990 and 31 percent in 1998. Latin America and Central Europe were the major recipients of international capital flows to the banking sector.

Table 5.1 shows current foreign participation in selected developed and emerging market banking systems. The table reveals that foreign banking is of great importance in Latin America and Eastern Europe. During the second half of the 1990s, the share of foreign ownership of banks in both regions increased significantly.[13] Figure 5.3 shows that foreign ownership of banking institutions grew notably between 1994 and 2001 in Latin America.

Most foreign investment in banking in Latin America comes from OECD country banks, particularly Spanish and U.S. institutions.[14] Table 5.2 shows the source of foreign banking grouped by world regions. Europe has the highest degree of intra-regional financial integration (15.9 percent), followed by Africa and the Middle East (7.7 percent), while Latin America has the lowest (0.6 percent).[15] Between regions, the major recipient of foreign participation has been Latin America, where OECD countries, Europe, the United States and Canada own 46.5 percent, 28.2 percent and 18 percent, respectively, of total assets of the regional banking system.

These numbers, however, underestimate the influence of foreign banks in Latin American economies. In most cases, foreign bank participation is accompanied by a very relevant role in managing private pension funds. Table 5.3 shows the share of foreign firms in pension funds in Latin American countries. The share is highest in Bolivia, Peru and Argentina, where foreign intermediaries account for nearly 85.3 percent, 78.5 percent and 73.6 percent of pension funds, respectively. In mature systems such as that of Chile, where the size of the system is nearly 54 percent of GDP, foreign firms manage 54.1 percent.

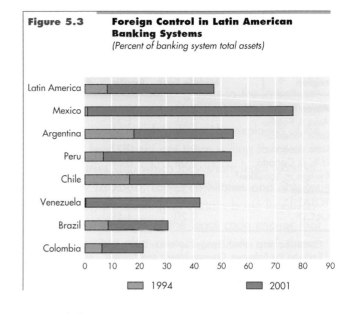

Figure 5.3 **Foreign Control in Latin American Banking Systems**
(Percent of banking system total assets)

Source: Galindo, Micco and Serra (2002).

What Determines Bank Location Abroad?

The location of foreign banks across the world is influenced by many factors. Investment decisions by banks take into account the profitability of investment, the development of the financial system, and the need to follow similar strategies as their competitors and maintain their market share. However, there are other crucial factors that influence decisions regarding expansion abroad. In particular, the decision appears to be strongly determined by other forms of integration.

---

[13] Several reasons led to this outcome. Restrictions on entry of foreign banks were removed as a part of the liberalization process; formerly, public banks were privatized and foreign investors participated in the process; and the banking sector used international funds to recapitalize after the sequence of external shocks that hit the region during the decade.

[14] Banco Bilbao Vizcaya Argentaria (BBVA) and Banco Santander Central Hispano (BSCH) have become the largest international players in Latin American retail banking markets. Banks from different regions have had different patterns in their expansion into Latin America. While U.S. banks have tended to focus exclusively on U.S. firms operating in the region, European banks have had a more retail oriented approach. See Guillén and Tschoegl (1999).

[15] Taking the region as a whole, the financial integration measure is a little higher (1.5 percent).

Micco and Serra (2002) estimate that when supervisory practices are similar, foreign participation is increased by nearly 19 percent. This finding also suggests that harmonizing regulations across countries can increase financial market integration even at the regional level by increasing the participation of external and national players in several markets simultaneously.

The Effect of Foreign Bank Penetration in Domestic Markets

Financial liberalization makes a financial system function better, in turn fostering growth, by improving system efficiency and under certain conditions increasing the availability of funds. In particular, the financial liberalization process in recent decades has allowed foreign banks to freely participate in local markets (Figure 5.3).

Overall empirical evidence on the impact of foreign banks on domestic markets is scarce. However, the fragmented evidence available suggests that the effects of internationalizing the banking system are positive, since banking systems increase their competitiveness and efficiency, in particular when foreign banks come from a more developed country.[19] However there is some controversy as to whether credit volatility is reduced by foreign banks.[20] On the one hand, some authors claim that foreign banks are able to stabilize credit because they have access to external funds, and, due to their reputation (brand name), they are able to stabilize local deposits. In addition, foreign bank entry may generate competitive pressure that leads to measures that guarantee future stability through more aggressive provisioning standards and higher capital ratios (Crystal, Dages and Goldberg, 2001). On the other hand, some economists claim that foreign banks are more sensitive to shocks in the host economy because they can substitute local assets with alternative investments abroad that are not easily available for local banks.

Foreign Banks, Efficiency and Regulatory Standards

Foreign banks traditionally have been associated with better resource allocation and higher efficiency. In particular, they have been linked with increased competition and the diffusion of new technologies. Foreign institutions improve the quality and availability of financial services by bringing new and better skills, management techniques, training procedures and technology. Moreover, Levine (1996) argues that the presence of foreign banks seems to lead to the development of better rating agencies, accounting standards and credit bureaus that acquire and process information, as well as better bank supervision and a more adequate legal framework. Foreign banks tend to follow prudential practices adopted in their home country. In the case of foreign banks from developed countries, these practices are usually more stringent than those of developing ones. In such cases, the increased security inspired by international banks leads domestic banks as well as supervisors to adopt international standards in order to ease competitive pressures coming from depositors searching for the safest institutions.

The presence of foreign institutions can boost competition and improve the operation of the domestic market (local banks), which in turn stimulates improvement in resource allocation and faster economic growth. In addition, international competition reduces interest rate margins and local banks' profitability.[21]

Credit and Deposit Stability and Foreign Banks

The huge increase in the number of foreign banks in Latin America, coupled with the region's credit crunch at the end of the last decade, have raised the question of whether the presence of foreign banks played a role in stabilizing domestic credit and deposits. This is a controversial issue in the literature. Some authors claim that foreign banks, due to their access to foreign liquidity, are less dependent on erratic local deposits, and therefore can stabilize credit in the host country. In addition, foreign banks, with their brand name (repu-

---

[19] See Levine (1996), Claessens, Demirgüç-Kunt and Huizinga (2001), Martínez Pería and Schmukler (2001).

[20] See Goldberg (2001) and Crystal, Dages, and Goldberg (2001).

[21] Foreign banks from non-Latin American countries located in Latin America tend to have higher profits, lower overhead costs, lower nonperforming loans, and fewer employees per loan than domestic banks.

tation), allow depositor-fly-to-quality to occur within the domestic market during financial turmoil, stabilizing both deposits and credit.[22]

On the other hand, others argue that foreign banks decrease their exposure to the country when domestic conditions deteriorate, increasing credit volatility.[23] Moreover, these banks can transmit shocks from their home countries. Changes in a foreign bank's claims at home or in other countries can spill over to the host country. In Latin America, most foreign banks come from developed countries that are also the main consumers of Latin American exports. Therefore, a contraction in these countries would affect Latin America not only through a contraction of external demand, but also through a reduction in local credit, amplifying the Latin American business cycle even more.

To test the validity of these two views, we study individual bank credit behavior after a change in deposits or in business opportunities. The measure of business opportunity is the change in external demand.[24] Appendix Table 5.2 shows that all bank credit reacts to changes in deposits, but this reaction is smaller for foreign banks. Foreign bank credit is 20 percent less sensitive to changes in domestic deposits than is domestic bank credit. With respect to bank reaction to business opportunities, after a contraction in external demand, all banks reduce their loans, but this reduction in credit is 50 percent smaller for domestic banks.

The results suggest that foreign banks would increase credit volatility if shocks were mainly changes in business opportunities in the host country, but would reduce it if the main source of credit volatility were the domestic supply of deposits. Which dominates remains an empirical question.

Foreign Banks and Market Segmentation

Despite the potential benefits of foreign bank penetration described above, some analysts have suggested that increased foreign bank penetration in developing countries might reduce access to credit to some segments of the market, particularly small and medium-sized firms that heavily depend on bank financing.

In general, foreign banks are large and organizationally complex financial institutions that find it difficult to lend to informationally opaque small and medium-sized firms.[25] Small businesses tend to have exclusive dealings with a single bank with which they have developed an "informal relationship" that reduces asymmetric information. Large foreign banks are likely to have difficulties developing these types of relationships. While large foreign banks are unlikely to replicate the lending method of small domestic banks, they can bring new technological innovations that foster credit to small and medium-sized firms. An example would be new credit scoring methodologies.[26]

Empirical evidence about the impact of foreign banks on the amount of credit to small businesses in developing countries is scarce and inconclusive. Some studies from Argentina associated foreign bank participation with a reduction of bank lending to small firms from around 20 percent of total lending in 1996 to 16 percent in 1998. However, during the same period, foreign banks increased both their propensity and their market share to this sector.

In an analysis of the behavior of foreign banks in four Latin American countries (Argentina, Chile, Colombia and Peru), Clarke et al. (2002) found that foreign banks generally lend less to small business than do private domestic banks. However, these results are mainly driven by small foreign banks, which were found in all four countries to lend less to small businesses than did similar domestic banks. The opposite is true for medium-sized and large foreign banks in Chile and Colombia, but not for Argentina and Peru. Finally, in Argentina and Chile, the two countries where the financial sector developed most during the study period, lending to small businesses by medium-sized and

---

[22] See IMF (2000).

[23] Caballero (2002) shows that local and foreign banks in Chile increased their positions in foreign assets during the 1998 recession, but this increase was substantially more pronounced for foreign banks.

[24] External demand is defined as the weighted average of the growth rate of trading partners.

[25] Goldberg (1992) shows that foreign banks in the United States tend to lend to large firms. See Berger and Udell (1995) for a discussion about the relationship between large banks and credit for small and medium-sized companies.

[26] Mester (1997) argues that there could be a U-shaped relationship between bank size and lending to smaller firms. One extreme would be small domestic banks using relationship-lending types of services, and the other would be large banks using more standard products for smaller businesses based on credit scoring.

large foreign banks was growing faster than lending to this sector by domestic banks. The authors speculate that the better institutional environments in Argentina and Chile allowed large foreign banks to use scoring methodologies, enabling them to increase their lending to smaller firms.

Foreign banking has increased significantly in Latin America since the 1990s. Empirical evidence tends to favor the advantages of foreign bank penetration over possible negative implications. Greater efficiency and less instability after deposit shocks from foreign banks have been noted in the region (except in major crisis episodes where all banks suffer equally). However, when idiosyncratic business opportunity shocks hit, foreign banks tend to move out in search of better opportunities in other countries. Evidence is inconclusive regarding foreign bank presence and lending to small and medium-sized enterprises. On balance, however, evidence is supportive of foreign bank participation in Latin American markets.

STOCK MARKET INTEGRATION

International listings almost entirely in the form of a North-South integration have been an important source to raise capital and expand the shareholder base for Latin American corporations. In 1994, Mexico was ranked third among countries with the most companies traded (in value terms) on the New York Stock Exchange (NYSE), with Argentina ranked fifth and Chile seventh. During the same year, Latin American companies trading in the United States in the form of ADRs (American Depositary Receipts) represented more than 50 percent of their local market indices. For Mexico and Brazil, this percentage reached respective levels of 87 percent and 71 percent. In the last decade, the amount of aggregate capital raised by Latin American firms in the ADR market has been a substantial portion of the capital raised in local stock markets. For example, Figure 5.5 shows that in 1996, Latin American corporations raised $22 billion in the form of ADRs and only $13 billion in local markets. Moreover, in contrast to ADRs from developed markets, those from emerging markets, and particularly Latin America, are usually traded more actively in the United States than in the domestic market.

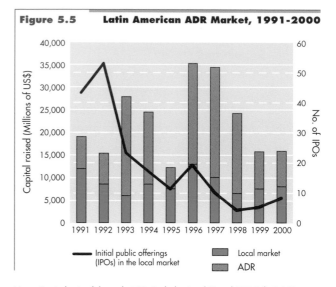

Figure 5.5 **Latin American ADR Market, 1991-2000**

Note: Capital raised through ADRs includes Level III and SEC Rule 144A programs.
Source: Moel (2001).

Firms that are able to issue ADRs on the NYSE reduce their credit constraints and are able to take advantage of foreign debt markets, reducing both their financial costs and their vulnerability to local market volatility. However, as shown by Moel (2001), the migration of these firms, generally the biggest ones, reduces the liquidity of local equity markets, increasing financial costs for local firms and reducing the incentive for new firms to enter in the local equity market.

Stock Market Integration in Latin America

There is little stock market integration in Latin American countries. Figure 5.6 shows the ratio of foreign firms hosted in domestic stock markets to stocks from domestic firms. The numbers for the region are extremely low compared to other parts of the world, meaning that very few foreign firms list on Latin American markets. Up until now, Latin American countries have been completely isolated from the world in this sense, as well as from other countries within the region itself. As seen in Figure 5.7 most Latin American firms list abroad, particularly the United States, and the degree of regional integration in Latin America is almost null. Aside from a few Argentine firms listing in Brazil, there is virtually no stock market integration within the region.

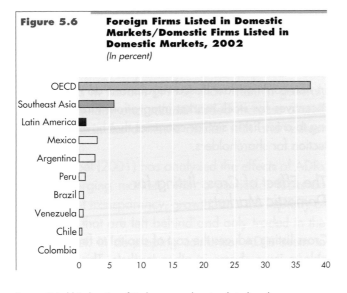

Figure 5.6 **Foreign Firms Listed in Domestic Markets/Domestic Firms Listed in Domestic Markets, 2002**

(In percent)

Source: World Federation of Exchanges and regional stock exchanges.

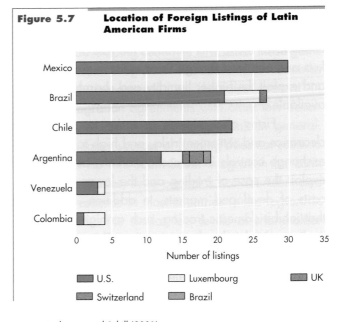

Figure 5.7 **Location of Foreign Listings of Latin American Firms**

Source: Sarkissian and Schill (2001).

What Determines the Decision to List Abroad?

Stock exchange investors are well known for investing in familiar assets.[27] There are many factors that reduce informational barriers and increase the degree of familiarity of an external asset. Empirical literature has shown that sharing several legal, cultural and geographical features reduces barriers for asset trading. Sharing a language, trading with the country where the asset is originated, and being geographically near that country are among others the factors that increase the likelihood of trading in another country's assets.[28] Taking advantage of these features allows foreign firms to list their stock in foreign stock exchanges.[29]

There are several advantages for firms from listing their stock abroad. Since capital markets are not fully integrated, businesses can benefit from lower capital costs by tapping external capital markets.[30] On the one hand, a premium for accessing restricted foreign securities can contribute to the lowering of capital costs; on the other, at the local level, the signaling effect of operating in international markets can increase the valuation of a firm's equity. From this perspective, diversifying to external listings can improve a firm's capacity to access cheaper forms of capital.

Tapping international stock markets also enables firms to access a higher shareholder base. A higher shareholder base leads to increased investor recognition, reduced information costs, and lower costs of capital for firms.[31] Listing abroad also provides liquidity gains, which is important because it allows firms to avoid reduction in funding when the home economy is hit by domestic shocks. In such cases, and if shocks are not completely symmetrical, an internationally diversified firm can continue to receive funding from its outside listings when domestic markets are contracting.

The quality of institutions is of great importance for firms when choosing where to list. La Porta, Lopez-de-Silanes and Shleifer (1997, 1998) have shown that countries differ substantially in their rules and regulations that protect the property of sharehold-

---

[27] For example, French and Poterba (1991) and Tesar and Werner (1995) discuss in detail the home bias feature.

[28] Grinblatt and Keloharju (2001) provide a detailed discussion on the impact of these variables on stockholdings and trading in Finland. Rauch (1999) has greater cross-country coverage and finds that colonial ties are also of great relevance.

[29] Empirical analysis by Sarkissian and Schill (2001) finds that the features noted in the text here are important determinants of cross-border listing. It also finds that better institutions, in the form of a stronger rule of law, attract foreign firms to local stock exchanges.

[30] See Errunza and Losq (1985).

[31] See Merton (1987) and Foerster and Karolyi (1999) for theoretical and empirical discussions.

management role, and the creation of new instruments for regulating and overseeing public services. The participation of the private sector through privatization and concession has helped meet crucial infrastructure needs. However, infrastructure demands remain large and ongoing, and the financial capacity to undertake new projects has clearly been affected by the financial crises in major economies of the region since the late 1990s.

Fay (2001) has forecast infrastructure needs in Latin America for 2000-2005 based on income levels. She projects a doubling of telephone mainlines per capita, a steady increase in electricity generating capacity, and steady expansion of road infrastructure, with rail transport becoming less important. Investments of $57 billion annually (roughly 2.6 percent of Latin America's GDP) will be needed over the period for electricity ($22 billion), roads ($18 billion), and telecommunications ($6 billion). Private investment exceeds predicted need for telecommunications (although the model did not include costs associated with the emergence of cellular phones), covers about half the demand for roads, and meets just a fraction of needs in power and water and sanitation. Moreover, these projections are likely to be on the low side because they cover new investments rather than rehabilitation or maintenance.

The fact that infrastructure networks remain incomplete limits the ability of some areas to participate in economic growth. In addition, insufficient capacity across all infrastructure sectors in major corridors linking the region's metropolitan areas has resulted in bottlenecks that create delays, raise costs, and limit potential gains from trade and development. Thus, the current situation might be viewed as a stage to complete, consolidate and extend the recent reforms.

CONCEPTUAL ISSUES IN REGIONAL INFRASTRUCTURE DEVELOPMENT

Trade, Infrastructure and Development

There is a well-established relationship across countries between income levels and the quality of infrastructure (IDB, 2001a). Infrastructure is an important determinant of productivity and development. Higher income levels and growth feed back into larger demands for transport, telecommunications and energy services. These linkages are particularly pronounced in facilitating trade that is critical for regional integration.

The opening up of Latin American economies has led to marked increases in international trade, financial capital and foreign direct investment. There has also been an upswing in regional trade: both the share and the growth rates of intra-regional trade in the 1990s grew much faster than extra-regional activity (see Chapter 2).

This growing commercial interdependence has been associated with various kinds of regional cooperation, especially in terms of regional trade agreements. Even the regional orientation to international markets has spurred greater specialization and intra-industry regional trade. This trade also has been in higher value-added goods and services. The higher value in turn requires higher quality infrastructure, especially in telecommunications, data transfer, roads and multimodal transport (Guasch and Kogan, 2001).

This expanded activity also has focused attention on the need for greater integration of trade infrastructure, both in terms of physical investments and institutional coordination. For example, border crossings remain a major impediment to transport connections within Latin America. Working to resolve these issues will not only make regional infrastructure linkages more effective, but also spur new opportunities for integration.

The level of regional trade depends critically on the quality of supporting infrastructure. Poor infrastructure represents 40 percent or more of transport costs in developing countries, with substantial effects on trade. But regional provision of infrastructure has lagged behind. Even with the investments in the 1990s, transport, telecommunications and electricity networks remain incomplete, with underdeveloped linkages across some borders, or with insufficient capacity in key corridors. Transport costs in the region remain high relative to the rest of the world (Guasch and Kogan, 2001). Moreover, improvements in infrastructure (ports, roads, telecommunications) in developing countries can help to significantly reduce inventory levels and thus the cost of doing business.

National Legacies, Regional Projects and Externalities

Regional integration flows are rarely channeled through specific infrastructure, but rather use networks that are shared with domestic and global traffic. In practice, services of differing geographical scope share segments of the same infrastructure network. For example, vehicles connected with interurban and international traffic use the same roads; domestic and international air passengers use the same airport; electricity, oil and gas share interconnection lines and pipelines; and local and international data can move over the same fiber optic network. As a result, infrastructure investment has tended to be viewed in national terms, both in the form of public provision and for private concessions.

Many of the infrastructure problems that constrain regional integration also hinder domestic development and international trade. These include the need to upgrade and complete service networks, such as electricity; add capacity to eliminate bottlenecks in key transport corridors, especially at border crossings; link transport modes at ports, airports and trucking terminals; expand oil and natural gas access; and increase access to Internet and telecommunications services.

Infrastructure projects generally are characterized by network and scale economies. For example, in Central America the small size of countries and national markets has prevented infrastructure investments from achieving scale and network economies, thereby raising the costs and associated required rates of return. These scale effects could also bring environmental benefits, because fewer physical sites are necessary for a given output level. Similarly, the extension and completion of regional infrastructure networks can help relieve congestion and improve environmental aspects associated with current patterns of concentrated development and urbanization.

Even when regional activity has been sizable, though, there has not been a shared vision of regional planning to develop a network of regional infrastructure. Indeed, this situation has become more complex, given the now-established role of private participation in most infrastructure sectors in the region. These new private stakeholders are likely to have different views about the needs and priorities for investment. They often operate under different legal, contractual and organizational structures, thereby making coordination and integration of national infrastructure networks more difficult.

Regional infrastructure projects present other issues as well. In addition to traditional domestic externalities, transnational projects are likely to have costs and benefits that are distributed asymmetrically across countries. This creates an incentive for a country to make individual decisions taking into account only costs and benefits within its borders. As a result, some potentially valuable regional projects are likely to be ignored or abandoned (Bond, 2001). A combination of factors makes the development of such projects difficult (Beato, Benavides and Vives, 2002). First, it is difficult for one country to identify the benefits it may obtain from a regional project. Second, even if benefits are known, for political reasons countries may be unwilling to pay for regional investments outside their borders even if the domestic benefits exceed these costs. Third, there currently are few socially acceptable institutional mechanisms to distribute regional benefits and costs across affected countries.

Another issue regarding regional infrastructure projects involves potential problems in establishing and managing a portfolio of regional projects (Beato, Benavides and Vives, 2002). Country authorities may view regional initiatives as a mechanism for low-cost financing of national projects. This also creates incentives to overestimate the regional benefits of predominantly national projects.

To date, there have been very few successful transnational infrastructure projects that were developed as such. The most successful projects have been those where key inputs are in one country while user markets are in another, such as the Brazil-Bolivia gas pipeline. Other successful efforts have involved linking existing network components by upgrading or expanding access to existing corridors. One such project is the road connecting Manaus, Brazil and Caracas, Venezuela. This is a "success story" with many lessons: each country knew exactly what it had to do and to gain; the money was provided by development funds and spent inside the countries; the construction companies liked it; the beneficiary states (as well as the national governments) were in favor of it; and the performance has met investment expectations (Guasch and Strong, 2001).

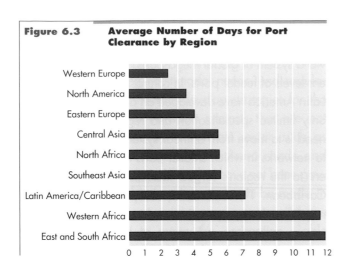

Figure 6.3 Average Number of Days for Port Clearance by Region

Source: Cámara Marítima y Portuaria de Chile (1999).

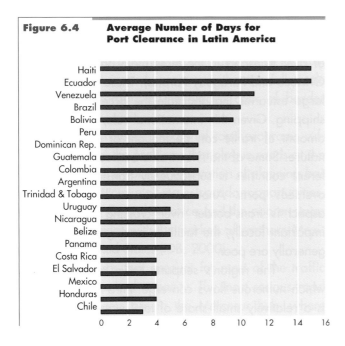

Figure 6.4 Average Number of Days for Port Clearance in Latin America

Source: IDB (2001).

Delays related to customs and port handling continue to be a major constraint to trade and integration. Figures 6.3 and 6.4 show that the regional average is over seven days for customs processing, with many countries even higher, ranking the region's processing time as among the highest in the world.

Although significant progress has been made in recent years, regulatory restrictions persist in river and maritime transport. The most important of these

has been the continuation of cargo reservation policies. In addition, river navigation regulations limit the size of convoys or impose service contracts for non-essential services.

Energy

Gas. Natural gas promises to grow in importance in world energy markets, given its relatively favorable reserve levels, lower transport costs, environmental advantages, wide range of uses, and technical advantages over other energy sources in certain applications. During the last decade, more than $12 billion was invested in 37 natural gas transportation projects (Izaguirre, 1999). The sharp increase in gas reserves and regional production has encouraged both public and private firms to develop regional gas transport links to neighboring countries. In the Southern Cone countries, 12 gas pipelines currently are operating or under construction, covering almost 8,000 kilometers and with a potential transportation capacity of 85 million cubic meters per day.[3] The two major pipeline networks run between Argentina, Brazil, Chile and Uruguay; and from Bolivia to Brazil. Additional projects have been proposed that would almost double both current longitude and capacity (7,000 kilometers and 75 million cubic meters per day).

In spite of this physical integration, serious institutional and regulatory problems impede the formation of a regional gas market. The lack of harmonized technical standards and the dominant power of some producers and transporters make integration difficult. For example, in Brazil, Petrobras has a dominant position in the importation and local production of gas, as well as being the main transporter of it. Similarly, Bolivian concession agreements give priority transport to the gas fields operated by Petrobras and Repsol-YPF (IDB, 2001b).

These market structures and preferences need to be addressed through greater harmonization of regulatory frameworks at the regional level. These national frameworks vary widely in their scope and effectiveness (Guasch and Spiller, 1999).

---

[3] Private sponsors have also participated in domestic transportation of natural gas in Colombia and Mexico.

Electricity. Regional integration can help to improve electricity services in a number of ways. Regional wholesale electricity markets make it easier to achieve scale economies and thus lower-cost generation projects, as in the case of the Central American Electricity Interconnection Project (SIEPAC). Interconnecting networks also allow for diversifying the energy sources used in generation. This reduces the risk of shortages by linking different hydrographic regimes or providing alternatives, such as balancing predominant hydroelectric systems with natural gas. However, physical integration is not sufficient to create a regional market and needs to be coupled with adequate institutional and regulatory frameworks.

The economic organization and ownership structure of the region's electricity sector underwent a radical transformation in the past decade, so that new electricity projects are almost exclusively operated by the private sector. The electricity sector undoubtedly has become an engine of economic integration in the Southern Cone, with clear potential to do so in the Andean and Central American subregions as well.

Structural reform and the privatization of public companies in the energy sector have enabled many countries in the region to begin to develop national energy markets. However, the nature, intensity and performance of sectoral reforms have varied by country. Given these differences, it is not surprising that the international projects currently underway to connect electricity networks stem mainly from bilateral agreements on interconnection and energy provision, rather than from open markets. Thus, the generation, transmission and distribution facilities are for specific use, limiting the sector to exchange and supply contracts.

Regional initiatives have traditionally been accomplished through bilateral agreements, such as the 1997 Brazil-Argentina agreement to integrate electricity markets. But these agreements tend to be through ad hoc contracts and not part of a plan to integrate markets. More recently, larger initiatives have been undertaken, such as the 1998 Mercosur Memorandum of Understanding on Electricity, which fosters the creation of an integrated electricity market in the Southern Cone. The Cartagena Agreement in the Andean region in 2001 also represents a positive step toward regional regulatory harmonization of transmission interconnections. The Regional Commission for Power Integration (CIER[4]) estimates that the economic benefits of electricity integration could reach $1 billion annually. The SIEPAC system in Central America is finally becoming a reality, spurred by the increased incentive of links to Southern Mexico.

Latin America's hydroelectric resources offer significant potential for power generation and opportunities for regional integration. Binational hydroelectric projects include the Itaipú project linking Brazil and Paraguay; the Yacyretá hydroelectric project linking Argentina and Paraguay; and the Salto Grande hydroelectric project linking Argentina and Uruguay. Transmission line connections exist between Colombia and Venezuela (the Cuatricentenario-Cuestecitas lines, El Corozo-San Mateo lines and Tibu-La Fria lines). Links also exist between Colombia and Ecuador via the Ipiales-Tulcan lines. Connections between Pasto and Quito and between Ecuador and Peru are in the planning stages.

Much larger benefits might be possible through the development of regional energy markets. The evolution of exchanges from binational deals to regional markets requires mechanisms regarding the use of the system of interconnection, operating security and the energy purchase-sale operations. A regional market would likely require common regulations for the international exchanges (Rufin, 2001). These requisite minimums involve an energy purchase-sale method based on economic principles with transparent rules, the elimination of subsidies (especially if there is prominent state participation), the application of nondiscrimination principles relating to export and access, and implementation of a regulatory structure for transmission covering use and payment of the internal network (European Commission, 1999).

Regulatory reforms instituted by Chile and Argentina illustrate the complexity of harmonizing national regulations. Chilean reforms include the elimination of monopolies and the corresponding deregulation of generation. Argentina mandates the

---

[4] CIER (Comisión de Integración Energética Regional) is a non-profit international organization that includes electric utilities and nonprofit entities linked with the national energy sectors of 10 South American countries.

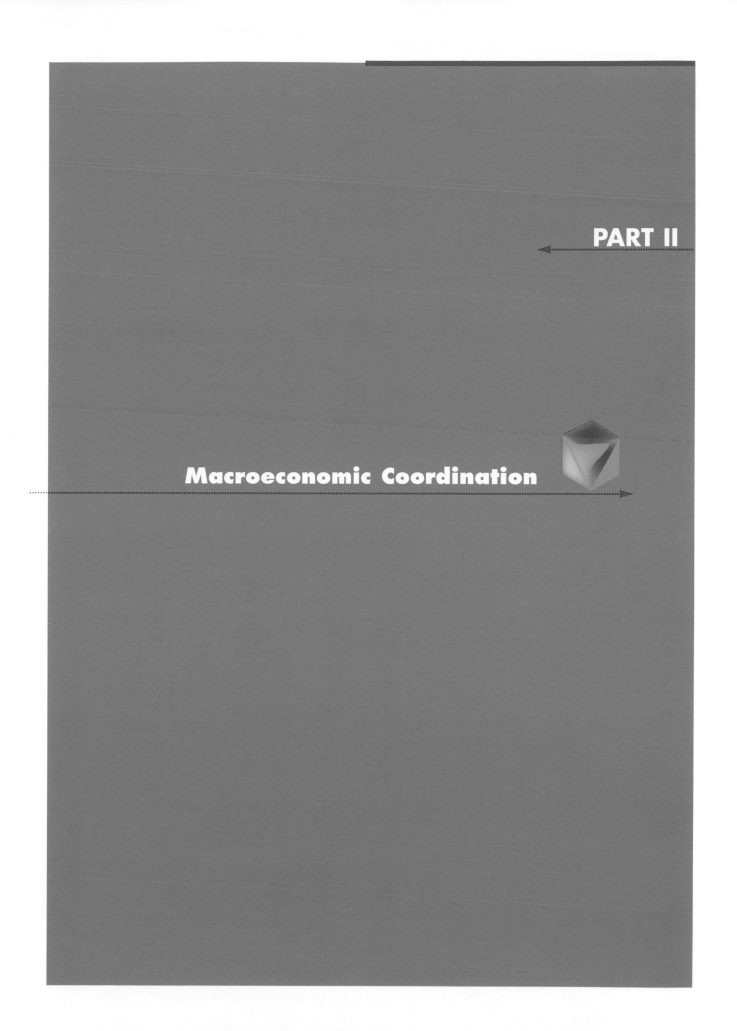

PART II

Macroeconomic Coordination

Chapter 7

MACROECONOMIC COORDINATION IN THE REGION

Macroeconomic coordination entails, by definition, a collective decision-making mechanism that reflects the interests of the parties involved. Imprecise terminology is often used to describe the different degrees of cooperation between countries. The terms policy convergence, coordination and harmonization are often used interchangeably, even though the concepts imply different levels of economic cooperation. According to Steinherr (1984), convergence policy is defined as a reduction of divergences between national objectives. Coordination requires national policies to be applied based on the acknowledgement of the policies and objectives of other countries and the effects of decisions by each country on the others. Harmonization is a process of steering towards a more uniform economic structure among countries that may lead to a unification of policies; that would occur, for example, when a single authority is responsible for bank supervision and regulation, or when monetary policy is unified under an independent central bank.

As the distinctions between these concepts are quite subtle, it is difficult to reach a consensus on their use that reflects different levels of cooperation. Consistent with the common practice, in this chapter, we shall use the concepts of cooperation and coordination interchangeably to refer to different levels of agreement in the macroeconomic arena, except when a precise distinction is required.

REASONS FOR COORDINATION

Macroeconomic coordination among the member countries of a trade bloc takes on a special meaning when policy decisions have a substantial effect on the trading partners. In this case, if the countries fail to consider the spillovers on other economies of making such decisions, the result can be less favorable to the parties as a whole than if a scheme of cooperative decisions were applied. In other words, cooperation may increase the well being of the overall group to the extent that externalities are present. Demand for coordination, then, is a direct function of the importance of these externalities to each country involved. This, in turn, depends on a set of factors that we shall analyze below.

Degree of Interdependence

A high level of interdependence implies that each county in the bloc is affected by the events in the other countries. By contrast, if Country A is dependent on the situation in Country B, but not vice versa, interdependence does not exist, reducing the possibilities for macroeconomic cooperation (Box 7.1).

In modifying import demand and export supply, domestic macroeconomic changes will affect the key trading partners through the impact of positive and negative cycles. There are two indicators used to measure trade interdependence between the members of a bloc: the share of regional trade in domestic product for each country, and the share of intra-regional trade

Box 7.1 Dependence and Interdependence

The figures below illustrate the level of dependence or interdependence in different regional agreements based on two indicators: intensity of reciprocal trade between the largest partner in each agreement and the rest of the bloc; and distribution of regional GDP. Both indicators show a lower level of dependence of the largest member, in the case of NAFTA and Mercosur, while interdependence is substantially greater under the other agreements.

There clearly may be other economic or political reasons beyond trade interdependence for coordination among members of an agreement. If trade dependence in the bloc varies substantially from country to country, however, it is reasonable to consider that there might be fewer incentives for the largest country to coordinate.

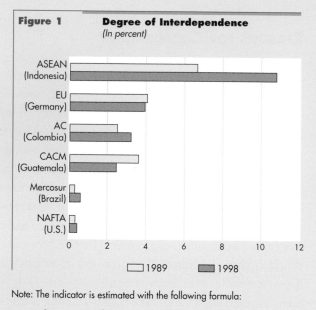

Figure 1 Degree of Interdependence
(In percent)

☐ 1989 ■ 1998

Note: The indicator is estimated with the following formula:

$$\psi_{int} = \left\{ \left(X_{jB}/X_{jTOT} \right) \Big/ \left(\sum_{\substack{n=i \\ j \neq i}} X_{ij} \Big/ \sum_{\substack{n=i \\ j \neq i}} X_{iTOT} \right) \right\}$$

which shows the ratio between the exports of the larger country j to the regional integration agreement B, and the sum of the exports of the rest of the country members i to the larger country j. In both cases, exports are normalized by the respective total exports. In parentheses, the left axis shows the larger country in terms of its share to regional GDP.
Source: IDB calculations based on IMF (2001a) and World Bank (2001).

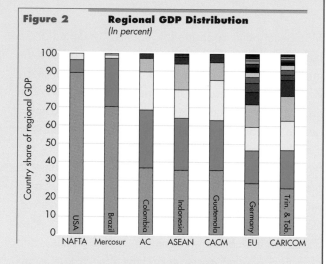

Figure 2 Regional GDP Distribution
(In percent)

Note: The distribution measures each country's GDP share of the 1990 average regional GDP.
Source: IDB calculations based on World Bank (2001).

in total trade. The impact of intra-regional trade on product reflects both the weight of intra-regional trade and the openness of the economy. Levels of intra-regional trade may be high as compared with total trade while, at the same time, insignificant in terms of product due to the fact that economies are relatively closed.[1]

What are the characteristics of Latin America and the Caribbean from this standpoint? The indicators

---

[1] A high level of intra-regional trade, however, makes a country more vulnerable to the situation in the region, particularly when such trade entails a substantial component of "regional goods," i.e., those not easily exported to the rest of the world (see Chapter 8).

Figure 7.1a **Degree of Interdependence by Regional Bloc for Intra-regional Exports**
(Percent of total exports)

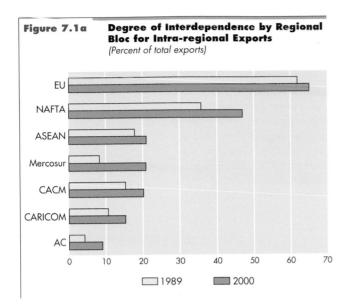

Figure 7.1b **Degree of Interdependence by Regional Bloc for Intra-regional Exports**
(Percent of regional GDP)

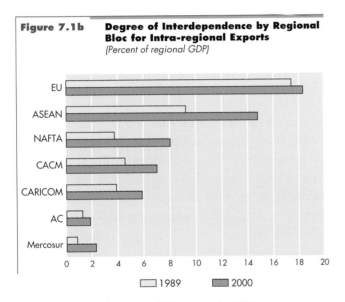

Note: For CARICOM, the latest available data are for 1997.
Source: IDB calculations based on IMF (2001a) and World Bank (2001).

show that interdependence in regional integration agreements (RIA) has increased substantially during the past decade. Nonetheless, the interrelationships within the different blocs are still less important than in other regions. These findings are evident when we analyze intra-regional trade with respect to total trade, and particularly intra-regional trade in terms of gross domestic product (Figures 7.1a and 7.1b). The results are primarily attributable to the openness of the countries, although the fact that regional agreements in Latin America represent a smaller relative share of world product also plays an important role.[2] Accord-

ingly, the low level of interdependence in Mercosur and the Andean Community (AC) is attributable primarily to the relative closure of the economies involved, while levels in the Central American Common Market (CACM) and the Caribbean Community (CARICOM) are higher, reflecting the intensity of intra-regional trade, and the fact that they are the most open blocs in the region. In any case, these values contrast with the greater importance of intra-regional trade in terms of product in Europe during the late 1980s, i.e., before the decision was made to create a monetary union, or the Association of Southeast Asian Nations (ASEAN) of today. The greater importance of intra-regional trade in the case of NAFTA is basically explained by the fact that it represents approximately 30 percent of GDP for Canada and Mexico.

While the topic of interdependence has been discussed generally from the standpoint of trade relations, the intense globalization of financial markets during recent years has led to greater financial interdependence and, through different channels, has generated contagion effects in critical situations.[3] Empirical studies have shown the existence of strong interconnections between financial markets in emerging countries that are clearly influenced by geographic proximity, trade links and economic policy similarities.[4]

Does membership in a given trade bloc increase financial contagion beyond the indirect impact through trade? There is evidence that a country's currency crises are more closely associated with

---

[2] The share of Mercosur, AC, CACM and CARICOM in world output is 3.3 percent, 0.8 percent, 0.15 percent and 0.07 percent, respectively, while the European Union accounts for 29 percent. The contrast with ASEAN, which accounts for a lower share of world product than Mercosur, demonstrates that an economy's openness, in addition to its size, is a fundamental factor in increasing regional interdependence.

[3] One exception is the absence of contagion in the final phases of the Argentine crisis. This could be attributed to the "absence of surprise" as events unfolded, which permitted investors to prepare themselves by reallocating their assets gradually. During the preceding months, however, there was an impact on other countries in the region, and during 2002 the crisis severely affected Uruguay. Although there are different definitions of contagion, references here are to a situation in which a crisis in another country increases the probability of crisis in the home country, after controlling for the economic fundamentals (Eichengreen, Rose and Wyplosz, 1996).

[4] See De Gregorio and Valdés (2001); Eichengreen, Hale and Mody (2000); Dornbusch, Park and Claessens (2000); Forbes and Rigobon (2000); Froot, O'Connell and Seasholes (2001); and Glick and Rose (1999).

exchange rate misalignments vis-à-vis the partners in a trade agreement than with the rest of the world.[5] When we measure contagion through the impact of a change in a country's capital flows on the other partners in an agreement, however, the evidence is more ambiguous.[6] These results are consistent with further empirical evidence that shows that interdependence in financial markets is manifested to a greater extent in price variations than in levels of capital flows.[7]

Political Support for the Degree of Integration

Greater demand for coordination is a function of the present level of interdependence, as well as the decision of governments to deepen the process of integration—that is, of future interdependence. For example, when the objective of the integration process is to achieve a monetary union, incentives to cooperate at the macroeconomic level increase substantially, as it is difficult to move forward in creating a single currency if inflation rates differ substantially between the countries, or if the fiscal deficit generates substantial growth in public debt. Integration processes in the region, particularly in recent years, have been characterized by the goal of going beyond free trade areas. This political willingness, however, is not always reflected in specific decisions in support of this objective. As macroeconomic cooperation has its costs, which we shall discuss below, in order to move forward governments must prove tangibly that the national agenda is giving way to the regional one.[8]

Reducing Volatility in the Bloc

Extent of volatility. By increasing uncertainty, macroeconomic volatility affects the rate of economic growth (see Box 7.2).[9] In recent decades, Latin American countries have evidenced a high degree of volatility, measured by the inflation rate and its variability, variations in the real exchange rate, and in part as a result of these factors, sharp variations in the growth rate. This volatility declined during the past decade, substantially as a result of more responsible fiscal and monetary policies that reduced the level and variability of the inflation rate, inducing a reduction in real exchange rate volatility.[10] In addition, while the rate of growth of GDP increased, its variability declined significantly. Still, volatility continues to be high, particu-

---

[5] Fernández-Arias, Panizza and Stein (2002). See Chapter 8 for a detailed discussion.

[6] Hernández and Mellado (2002) find no significant contagion, other than that generated by trade, from changes in capital flows from one country to the others in the bloc, with the exception of portfolio investment in some trade blocs.

[7] See Eichengreen, Hale and Mody (2000) and Froot, O'Connell and Seasholes (2001). Changes in the value of shares, fluctuations in the cost of indebtedness in domestic and international markets, or changes in the exchange rate could affect growth to an extent equal to or greater than changes in capital flows.

[8] This is demonstrated by adoption of a common external tariff, elimination of non-tariff barriers to intra-regional trade, and gradual progress toward establishment of supranational institutions.

[9] IDB (1995) analyzes the negative impact of volatility on growth.

[10] Except in CARICOM countries, where both inflation and volatility remained at similar low levels throughout the period.

Table 7.1 | **Macroeconomic Volatility**

	Standard deviation[2]							
	Annual rate of Inflation[1]		Quarterly inflation rate		Annual GDP growth		Multilateral real exchange rate	
	1991-2001	1971-2001	1991-2001	1971-2001	1991-99	1971-99	1991-2001	1980-2001
AC	32.22	90.05	3.06	16.84	1.84	1.67	1.65	7.85
	31.51	142.51	4.93	30.04	2.65	3.06	5.40	14.90
CARICOM	11.66	8.84	1.53	1.29	0.71	1.78	2.28	2.33
	13.89	9.01	3.06	2.93	3.06	5.15	3.78	4.77
CACM	37.42[3]	98.60	4.26	5.50	1.29	1.72	2.08	3.72
	78.36	215.17	15.44	23.13	2.21	4.40	6.75	15.29
Mercosur	393.66[4]	367.60	40.94	46.58	1.55	2.56	4.26	5.32
	155.57	196.92	17.92	31.64	3.36	4.84	3.85	7.81
ASEAN	7.50	8.44	2.22	1.86	2.23	2.11	4.41	3.43
	11.20	11.29	2.97	3.37	3.65	4.16	5.50	7.51
EU	2.69	5.47	0.33	0.90	0.90	1.34	1.05	0.86
	3.19	6.33	0.65	1.38	1.75	2.25	2.37	2.25

[1] Cells in red show the average across countries' annual inflation rate weighted by the countries' GDP, and in blue the simple average.

[2] Cells in red show volatility across countries' average change in absolute value weighted by the GDP, and cells in blue show the simple average of the countries' volatility.

[3] Excluding 1991 (high inflation in Nicaragua), the average inflation rate decreases to 12.03 percent.

[4] Since 1995, the average inflation rate for Mercosur has decreased to 11.49 percent.

Source: IDB calculations based on IMF (2001b) and World Bank (2001).

larly in comparison with the European Union, although certain indicators register levels similar to ASEAN (Table 7.1).

This higher level of volatility not only affects the rate of investment and growth in the country directly exposed to it, but also those rates in the interconnected countries. High and variable inflation rates and substantial variability in GDP make the partner unpredictable, although the most relevant issue among regional partners, for reasons discussed below, is exchange rate variability. Figure 8.2 in Chapter 8 shows that the variability in the intra-regional exchange rate has been considerably higher for all agreements in Latin America than for the European Union or ASEAN. In the region, Mercosur, followed distantly by the AC and CACM, register the highest levels of volatility.

Effects. As economic agents are typically risk adverse, the increase in uncertainty usually associated with volatility can be expected to have a negative impact on economic activity. While a country's volatility affects its partners in different ways, exchange rate

volatility typically attracts the most attention due to its effects on trade and on the political economy of the integration process.

Most empirical studies that have analyzed the impact of exchange volatility on trade flows have found ambiguous or slightly negative effects that can be explained by the existence of exchange risk hedging mechanisms.[11] The absence of a stronger negative effect is strengthened by the fact that these studies primarily used data from developed countries in which exchange coverage mechanisms are more advanced.[12] As developing countries began to be incorporated into the studies, volatility had a greater negative impact on exports.[13] It is not surprising, then, that a monetary

[11] From a theoretical standpoint, models with agents neutral to risk or risk lovers can also be constructed. See Mckenzie (1999).

[12] The estimates show a lower impact of volatility with improvement in coverage instruments for transactions in foreign exchange (Frankel and Wei, 1998).

[13] See Estevadeordal, Frantz and Sáez (2001) and Giordano and Monteagudo (2002).

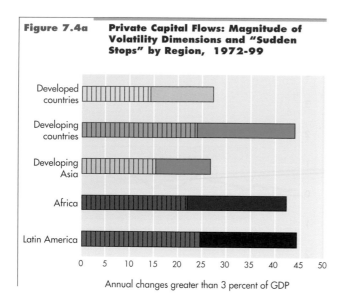

Figure 7.4a   **Private Capital Flows: Magnitude of Volatility Dimensions and "Sudden Stops" by Region, 1972-99**

Annual changes greater than 3 percent of GDP

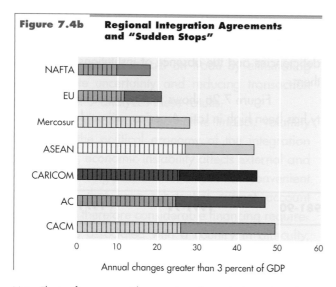

Figure 7.4b   **Regional Integration Agreements and "Sudden Stops"**

Annual changes greater than 3 percent of GDP

Notes: The two figures present the percentage of annual observations when net private capital flow changes are greater than 3 percent of current GDP, based on country data. The bars with vertical lines present sudden stops, which are cases when the negatives changes were greater than 3 percent of current GDP.
Source: IDB calculations based on World Bank (2001) and IMF (2001c).

flows in emerging regions have been substantial, particularly when foreign direct investment is excluded. Similarly, Table 7.2 shows that this volatility has been greater in all the Latin American blocs than in Europe.[16]

To illustrate the magnitude of this volatility, a sample of 121 countries (23 developed and 98 developing countries, according to the IMF classification) is used to calculate cases in which annual variations in net private capital flows exceeded 3 percent of GDP in the receiving country over 1972-99. Figure 7.4a shows that for all developing countries, this level is exceeded in 44 percent of the observations, although it drops to 38 percent when developing countries having income levels below $20 billion (in 1995) are excluded.[17] The same coefficient is 27 percent for developed countries, and 6 percent when only the G-7 countries are considered. Given the impact that sharp reductions in capital flows have on GDP and on the exchange rate (Calvo, 2001), the same figure also shows how many of these variations correspond to reductions exceeding 3 percent of the countries' GDP. In developed and developing countries, there are approximately the same number of cases of sudden stops as sudden starts of capital flows, which would seem to imply that the sudden whims of the markets occur in both directions.[18] Figure 7.4b presents the same information by regional integration agreement. With the exception of Mercosur, in all of the remaining agreements in Latin America, the cases where changes in annual capital flows exceed 3 percent of GDP are around 45 percent.

While for closed economies fluctuations in capital flows as a percentage of GDP could be low, the impact in terms of variation in GDP and the real exchange rate required to adjust the current account

are not much different from the volatility within ASEAN, despite that region's greater diversification of exports.[15] Figure 7.2b shows the impact of this volatility in terms of product, which depends crucially on the economy's openness and explains its relatively low impact in Mercosur.

During the past few years, however, volatility in the region and in emerging countries in general has mainly come from changes in private capital flows. Figures 7.3a and 7.3b show that oscillations in capital

---

[15] Volatility is calculated for the past three decades, a period during which the export structure is not uniform. In fact, volatility in terms of trade decreases substantially for ASEAN when only the past decade is considered.

[16] For Mercosur, however, this is true only when the indicator is weighted by country size. NAFTA is found to have volatility similar to Europe.

[17] The maximum values for developing countries are found in Latin America (44 percent) and Africa (42 percent).

[18] Sharp increases in capital inflows tend to produce a substantial increase in product and appreciation in the exchange rate, which, in many cases, is indicative of future crisis.

may exceed that required in more open economies. This is the case of Mercosur compared to other agreements in Latin America. In fact, when the number of observations in which the annual fluctuations in capital flows exceed 20 percent of exports, Mercosur is found to have a higher level of volatility than other blocs, as observations with these characteristics amount to 39 percent of the total, as compared to 29 percent for the AC and 23 percent for CACM.

All of this represents further proof of the magnitude of the region's financial volatility—volatility that is not only the result of changes in the external context, but also of internal factors that traditionally have shown great instability in emerging countries.

In summary, while volatility declined during the past decade, subregional blocs still exhibited macroeconomic instability, explained by both domestic and external factors. There is, accordingly, broad scope to establish policies that reduce the impact of external shocks (for example, through diversification of exports and adoption of measures to reduce the impact of the variability of capital flows). There are also opportunities for cooperation to address these external shocks, such as by creating regional financing mechanisms. Volatility of internal origin might be reduced through coordination of macroeconomic policies, mainly in the monetary and fiscal areas.

Discipline under Domestic Pressure

Regional agreements can serve to implement measures that generate domestic resistance. An international agreement may strengthen certain actions by associating them with a consensus with other countries, therefore making them less subject to a decision of the national authorities. To date, in countries of the region, the external discipline mechanism has been introduced under agreements with international financial institutions rather than under coordination agreements with the regional partners. The advantage of a regional agreement, however, is that it typically is viewed as a choice by the country, over which it normally has some degree of control, while agreements with international organizations are often considered to be imposed by outside interests.

In any case, the importance of regional agreements in imposing some degree of internal discipline

depends on whether the agreement is perceived as advantageous to the country. While this has been true for Europe, it has not necessarily been so for Latin America. As a result, there is a risk that implementation of unpopular economic policies will be viewed as the result of an agreement whose benefits are not clear, therefore generating incentives for its termination.

Increasing Credibility

Coordination of macroeconomic policies with partners that enjoy a good reputation can generate positive externalities. In an extreme case, even if there are not conditions to create a monetary union, coordination could lead to the adoption of a single currency with a view to gaining further credibility. Similarly, the countries may decide to adopt the currency of a country outside the region if it is believed that the benefits of that country's reputation may offset the costs associated with the absence of monetary policy.

Unlike Europe, where coordination is viewed as a responsible policy given the reputation of some of the partners, the absence in Latin America of countries with a tradition of monetary stability implies that the qualification of a country as "responsible" in macroeconomic policy management has little to do with honoring commitments with the country's partners. Coordination between countries without reputation can generate credibility gains if it enables more responsible economic policies to be implemented—among other reasons, because it can help reduce domestic pressures. For coordination to be credible, however, there must be some costs associated with noncompliance.

Eliminating Distortions and Reducing Fiscal Costs

As countries eliminate tariff barriers, reduce exchange rate volatility, and advance in their level of interrelations, distortions in competition resulting from different tax systems generate increasing costs, and therefore also incentives to coordinate policies in the area.

Elimination of barriers to the flow of goods and services—a minimum level of integration to which all modern second-generation agreements aspire—increasingly requires establishment of trade-neutral

Third, progress was gradual and resulted from mutual trust created between national representatives, fostered by periodic meetings between the key policy and economic players and the functioning of technical groups that included members from the different countries involved. This approach and compliance with certain agreements reduced the risk that the parties would engage in opportunistic behaviors.

Fourth, the experience of the 1980s clarified the need for the assessment of compliance with the agreements not to be limited to the policy authorities of the countries. Rather, the assessments should be broadly disseminated, as should the recommendations provided by the members of the agreement or the supranational organizations regarding how to correct imbalances. This approach allows for oversight of the policy authorities by their own citizens and the international community (countervailing powers). At the same time, it improves the market credibility of the agreements so that countries can be rewarded or punished accordingly.

Finally, supranational organizations play an important role in enabling criteria shared by the parties to be established, ensuring some degree of independence in assessing national policies, and providing recommendations on how to correct economic policy deviations. In this area, as in many others, it is advisable to make progress incrementally, beginning with institutional rules that do not significantly reduce the autonomy of the countries.

Perhaps the most important lesson from the European Union is that the attempts at macroeconomic cooperation consistently complemented progress toward integration. In other words, interdependence provided incentives for coordination, and macroeconomic cooperation, particularly in the area of exchange rate arrangements, allowed enhanced interdependence.[42]

What can be said about macroeconomic coordination efforts in Latin America? Box 7.4 shows that some integration agreements have attempted to follow European convergence criteria (Maastricht). Mainly because there were no incentives for compliance, these attempts were not very significant. However, beyond the absence of agreements to achieve a certain degree of macroeconomic convergence, the different blocs and the region as a whole have con-

verged toward more responsible macroeconomic policies. Figures 7.8a-d show a decline in inflation levels and its dispersion among the member countries of different agreements during the 1990s.

In the area of exchange rate policy, there have been few coordination efforts. This is of course explained by the existence of different exchange regimes within some blocs, and by problems in defending the value of the local currency against speculative attacks. Clearly, it is difficult to coordinate exchange rate policies when economies have "polarized" exchange rate schemes, such as convertibility or dollarization, and floating exchange regimes. Figure 7.9 shows the differences in exchange rate regimes within the different blocs.[43]

WHAT OPTIONS ARE AVAILABLE?

Progress in macroeconomic coordination under integration agreements is complex from the economic and political standpoints. The scarce progress in Latin American subregional agreements is a clear manifestation of these difficulties. From the economic standpoint, although trade interdependence increased during the 1990s, it is still considerably lower than the levels in other regional agreements. While levels of financial interdependence are much higher than they were a decade ago, attempts by countries to differentiate themselves from a partner have been decisive in moments of crisis, aggravating political problems and undermining progress in the integration process. The perception that coordination with regional partners generates more negative than positive externalities is crucial to explain this attitude. In turn, it leads to the increasing conviction that the partner will behave in an uncooperative manner, which further weakens the prospects for progress in macroeconomic policy coordination.

---

[42] Europe is also a case in which macroeconomic cooperation was accompanied by coordination in other areas (policy on labor, income, mobility of goods and services, capital markets, etc.), which helped increase interdependence.

[43] The IMF classification used has the problem that some schemes appear to be floating regimes, but perform otherwise. See Calvo and Reinhart (2002).

Box 7.4   Macroeconomic Cooperation in Practice

• Andean Community (AC)

1997: An advisory council was created for central bank governors and treasury ministers.
1999: Inflation convergence criteria were adopted.
2001: The target of single-digit inflation was agreed upon for December 2002. Fiscal convergence criteria were adopted (ratio between deficit and GDP and public debt and GDP not to exceed 3 percent and 50 percent, respectively). A community monitoring system was established in compliance with targets.

• The Caribbean Community (CARICOM)

1997: The Council for Finance and Planning was established, indicating a willingness to coordinate fiscal and monetary policies, and particularly interest rates, exchange rates, tax structures and budget deficits.
Late 1990s: Convergence criteria were established to determine eligibility for monetary union, consisting of a rule on exchange rates, reserve coverage, and a debt service to export ratio.

• Central American Common Market (CACM)

1960s-80s: A region-wide policy of exchange rates pegged to the U.S. dollar was pursued, creating an implicit monetary area and achieving some degree of convergence.
1998: Objectives to control inflation were announced through budget deficit regulation and gradual elimination of the quasi-fiscal deficit.
Late 1990s: Reciprocal consultations were increased between monetary authorities and financial system regulators.

• Southern Cone Common Market (Mercosur)

2000: The Macroeconomic Monitoring Group was established to harmonize statistical processes for calculation of certain key indicators (consumer price indices, budget deficit, and net debt of the consolidated public sector). A quarterly publication providing these indicators was introduced. A two-phase convergence mechanism was established as a transition through which countries would announce their objectives in terms of the indicators.

2002: Adoption of common objectives that would include a maximum of 5 percent inflation and targets for fiscal variables.

• North American Free Trade Agreement (NAFTA)

The growing interconnections between the economies involved as a result of NAFTA has led to an enhanced exchange of information and more effective informal contacts among the authorities.

• European Union (EU)

1970s: Coordination mechanisms were consolidated in light of the instability following the breakdown of the Bretton Woods agreement. The Werner Report (1970) proposed a monetary union. The currencies of the European Economic Community were tied through the European mechanism for managing currency fluctuations beginning in 1972, although the macroeconomic instability that characterized the first half of the 1970s made convergence impracticable. The European Monetary System (EMS) was established in 1978 and the currencies of eight countries were linked through the Exchange Rate Mechanism (ERM), which permitted fluctuations within pre-established limits. Between 1979 and 1987, there were 11 realignments, although the parities were maintained under the agreement from that time until 1992, when Great Britain left the system. Other currencies followed suit.
1993: Convergence criteria proposed in the Maastricht Treaty were adopted.
1999: Creation of the Monetary Union.
2002: The euro entered circulation.

• Association of Southeast Asian Nations (ASEAN)

During the late 1990s, a process was established to monitor the region's macroeconomic development and to stimulate adoption of transparent policies through a policy of revision. An initiative was also approved to provide support in the event of balance of payments crises.

The difference in the European experience is significant. In Europe, there are at least three types of incentives to comply with the objectives established under the Maastricht agreement and the Stability Pact. First, being considered a responsible country;[44] sec-

ond, the gains associated with elimination of exchange rate volatility with key trading partners; and third, the

---

[44] For countries with better reputations, there are incentives to eliminate opportunistic behavior by the other members.

Figure 7.8   Convergence in Latin America

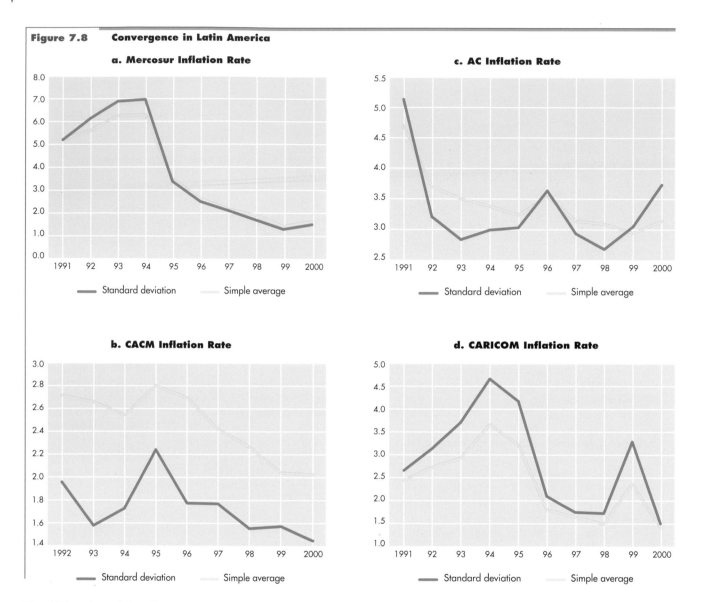

a. Mercosur Inflation Rate

c. AC Inflation Rate

b. CACM Inflation Rate

d. CARICOM Inflation Rate

Standard deviation   Simple average

Note: All the series are in logarithms.
Source: IDB calculations based on IMF (2001b).

existence of a system of penalties for countries that fail to meet fiscal targets.[45] These factors have not been present in South-South regional agreements, and particularly in Latin America. Under these agreements, qualifying countries as "responsible" in macroeconomic policy management for now and in the near future has nothing to do with meeting commitments within the area. Rather, it involves agreements with multilateral credit institutions, and particularly, with the International Monetary Fund. Although intra-bloc exports are substantial in a number of regional agreements, the levels registered in the European Union have not been

attained by any of them. Finally, the countries of the region have not established mechanisms to levy penalties for noncompliance with the proposed objectives.

The relevant question then is whether it makes sense to attempt to coordinate macroeconomic policies under regional integration agreements in Latin America. One answer is that this depends on the intended level of integration. If the agreement's objective is a

[45] Penalties should be commensurate with the purpose. In some cases, penalties entailing publication of slippages might be more effective than pecuniary fines.

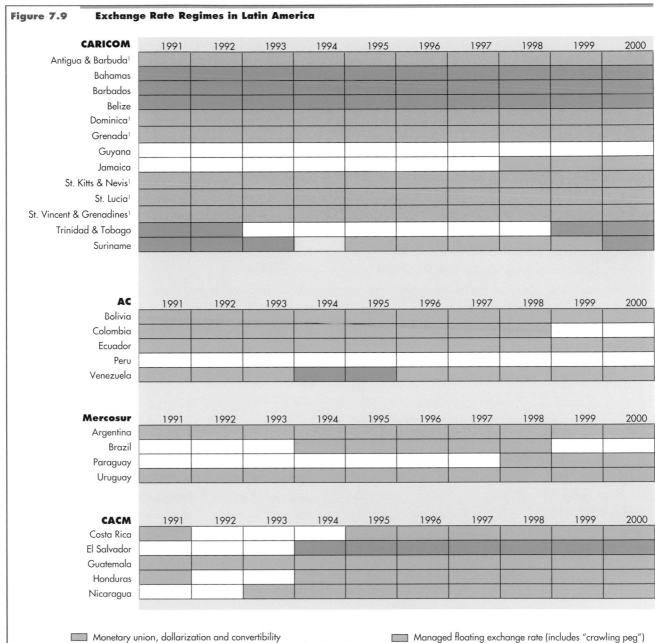

Figure 7.9   Exchange Rate Regimes in Latin America

CARICOM	1991	1992	1993	1994	1995	1996	1997	1998	1999	2000
Antigua & Barbuda[1]										
Bahamas										
Barbados										
Belize										
Dominica[1]										
Grenada[1]										
Guyana										
Jamaica										
St. Kitts & Nevis[1]										
St. Lucía[1]										
St. Vincent & Grenadines[1]										
Trinidad & Tobago										
Suriname										

AC	1991	1992	1993	1994	1995	1996	1997	1998	1999	2000
Bolivia										
Colombia										
Ecuador										
Peru										
Venezuela										

Mercosur	1991	1992	1993	1994	1995	1996	1997	1998	1999	2000
Argentina										
Brazil										
Paraguay										
Uruguay										

CACM	1991	1992	1993	1994	1995	1996	1997	1998	1999	2000
Costa Rica										
El Salvador										
Guatemala										
Honduras										
Nicaragua										

    Monetary union, dollarization and convertibility   Managed floating exchange rate (includes "crawling peg")
    Fixed exchange rate (includes fixed exchange rate within a band)   Floating exchange rate

[1] Members of a monetary union whose currency is fixed with the dollar.
Source: IMF, *Exchange Rate Agreements, Annual Reports*, various years.

free trade area, it would not seem necessary to move forward with significant forms of coordination, except perhaps efforts designed to avoid tax wars between the member countries. Even for agreements that attempt to move toward higher forms of integration, it might be argued that macroeconomic coordination should be the result of greater independence. For instance, if volatility of members creates problems

under the agreement, a need for coordination would arise in due course. However, as mentioned, the absence of macroeconomic coordination mechanisms weakens the process of integration. While the example of Europe is commonly used to affirm that demand for coordination increases with the level of interdependence, the European case shows that there is an interactive process between coordination and interdependence that makes them complementary. Therefore, the need arises to move forward jointly on both fronts.

Due to the magnitude of the external shocks and the absence of an exogenous coordination mechanism similar to the one provided for the exchange rate under the Bretton Woods agreement during the early years of European integration, Latin America faces greater difficulties than Europe in coordinating its macroeconomic policy.[46] What type of coordination is possible, then, in the subregional agreements in Latin America? Clearly, this will depend on the specific characteristics of each agreement, although certain general criteria can be established considering the international experience and the reality of the region. The European experience shows that there has been convergence as a result of establishing limits to the level of disequilibrium in the public accounts and inflation rates, as well as through the different attempts to coordinate exchange rate policy that culminated in the adoption of a single currency. The fact that Europe has not been willing or able to move forward toward higher levels of fiscal coordination might help to establish certain criteria for Latin America. It has been argued, however, that progress in areas that involve institutional change—such as independence for central banks and price and wage flexibility—would be more important than establishing goals for certain variables (Eichengreen, 1998). This is true to the extent that inflation and budget deficit reductions can be transient, and therefore it is better to emphasize the structural changes, such as independence of the central bank, which would make possible low long-term inflation rates. Regarding prices and wages, flexibility would make it easier to cope with asynchronous perturbations in a context of macroeconomic coordination.[47] However, there is no way to ensure that the institutional changes will be permanent, as many of them are based on a law.[48] Further, to the extent that the cooperative scheme requires generating confidence between the different countries involved, it would seem that this should be achieved by reducing volatility for a prolonged period of time so that stability becomes a public asset that instills confidence in the partners and will transcend the current government. Creating institutions that help maintain this stability in the medium term is of greater importance, and, accordingly, the institutions must be complementary with, rather than

substitute for, macroeconomic convergence. Similarly, creation of the institutions that facilitate flexibility in nominal variables would certainly support any coordination effort.

In addition to macroeconomic convergence and the institutional reforms necessary to help sustain it in the long term, moving toward mechanisms of exchange rate coordination would also be advisable. Exchange rate volatility not only weakens the possibility of enhanced trade integration, but also generates policy tensions within the agreement.

Macroeconomic convergence. No one wants to associate with an unstable country. Besides, it is difficult to imagine that macroeconomic policies could be coordinated with a highly volatile partner. Macroeconomic stability is therefore vital in order to make progress in the integration process. This is where macroeconomic convergence matters: there are certain economic criteria essential to achieve stability, which is crucial for any integration agreement to function. Stability is therefore an objective shared by each country and by the regional bloc as a whole. A realistic mechanism for regional coordination, therefore, is convergence of fiscal policies (deficit and debt) and inflation rates. The European experience has shown that the acceptable fiscal disequilibrium should entail the structural deficit rather than the current one, i.e., the deficit adjusted by the level of economic activity.[49] The history of Latin America suggests that the level of this deficit should be considerably lower than it is in Europe. Given the region's exposure to external shocks, a maximum level of current account disequilibrium, or at least

---

[46] This does not imply that the region has no other mechanisms for exogenous coordination, such as the impact on financial regulations and supervision mechanisms for substantial foreign investment flows in the financial area.

[47] From the standpoint of the change in relative prices, full price and wage flexibility would mean that changes in nominal exchange rates would not be necessary. Of course, in the case of contracts with nominal interest rates denominated in domestic currency, price deflation generates problems in the financial system beyond those produced by a flexible exchange rate.

[48] Argentina is one case where it can be argued that the low inflation rate for a decade ultimately proved to be transient. However, Argentina also showed that institutional reforms (such as the loss of the central bank's independence in 2001) also ultimately proved transient.

[49] Establishing the structural budget deficit as a target would eliminate objections involving the difficulty of implementing anticyclical fiscal policies, as has been the case in Europe.

of short-term external indebtedness, should also be considered.[50] Furthermore, as the weakness of financial systems in emerging countries has been one of the main reasons for instability, it is important to achieve minimum harmonization criteria in the areas of financial regulation and supervision.

In addition to moving forward with these criteria, it is important to know how to convert a regional macroeconomic convergence agreement and the appropriate institutional reforms for long-term stability into a relevant instrument within the region and within the international framework. To that end, beyond the incentives generated by agreements with the international credit institutions—which in any case function as "exogenous coordination" mechanisms—the region should set its own incentives. One possibility is to assign more importance to convergence agreements, for example, through public dissemination of the results and recommendations to be made by a group of technical experts to countries that have not observed the agreed-upon guidelines. Another possibility, which may be complementary, would be to create a regional fund for which access would be authorized, among other requirements, when the countries meet the conditions established under the macroeconomic convergence agreements. As noncompliance with the agreed terms would generate additional regional costs, the rules of macroeconomic convergence—and the related institutional reforms—would receive more serious consideration from the members, and from the international community.

Since coordination in complementary areas favors the integration process, which will increase the demand for macroeconomic coordination, it would be advisable for international organizations to support regional proposals aimed at that objective. The incentives that these organizations might provide, in addition to technical cooperation, include rapid-disbursement loans to support the implementation of common policies (rules of competition, trade standards, an institutional dispute settlement framework, establishment of regional technical agencies, regulation and supervision of the financial system, etc.) and institutional reforms that would help macroeconomic policy coordination (independence of central banks, labor regimes, relations between the national and subnational governments, the social security system, etc).

Exchange rate coordination. The literature on currency crises offers a number of explanations for exchange rate variability, and therefore its volatility within a bloc. In addition to these explanations, the existence of large external shocks and different exchange rate regimes within integration agreements must be considered. So far, we have discussed external shocks and synchronism in economic cycles. When different exchange regimes are involved, an external shock that has the same effect on the equilibrium exchange rate of two countries can change the current bilateral exchange rate between them, as is evident in the extreme case when one country has a fixed exchange rate and another a floating rate. Therefore, the existence of similar exchange regimes should eliminate at least one of the reasons for exchange rate variability within the bloc. When countries adopt managed floating regimes, coordinating exchange rates will require, in addition to macroeconomic convergence, substantial international reserves or the capacity to borrow in critical situations. This introduces limitations to those schemes aimed to reducing exchange rate volatility through the establishment of floating bands (the "European way"). However, this is particularly difficult, since there is greater capital mobility than during the 1970s and 1980s, and since, unlike Europe, there are no loan agreements between countries in the event of critical situations, and none of the currencies in the region can function as a reserve currency. On the other hand, the alternative of adopting a fixed exchange system, or even dollarization, entails significant costs in terms of flexibility to adjust to external shocks, as the recent Argentine experience shows. Thus, the decision to adopt a mechanism with these features cannot be based only on the attempt to reduce exchange rate volatility to promote trade integration.

In light of these observations, and the fact that the domestic dollarization component plays a central role in selecting an exchange regime or in the exchange rate variability that countries are prepared to accept in floating schemes, it does not appear realistic at this stage to propose exchange rate coordination mechanisms, unless sufficiently broad bands are involved. To the extent that different blocs must coexist

---

[50] See Zahler (2000).

$$Protection_i = \sum_{j=1}^{n-1} t_{j,1995} \times \frac{trade_{ij}}{\sum_{j=1}^{n} trade_{ij}}$$

where $trade_{ij}$ is the average trade between country i and country j between 1989 and 2000, $t_{j,1995}$ is the average external tariff of country j in 1995, and n is the number of countries that form the RIA of which country i is a member. The trade data are from the IMF and the tariff data from the World Bank.

Next we compute the sample mean of the protection index and generate the high protection dummy variable that assigns the value of 1 to countries that have RIA partners with average protection above the sample mean, and 0 to countries that have average protection below the sample mean. As a result of this calculation, the following countries were classified as belonging to highly protected RIAs: Argentina, Bolivia, Brazil, Colombia, Costa Rica, Ecuador, El Salvador, Guatemala, Honduras, Nicaragua, Paraguay, Peru, Singapore, Uruguay and Venezuela. Note that with the exception of Singapore, all are developing countries. Likewise, we generate the low protection dummy variable.

REGRESSION RESULTS

Appendix Table 8.1 | Exports and Real Exchange Rate Misalignments: Regression Results

	Dependent variable: Exports (log)				
	Reg. 1 All countries	Reg. 2 All countries	Reg. 3 Developing countries	Reg. 4 Developed countries	Reg. 5 All countries
Log(GDP)	0.433 (6.89)***	0.433 (6.85)***	0.23 (1.93)*	0.42 (7.30)***	0.429 (6.81)***
Total misalignment	0.613 (3.09)***				
(a) Regional misalignment		1.449 (2.19)**	2.649 (2.31)**	0.602 (1.20)	
(b) Nonregional misalignment		0.347 (1.35)	-0.115 (0.30)	-0.304 (0.86)	0.321 (1.25)
(c) High protection * Regional misalignment					2.9 (2.93)***
(d) Low protection * Regional misalignment					0.572 (0.72)
Constant	-1.263 (0.81)	-1.255 (0.80)	2.772 (0.98)	-0.01 (0.01)	-1.159 (0.74)
No. of observations	394	394	208	185	394
No. of pairs	36	36	19	17	36
R²	0.79	0.8	0.79	0.91	0.8
Tests on difference between coefficients					
(a)-(b)		1.102 [0.09]*	2.764 [0.02]**	0.906 [0.09]*	
(c)-(d)					2.328 [0.025]**
(c)-(b)					2.579 [0.009]***
(d)-(b)					0.251 [0.39]

Notes: Absolute value of t-statistics in parentheses, one tail p-values in brackets. Year dummies and country fixed effects included in all regressions not reported.
* Significant at 10% level.
** Significant at 5% level.
*** Significant at 1% level.
Source: Fernández-Arias, Panizza and Stein (2002).

Appendix Table 8.2 | **FDI and Real Exchange Rate: Regression Results**

Independent variables	Dependent variable: FDI$_i$/FDI$_j$ (log)			
	Reg. 1 All countries	Reg. 2 South-South	Reg. 3 North-South	Reg. 4 North-North
GDP difference	1.5169	1.1501	1.7225	2.0372
	(16.386)***	(5.843)***	(13.513)***	(10.031)***
Openness difference	0.001	-0.0127	0.0036	0.0143
	(1.005)	(6.829)***	(2.650)***	(6.488)***
(a) Same RIA * Real exchange rate	1.2991	0.7891	0.7142	1.8943
	(5.973)***	(2.604)***	(0.639)	(5.234)***
(b) Not same RIA * Real exchange rate	0.119	0.097	0.304	0.4806
	(1.174)	(0.552)	(2.097)**	(1.227)
Constant	-1.8293	-1.0844	-1.7156	-6.6943
	(3.690)***	(1.329)	(2.385)**	(4.482)***
No. of observations	6,120	1,654	3,139	13,27
No. of pairs	630	171	323	136
R^2	0.094	0.096	0.127	0.107
	Tests on difference between coefficients			
(a) - (b)	1.18	0.69	0.41	1.41
	[0.000]***	[0.010]***	[0.355]	[0.000]***

Notes: Absolute value of t-statistics in parentheses, one tail p-values in brackets. Year dummies and country fixed effects included in all regressions not reported.
* Significant at 10% level
** Significant at 5% level
*** Significant at 1% level.
Source: Fernández-Arias, Panizza and Stein (2002).

Appendix Table 8.3 | **Real Misalignments and Currency Crisis: Probit Regression Results**

Independent variables	Dependent variable:					
	A crisis is a real devaluation greater than 5%			A crisis is a real devaluation greater than 10%		
	Reg. 1	Reg. 2	Reg. 3	Reg. 4	Reg 5	Reg 6
(a) Multilateral misalignment	-0.2288			-0.127		
	(8.180)***			(6.591)***		
(b) Regional misalignment		-0.4046			-0.3388	
		(4.183)***			(3.800)***	
(c) Nonregional misalignment		-0.1652			-0.0598	
		(4.285)***			(2.298)**	
(d) Dummy regional misalignment			0.1459			0.1242
			(6.435)***			(5.146)***
(e) Dummy nonregional misalignment			0.0719			0.0457
			(7.835)***			(6.375)***
(f) Access to foreign credit	-0.0194	-0.0188	-0.0172	-0.0049	-0.0035	-0.0027
	(3.040)***	(2.977)***	(2.888)***	(1.075)	(0.868)	(0.845)
(g) Government change	0.0157	0.0166	0.0162	0.0162	0.0147	0.0136
	(1.486)	(1.563)	(1.623)	(1.817)*	(1.814)*	(1.997)*
No. of observations	3,848	3,848	3,848	2,716	2,716	2,716
No. of groups	28	28	28	19	19	19
R^2	0.1368	0.137	0.173	0.1436	0.1577	0.2248
	Tests on difference between coefficients					
(b) - (c)		-0.24			-0.28	
		[0.023]**			[0.005]***	
(d) - (e)			0.07			0.08
			[0.069]*			[0.090]*

Notes: The coefficients reported in the table are marginal effects. Absolute value of t-statistics in parentheses, one tail p-values in brackets. Year dummies and country fixed effects included in all regressions not reported.
* Significant at 10% level.
** Significant at 5% level.
*** Significant at 1% level.
Source: Fernández-Arias, Panizza and Stein (2002).

Box 9.2   Recent Experiences with Dollarization: Ecuador and El Salvador[1]

In recent years, a small but varied group of Latin American countries has seriously considered the option of fully dollarizing its economies. In Ecuador and El Salvador, dollarization was actually adopted, although under very different circumstances.

There are, of course, costs and benefits associated with full dollarization. As in the case of currency unions, a country that adopts the currency of another country sacrifices an independent exchange rate and monetary policy. However, this loss is more important in the case of dollarization, since the United States or any other "anchor" country would not take economic conditions in dollarizing countries into account when conducting its monetary policy. In addition, dollarization implies the loss of seigniorage revenues, which can be substantial, and restricts the ability of the central bank to act as a lender of last resort in case of widespread bank runs.[2]

On the positive side, dollarization maximizes the gains from credibility, representing the strongest commitment to a stable currency from a country with a sound reputation for monetary policy management, and eliminates the scope for currency crises. These credibility gains cannot be matched by the formation of a currency union among emerging economies. Moreover, in the case of countries with a high degree of de facto dollarization, the elimination of currency risk associated with full dollarization may result in the reduction of country risk, as it eliminates important currency mismatches in the balance sheets of the financial, private and public sectors.[3]

Ecuador: Dollarization as Crisis Resolution

In the early 1990s, Ecuador benefited from a successful stabilization program, higher oil prices and large capital inflows. But the boom turned to bust in 1995-96. A "sudden stop" in capital inflows, coupled with a banking sector that was undergoing rapid liberalization but had weak regulatory oversight, created problems in several financial institutions. Things got worse in 1997-98, given the lack of decisive action on problem banks and compounded by El Niño, contagion from the Russian default, and sharp declines in oil prices.

The failure to maintain the exchange rate within a band, coupled with high levels of dollar debts, generated a spiral of corporate default, capital flight and devaluation. The exchange rate depreciated to over 5,000 sucres per U.S. dollar by the end of 1998 and more than 10,000 by June 1999. The banking and currency crisis was accompanied by a major fiscal crisis as the real economy imploded. In September 1999, Ecuador deferred payments on its Brady bonds. A deposit freeze stabilized the sucre through July 1999,

but further runs, sparked by the fear of default, sent the sucre into a tailspin that reached 26,000 per U.S. dollar in January 2000.

The full dollarization announced in January 2000 to stabilize the exchange rate and bring back confidence was implemented through the Economic Transformation Law passed several months later. The law prohibited new issues of sucres, required the central bank to exchange sucres for dollars at the exchange rate of 25,000, and forced companies to convert their accounts into dollars. By Latin American standards, Ecuador had neither a high degree of trade integration with the United States nor a business cycle highly correlated with that country. It did have important de facto dollarization, and was in desperate need of stability and credibility.

Dollarization, by definition, stabilized the currency market. The surprise, for many observers, was how the Economic Transformation Law calmed the nerves of depositors in the banking system, even though the bank resolution process was by no means complete.[4] The law included other important policy changes such as fiscal and labor market reforms, and led to an IMF agreement in April 2000.[5] In addition, Ecuador finally had some good luck, since oil prices through the first quarter of 2001 rose dramatically. Finally, Ecuador's default was resolved relatively quickly and perhaps more smoothly than many anticipated.

The rate of 25,000 sucres per dollar implied that the real exchange rate was very significantly undervalued, and ensured that the central bank had "excess reserves" to provide liquidity to the banking system in dollars if needed. Interest rates declined to around 20 percent, which, coupled with the slow decline in inflation, implied continuing negative real interest rates through the transition. These factors helped the real economy, in particular corporate borrowers who saw their profitability rates rise and their debt diluted.[6]

Ecuador still faces many challenges. The banking system has improved but could be strengthened further and the fiscal situation remains a concern. Dollarization did not and cannot provide a solution to these issues. While there were many other factors at play, the preliminary conclusion is that dollarization, coupled with other appropriate policy reforms and some good luck, did appear to help to put Ecuador back on the road to economic stability.

El Salvador: Dollarization to Consolidate Economic Success

El Salvador had relative economic success through the 1990s. Since 1993, the exchange rate has been fixed and constant. Growth averaged 3.9 percent annually over 1995-98, and although it declined for 2000 and 2001, this was largely a result of significant external shocks and the country's devastating earthquakes. Moreover, with a fiscal deficit that hovered around 1.5 percent of GDP from 1993 to 1999 and with both monetary and financial stability, the country obtained a much prized investment grade credit rating.

The motivation for dollarization was at least threefold. First, perceived devaluation risk persisted, as evidenced by a spread between colon and dollar interest rates. By dollarizing, the authorities hoped to bring down domestic interest rates, increasing investment and growth. Second, dollarization was seen as a way to reduce transaction costs and enhance integration. El Salvador's exports to the United States and to the dollarized trading regime of Central America represent 70 percent of total trade, local companies have been borrowing directly from international banks, and El Salvador benefits hugely from substantial remittances from the United States. A third motivation may have been more political: the government had been pushing through a radical reform program, and dollarization may have been seen as a way of locking in those reforms.

Dollarization commenced at the start of 2001 when the Monetary Integration Law made the U.S. dollar legal tender and all new financial contracts became denominated in them. The central bank started to exchange colons for dollars, voluntarily, at the rate of 8.75 colons per U.S. dollar. After one year, more than 50 percent of colons in circulation had been retired.

Colon interest rates have ceased to exist and dollar rates, which are comparatively lower, have implied a significant fall in the cost of financing.[7] There is also evidence of an increase in the availability of different forms of credit. In particular, mortgages are now available at maturities of 15 years and longer, and at interest rates of 10.5 percent, benefiting both the household and the corporate sector. Credit from foreign banks extended directly to local companies has grown substantially, more than compensating for a decline in domestic credit. This suggests that dollarization has had a large impact on financial integration.

It is difficult to assess the effect of full dollarization on the real economy, in part because the process is not yet complete. Through 2001, El Salvador was hit by a series of negative shocks: earthquakes, a significant fall in coffee prices, a severe drought, and finally the effects of the terrorist attacks on the United States in September. These developments have raised concerns regarding both competitiveness and the country's fiscal position, as lower growth and reconstruction efforts have placed pressure on the budget. The government must continue to enhance perceptions of fiscal sustainability and the economy needs to be highly flexible to respond to these and other shocks in order to reap the full benefits of dollarization.

---

[1] This box was written by Andrew Powell.

[2] Calvo (1999) argues that countries that provide effective services as lenders of last resort are those that are able to borrow in such times, rather than just print money.

[3] For a discussion of the link between currency risk and country risk, see Powell and Sturzenegger (forthcoming).

[4] Bank deposits rose gradually from $2.7 billion in January 2001 to $4.4 billion by mid-2001.

[5] The IMF was not consulted on the decision to dollarize. See Fischer (2000) for an account of the relations between Ecuador and the IMF.

[6] See de la Torre, Garcia Saltos and Mascaro (2001) for an account of the "inflation hump and dilution of debts."

[7] Interestingly, dollar rates did not fall. This follows academic predictions, given that the country was not particularly dollarized previously and had high credibility, as evidenced by its investment grade rating. See Berg and Borensztein (2000) and Powell and Sturzenegger (forthcoming).

Existence of alternative adjustment mechanisms. Exchange rate adjustment is not the only mechanism to restore equilibrium in case of asymmetric shocks. Other possible mechanisms are wage flexibility and labor mobility. If wages are perfectly flexible, restoring equilibrium through depreciation is almost equivalent to achieving this effect through a reduction in wages. In contrast, when wages are downwardly inflexible, adjustment through wage reductions is much slower and more costly, as it leads to extended periods of high unemployment. Wage inflexibility thus makes exchange rate flexibility and monetary independence more desirable.[24]

---

[24] Eichengreen (1996) has argued that the emergence of universal suffrage and increasing unionization led to the collapse of the Gold Standard, as it became politically difficult for countries to sustain the extended periods of unemployment associated with the lack of monetary independence.

Box 9.3   Labor Mobility in the European Union[1]

The goal of full mobility of labor within the European Union was already stated in the Treaty of Rome and formally embodied in European law in 1968. However, just as for the mobility of goods, many barriers remained. It was not until the European Act of 1986, which was implemented in 1992, that precise steps were taken to practically implement labor mobility within the EU. Such steps include detailed directives about harmonization of labor standards and mutual recognition of qualifications, as well as the establishment of a cross-border European Employment Service (EURES).

Prior to 1992, however, there were some multilateral agreements that guaranteed labor mobility among a subset of European countries. For example, the Common Nordic Labor Market established between Denmark, Finland, Norway and Sweden in 1954 allowed nationals from any of these countries to work in any other Nordic country without a work permit. Similarly, in 1958, the Benelux countries (Belgium, Netherlands, and Luxembourg) signed an economic integration treaty that went much further than the European Community. Nationals of any Benelux country could freely enter any other Benelux country to engage in any economic activity. The Benelux treaty guaranteed that they would be treated on par with nationals of the host country. Finally, in 1990, free movement was extended beyond the EU's border, since it was granted to countries of the European Economic Area.[2]

That the 1968 agreement was not sufficient to remove barriers to mobility, and that such a right had to be repeatedly reasserted in European treaties since then,[3] shows that progress in establishing full labor mobility has not been as rapid as expected.

Euro-law does not prevent national governments from establishing some subtle barriers. For example, it does not prevent border controls. For that reason, a subset of European countries has signed the Schengen Agreement, which goes further than the Maastricht Treaty by abolishing border controls among members. This treaty came into effect in 1995 and currently includes all EU countries except the United Kingdom and Ireland.

Euro-law does not guarantee the free movement of people. Thus, one may move to seek work, but not just to settle or to be on welfare—typically, unemployed persons are allowed to move only if they can prove financial autonomy. In practice, this means that job seekers are allowed a three-month stay. While the European Court recently stated that longer periods were appropriate, this is a potential source of conflict. Furthermore, given the traditionally long duration of unemployment in most European labor markets, three or even six months is not a long period relative to the time it takes to find a job. Thus, such limitations, which are motivated by the need to discourage "welfare shopping," may also act as a barrier to labor mobility.

More serious barriers come from a lack of recognition of professional qualifications. Given the convergence in income levels, and the linguistic barriers to mobility, intra-EU migrants would be expected to be mostly skilled. Consequently, inadequate recognition of qualifications can be a very effective barrier to labor mobility. The European Commission states: "The rights of EU citizens to establish themselves or to provide services anywhere in the EU are fundamental principles of European Union law. Regulations which only recognise professional qualifications of a particular jurisdiction present obstacles to these fundamental freedoms." As a result, the European Commission has issued 17 directives in order to ensure mutual recognition of professional qualifications.

Since the establishment of the single market, many court cases have come up regarding failures of member states to implement such directives. Examples include art restorers, school doctors, architects, hairdressers, nurses, lawyers and ski instructors. In each of these cases, someone from one of the professions was barred from working in another EU country because his or her degree or professional experience was not recognized by the host country. As recently as April 2002, that is, 10 years after the Maastricht Treaty, the commission launched an infringement procedure against 11 member states for failing to implement an EC directive relating to mutual recognition in some areas.

These cases suggest that progress in implementing the labor mobility part of the Single European Act has been slow. A person considering working in another member country faces substantial uncertainty regarding whether he or she will actually be allowed to do so by the host country's government. Such uncertainty remains a significant barrier to labor mobility.

One reason why the process is slow is that the EC has opted for a piecemeal approach, issuing specific directives for specific sectors and professions. Given the large numbers of countries and professions, this involves complex regulations and opportunities for cheating. Alternatively, the EC could have tried a more liberal and ambitious approach by challenging the very principle of recognition as a prerequisite for being allowed to work. Under such an approach, national governments would issue certifications rather than authorizations. Such certifications would be a signal of quality, and workers with different certifications by different governments (or by any private certification agency) would be allowed to freely compete in the same territory. This is, after all, what prevails for the bulk of wage earners.

While the administrative tradition prevailing in the EC makes it unlikely that it will evolve toward such a view (which might also be blocked by some member states), the community has nevertheless recognized that "over the years the legal environment for the recognition of professional qualifications has become more and more complex," and, in the aftermath of the Stockholm European Council, has launched a consultation to put forward a more uniform, transparent and flexible system.

Another important impediment to mobility is lack of pension portability. This involves two main issues. The first is whether previous contributions in another member country can be validated when computing the pensions. This will not be the case if eligibility is conditional on a minimum contribution period and if mobility takes place before that period has elapsed. The second issue is whether differences in tax practices—such as taxation at the date of contribution in one country versus the date when pension income is paid in another—can be offset to prevent double taxation of mobile workers' pensions. While main pension schemes were made transferable in the European Union Treaty, this is not the case for supplementary schemes, which represent a substantial portion of skilled workers' pensions. In the aftermath of the Stockholm Council, the commission has pledged to make proposals to increase supplementary pension portability.

The European Union also has a piecemeal and discretionary approach when considering enlargement. Newcomers need not be fully integrated within the EU's legal framework overnight. For example, in the case of the accession of Greece (1981), Portugal and Spain (1986), a transition period of seven years was imposed before full labor mobility was granted. The European Commission proposed a similar transition period in 2001 for the next wave of enlargement, which will include 10 Central and Eastern European countries. The philosophy behind such restrictions is probably to ensure, in order to avoid being flooded by migrants from newly admitted countries, that enough convergence in income levels has taken place before boundaries are fully open. Indeed, such provisions were not imposed in 1995 when three wealthy countries joined (Austria, Finland and Sweden), nor in 1971, when Denmark, Ireland and the UK joined. Finally, according to EC plans, two accession candidates with small populations, Cyprus and Malta, will be able to bypass the seven-year transition period for labor mobility.

Labor mobility in the European Union is traditionally low and is not very elastic to economic conditions. This is true for interregional as well as cross-border mobility. In France and Germany, among foreign residents only 37 percent and 25 percent,

respectively, are EU nationals. In terms of flows, in 1997, Germany still had a large inflow of about 150,000 EU residents, while the UK had 61,000 and France only had 6,400 and Italy 9,200.[4] Presumably, the large influx of foreign EU residents in Germany is due to longstanding migration channels of unskilled workers from the south of Italy, while the UK benefits from having a virtually universally spoken language. By contrast, the French and Italian figures suggest that, absent these factors, cross-border EU migration is minute. It is also estimated that if unemployment goes up by 100 people in a particular area, only 30 of them would leave if that area were in Germany, only 8.4 in France, and only 3.7 in Italy.[5]

From an economic perspective, there is a large degree of complementarity between the European Monetary Union and closer integration of labor markets. Because of the EMU, individual countries can no longer offset an adverse shock by depreciating their currency. Alternative options are increasing price and wage flexibility, which requires painful structural reforms, or increasing cross-border labor mobility. If labor mobility is high, then when a region or country faces an adverse shock, people will move to other places with more favorable labor market conditions. This allows adjustment in the absence of movements in relative prices. However, the evidence of low cross-border migration, and low responsiveness of migration to shocks, suggests that this mechanism will be weak and that asymmetric shocks will generate tensions within the EMU.

For these reasons it is important to remove remaining barriers to labor mobility within the Euro-area, such as the legal barriers that are described above. However, this is likely to be insufficient in light of the importance of linguistic barriers and the fact that even intra-country and interregional migration are low in Europe.

---

[1] This box was written by Gilles St. Paul.

[2] That area now only includes Iceland, Liechtenstein and Norway. EEA membership in effect is equivalent to EU membership, but excludes participation in the Common Agricultural Policy.

[3] For example, in the Single European Act of 1986, the Social Charter of 1990, and the 1998 Treaty of Amsterdam.

[4] See Bruecker et al. (2001).

[5] See Puhani (2001).

Appendix Table 9.4 | **Business-Cycle Synchronization and Trade Integration:**
Panel Data Regression Analysis
The Effect of Regional Integration Agreements Sample of all Country Pairs, 1960-99

Independent variables	Dependent variable: Business cycle synchronization All countries		
	Model 1	Model 2	Model 3
I. Bilateral trade intensity (as a ratio of total trade in the country pair)			
Non-RIA member	29.715	30.011	28.055
	(5.25)**	(4.46)**	(3.60)**
RIA member	14.066	11.406	12.805
	(8.74)**	(6.36)**	(6.48)**
R^2	0.02	0.01	0.01
No. of observations	15460	12378	9533
II. Bilateral trade intensity (as a ratio of output in the country pair)			
Non-RIA member	28.527	25.472	27.995
	(9.04)**	(7.11)**	(7.08)**
RIA member	66.153	62.914	68.814
	(5.16)**	(4.12)**	(4.19)**
R^2	0.02	0.02	0.01
No. of Observations	16,647	12,652	9,760

Note: Instrumental variables panel estimation. Numbers in parentheses represent t statistics. Time dummies for each decade included in all regressions are not reported. Cyclical output is computed using Band-Pass filter. In Model 1, we do not include the index of similarity; in Model 2 we include the 3-sector index of similarity, and in Model 3 we use the 9-sector index of similarity. For Figure 9.7 we use the bilateral trade intensity as a ratio of output in the country pair and Model 3 (9-sector index of similarity). The standard deviation of the bilateral trade intensity of the country pairs is: 0.001566 for RIA members, and 0.000959 for non-RIA members.
* Significant at 10% level.
** Significant at 5% level.
*** Significant at 1% level.
Source: Calderón, Chong and Stein (2002).

Appendix Table 9.5 | **Business-Cycle Synchronization and Trade Integration:**
Panel Data Regression Analysis
The Effect of Regional Integration Agreements by Country Pair
Sample of all Country Pairs, 1960-99

Independent variables	Dependent variable: Business cycle synchronization All countries		
	Model 1	Model 2	Model 3
I. Bilateral trade intensity (as a ratio of total trade in the country pair)			
(Industrial-industrial) with non-RIA member	35.525	28.715	36.774
	(8.58)**	(4.19)**	(3.20)**
(Developing-developing) with non-RIA member	9.744	10.478	12.021
	(5.19)**	(5.37)**	(5.79)**
(Industrial-developing) with non-RIA member	14.573	11.472	14.327
	(4.70)**	(3.04)**	(2.93)**
(Industrial-industrial) with RIA member	28.328	31.59	37.655
	(5.15)**	(4.86)**	(4.88)**
(Developing-developing) with RIA member	10.333	8.823	14.187
	(1.35)	(1.03)	(1.58)
RIA	−0.009	0.011	−0.03
	(0.17)	(0.18)	(0.47)
R^2	0.02	0.02	0.01
No. of observations	15,460	12,378	9,533
II. Bilateral trade intensity (as a ratio of output in the country pair)			
(Industrial-industrial) with non-RIA member	84.194	68.663	103.588
	(8.39)**	(3.78)**	(3.07)**
(Developing-developing) with non-RIA member	18.816	22.4	25.497
	(5.20)**	(5.76)**	(6.14)**
(Industrial-developing) with non-RIA member	37.14	32.911	38.352
	(6.44)**	(4.60)**	(4.22)**
(Industrial-industrial) with RIA member	62.158	65.586	84.14
	(5.15)**	(4.56)**	(5.44)**
(Developing-developing) with RIA member	0.89	23.305	40.575
	(1.97)*	(1.40)	(2.35)*
RIA	-0.064	-0.034	-0.116
	(1.05)	(0.46)	(1.52)
R^2	0.02	0.02	0.01
No. of observations	16,647	12,652	9,760

Note: Instrumental variables panel estimation. Numbers in parentheses represent absolute values of t statistics. Time dummies for each decade included in all regressions are not reported. Cyclical output is computed using Band-Pass filter. In Model 1 we do not include the index of similarity; in Model 2 we include the 3-sector index of similarity, and in Model 3 we use the 9-sector index of similarity. For Figure 9.7 we use the bilateral trade intensity as a ratio of output in the country pair and Model 3 (9-sector index of similarity). The standard deviation of the bilateral trade intensity of the country pairs is: 0.001349 for Industrial-industrial with RIA member, 0.001571 for Developing-developing with RIA member, 0.001062 for Industrial-industrial with non-RIA member, and 0.001003 for Developing-developing with non-RIA member.
* Significant at 10% level.
** Significant at 5% level.
*** Significant at 1% level.
Source: Calderón, Chong and Stein (2002).

REFERENCES

Anderson, J., and E. van Wincoop. 2001. *Gravity with Gravitas: A Solution to the Border Puzzle.* NBER Working Paper no. 8079.

Baliño, Tomás, Adam Bennett, and Eduardo Borensztein. 1999. *Monetary Policy in Dollarized Economies.* IMF Occasional Paper 171, International Monetary Fund, Washington, DC.

Barro, R., and D. Gordon. 1983. A Positive Theory of Monetary Policy in a Natural Rate Model. *Journal of Political Economy* 91: 589-610.

Baxter, M., and R. G. King. 1999. Measuring Business Cycles: Approximate Band-Pass Filters for Economic Time Series. *The Review of Economics and Statistics* 81: 575-93.

Berg, Andrew, and Eduardo Borensztein. 2000. *The Pros and Cons of Dollarization.* IMF Working Paper WP/00/50, International Monetary Fund, Washington, DC. March.

Bernanke, Ben, Thomas Laubach, Frederic Mishkin, and Adam Posen. 1999. *Inflation Targeting.* Princeton, NJ: Princeton University Press.

Bruecker, H., G. Epstein, B. McCormick, G. Saint-Paul, A. Venturini, and K. Zimmermann. 2001. Managing Migration in the European Welfare State. Milan: Fondazione Rodolfo De Benedetti.

Calderón, C., A. Chong, and E. Stein. 2002. Does Trade Integration Generate Higher Business Cycle Synchronization? Inter-American Development Bank, Washington, DC. Mimeo.

Calvo, G. 1999. On Dollarization. University of Maryland, College Park, MD. Mimeo.

Calvo, G., and C. M. Reinhart. 2001. Fixing for Your Life. In Susan M. Collins and Dani Rodrik (eds.), *Brookings Trade Forum.* Washington, DC: Brookings Institution Press.

———. 2002. Fear of Floating. *Quarterly Journal of Economics* 117(2): 379-408.

Carrera, J., and F. Sturzenegger. 2000. Coordinación de políticas macroeconómicas en el Mercosur. Fondo de Cultura Económica, Mexico. October.

Cecchetti, S., and M. Ehrmann. 1999. *Does Inflation Targeting Increase Output Volatility? An International Comparison of Policymakers' Preferences.* NBER Working Paper no. 7426.

Chang, R., and A. Velasco. 2001. Dollarization: Analytical Issues. Rutgers University, Harvard University and NBER. December.

Clark, T., and E. van Wincoop. 2001. Borders and Business Cycles. *Journal of International Economics* 55(1) October: 59-85.

Deardorff, A.V. (ed.). 1998. Determinants of Bilateral Trade: Does Gravity Work in a Neoclassical World? In J.A. Frankel, *The Regionalization of the World Economy.* Chicago: University of Chicago Press.

de la Torre A., R. Garcia Saltos, and Y. Mascaro. 2001. Banking, Currency, and Debt Meltdown: Ecuador Crisis in the Late 1990s. World Bank, Washington, DC. Mimeo.

De Grauwe, P. 1994. *The Economics of Monetary Integration.* Oxford, UK: Oxford University Press.

Edison, H., and M. Melvin. 1990. The Determinants and Implications of the Choice of an Exchange Rate System. In W. Haraf and T. Willet (eds.), *Monetary Policy for a Volatile Global Economy.* Washington, DC: AEI Press.

Eichengreen, Barry. 1996. *Globalizing Capital: A History of the International Monetary System.* Princeton, NJ: Princeton University Press.

———. 1997. Free Trade and Macroeconomic Policy. In S. Burki, G. Perry and S. Calvo (eds.), Trade: Towards Open Regionalism. Paper presented at the LAC ABCDE Conference, World Bank, Montevideo, Uruguay.

———. 1998. Does Mercosur Need a Single Currency? Institute of Business and Economic Research, Center for International and Development Economic Research, University of California, Berkeley.

Estevadeordal, Antoni, Brian Frantz, and Raúl Sáez. 2001. Exchange Rate Volatility and International Trade in Developing Countries. Inter-American Development Bank, Washington, DC. Mimeo.

Estevadeordal, A., B. Frantz, and A. Taylor. 2002. The Rise and Fall of World Trade, 1870-1939. Inter-American Development Bank, Washington, DC. Mimeo.

Fatas, A. 1997. EMU: *Countries or Regions? Lessons from the EMS Experience.* Centre for Economic Policy Research Discussion Paper no. 1558.

Fernández-Arias, E., and E. Talvi. 1999. Devaluation or Deflation? Adjustment under Liability Dollarization. Inter-American Development Bank, Washington, DC. Mimeo.

Fischer, I. 1933. The Debt-Deflation Theory of Great Depressions. *Econometrica* 1(4) October: 337-57.

Fischer, S. 2000. Ecuador and the IMF. Hoover Institution Conference on Currency Unions, Palo Alto, CA. May.

Frankel, J. A., and A. K. Rose. 1997. Is EMU More Justifiable Ex Post than Ex Ante? *European Economic Review* 41: 753-60.

____. 1998. The Endogeneity of the Optimum Currency Area Criteria. *The Economic Journal* 108: 1009-25.

____. 2002. An Estimate of the Effect of Common Currencies on Trade and Income. *Quarterly Journal of Economics.*

Frankel, J. A., and S. J. Wei. 1997. Open versus Closed Trade Blocs. In Takatoshi Ito and Anne Krueger (eds.), *Regional versus Multinational Trade Arrangements.* Chicago: University of Chicago Press.

Fratianni, M., and A. Hauskrecht. 2002. A Centralized Monetary Union Mercosur: Lessons from EMU. Conference on Euro and Dollarization: Forms of Monetary Union in Integrated Regions, Fordham University and CEPR, New York, April 5-6.

Giambiagi, Fabio. 1999. Mercosur: Why Does Monetary Union Make Sense in the Long Term? *Ensaios BNDES* 12. December.

Giavazzi, Francesco, and Marco Pagano. 1988. The Advantage of Tying One's Hands, *European Economic Review* 32: 1055-82.

Giordano, P., and J. Monteagudo. 2002. Exchange Rate Volatility, Trade and Regional Integration: Evidence from Latin America. Inter-American Development Bank. Mimeo.

Glick, R., and A. Rose. 2001. *Does a Currency Union Affect Trade?* The Time Series Evidence. NBER Working Paper no. 8396.

Hausmann, R., and B. Eichengreen. 1999. *Exchange Rate and Financial Fragility.* NBER Working Paper no. 7418.

Hausmann, R., and A. Powell. 1999. Alternative Exchange Rate Regimes for the Region. Inter-American Development Bank. July.

Hausmann, R., U. Panizza, and E. Stein. 2001. Why Do Countries Float the Way they Float? *Journal of Development Economics.* December.

Heckman, James, and Carmen Pagés. 2000. *The Cost of Job Security Regulation: Evidence from Latin American Labor Markets.* Inter-American Development Bank Research Department Working Paper no. 430, Washington, DC. August.

International Monetary Fund. 2000. *Direction of Trade.* Washington, DC: IMF.

____. 2001. *World Economic Outlook: The Information Technology Revolution.* Washington, DC: IMF.

Krugman, P. 1991. *Geography and Trade.* Leuven, Belgium: Leuven University Press; and Cambridge MA: MIT Press.

Lavagna, R., and F. Giambiagi. 1998. Hacia la creación de una moneda común. Una propuesta de convergencia coordinada de políticas macroeconómicas en el Mercosur. BNDES.

Levy Yeyati, E. 2001. On the Impact of a Common Currency on Bilateral Trade. Universidad Torcuato Di Tella, Buenos Aires.

Licandro Ferrando, G. 2000. Monetary Policy Coordination, Monetary Integration and Other Essays. University of California at Los Angeles. Ph.D. Dissertation.

López-Córdova, E., and C. Meissner. Forthcoming. Exchange-Rate Regimes and International Trade: Evidence from the Classical Gold Era. *American Economic Review.*

McKinnon, R. I. 1963. Optimum Currency Areas. *American Economic Review* 53: 717-24.

Micco, A., E. Stein, and G. Ordoñez. 2002. The Currency Union Effect on Trade: Early Evidence from the European Union. Inter-American Development Bank. Mimeo.

Mundell, R. 1961. A Theory of Optimum Currency Areas. *American Economic Review* 51: 509-17.

Nitsch, V. 2001. Honey, I Just Shrank the Currency Union Effect. *The World Economy.*

Padoa Schioppa, Tommaso. 1999. EMU and Banking Supervision Lecture delivered at the London School of Economics, February 24.

Panizza, Ugo. 2000. *Monetary and Fiscal Policies in Emerging Markets.* Egyptian Center for Economic Studies Working Paper no. 50.

Panizza, U., E. Stein, and E. Talvi. 2002. Assessing Dollarization: An Application to Central American and Caribbean Countries. In E. Levy Yeyati and F. Sturzenegger (eds.), *Dollarization.* Cambridge, MA: MIT Press.

Persson, T. 2001. Currency Union and Trade: How Large is the Treatment Effect? *Economic Policy: A European Forum* 33: 433-48.

Powell, A., and F. Sturzenegger. Forthcoming. Dollarization: The Link between Devaluation Risk and Default Risk. In E. Levy Yeyati and F. Sturzenegger (eds.), *Dollarization.* Cambridge, MA: MIT Press.

Puhani, Patrick A. 2001. Labour Mobility: An Adjustment Mechanism in Euroland? *German Economic Review* 2(2) May: 127-40.

Rose, A. 2000. One Money, One Market: Estimating the Effect of Common Currencies on Trade. *Economic Policy* 30: 7-45.

Rose, A., and E. van Wincoop. 2001. National Money as a Barrier to International Trade: The Real Case for Currency Union. *American Economic Review* 91: 386-90.

Stein, E., and D. Weinhold. 1998. Canadian-U.S. Border Effects and the Gravity Equation Model of Trade. Inter-American Development Bank, Washingto, DC. Mimeo.

Tenreyro, S. 2001. On the Causes and Consequences of Currency Union. Harvard University, Cambridge, MA. Mimeo.

Wei, S.J. 1996. *Intra-National versus International Trade: How Stubborn Are Nations in Global Integration?* NBER Working Paper no. 5531. April.

Worrel, Marshall, and L. Smith. 1998. The Political Economy of Exchange Rate Policy in the English-Speaking Caribbean. Institute of Social and Economic Research, University of the West Indies, Bridgetown, Barbados, July.

Wyplosz, Charles. 1999. Economic Policy Coordination in EMU: Strategies and Institutions. Graduate Institute of International Studies, Geneva. Mimeo.

Zhaler, R. 1999. El Euro y su impacto internacional. Paper presented at the Annual Meeting of the Inter-American Development Bank and the Inter-American Investment Corporation, 15-17 March, Paris.

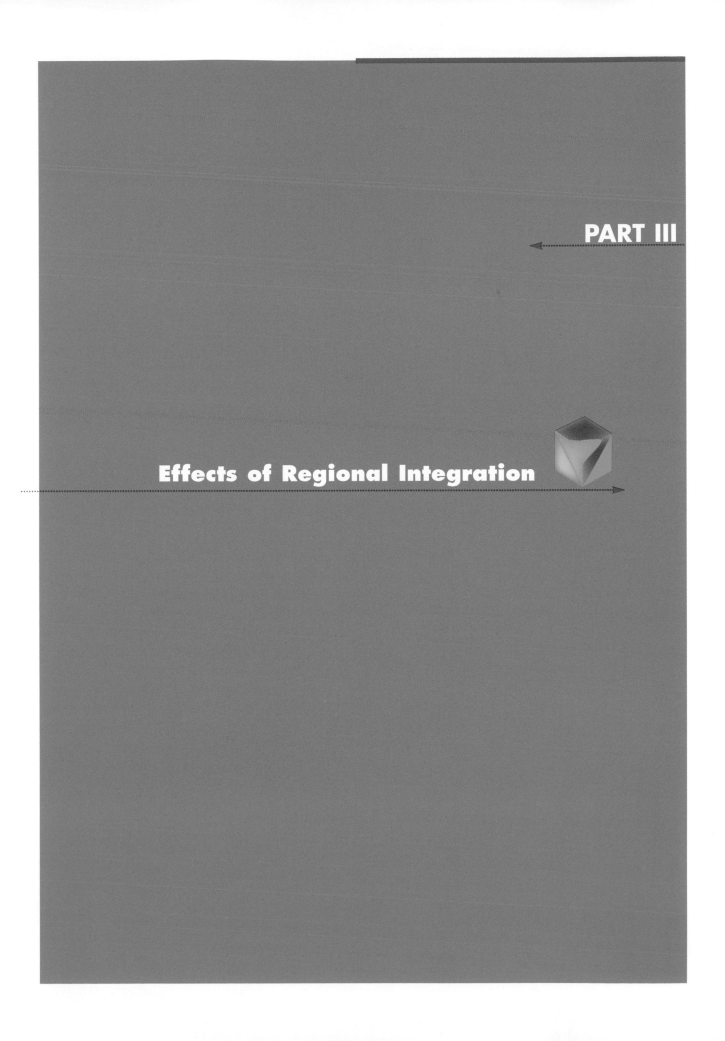

PART III

Effects of Regional Integration

Chapter 10

REGIONAL INTEGRATION AND FOREIGN DIRECT INVESTMENT

Just as there has been a proliferation in the number and depth of regional integration agreements worldwide over the past two decades, there has also been a dramatic surge in flows of foreign direct investment (FDI). While world trade has increased over the period by a factor of two, flows of FDI have increased by a factor of ten. The increased FDI has flowed toward both developed and developing countries, and in fact has become the main source of foreign financing by a large margin for emerging markets, and particularly for Latin America and the Caribbean.

In light of these developments, the role of regional integration agreements (RIAs) as a determinant of the location of FDI has become a key issue for emerging economies. For Latin America, the concern regarding the impact of RIAs on FDI is related to a wide range of initiatives, including subregional agreements, South-South arrangements, and agreements with the European Union (EU). The most wide-ranging agreement, of course, will be the Free Trade Area of the Americas (FTAA), which raises a number of important questions. What effect will the FTAA have on FDI from the United States and Canada to Latin American countries? How will it affect FDI from the rest of the world? What are the implications for a country such as Mexico, whose preferential access to the United States may be diluted? Should we expect to see winners and losers? What determines whether a particular country will win or lose?

RECENT FDI TRENDS IN LATIN AMERICA AND THE WORLD[1]

While FDI has been increasing rapidly for the last 20 years, the surge in multinational activity around the world was most dramatic during the second half of the 1990s, when FDI flows increased by more than 30 percent per year. FDI flows to Latin America followed a similar trend through 1999, but fell by nearly 20 percent during 2000 following seven years of steady growth (Figure 10.1).[2]

The spectacular rise in FDI in Latin America has resulted in a substantial increase in its importance, as measured by the stock of FDI as a share of GDP (Figure 10.2). While FDI stock represented less than 10 percent of GDP as recently as 1990, today it stands at around 23 percent. This is a far cry from the 60 percent share it represents for East Asia, but it is quite a bit larger than the corresponding figure for the industrial countries, which is on the order of 14 percent. Latin America has not been alone in terms of the significant increase in multinational activity: Figure 10.2 shows all regions in the world have experienced the same phenomenon.

---

[1] For a more detailed analysis of recent FDI trends, see ECLAC (2000) and UNCTAD (2001).

[2] It is not clear yet whether this fall marks a change in the trend, or whether it is just associated with the lumpy character of FDI. Some $15 billion of the $80 billion of FDI flows into Latin America in 1999 corresponded to a single operation: the purchase of Argentina's oil company by Spain's Repsol. Yet the downturn could also be explained by the fact that there is little left to privatize.

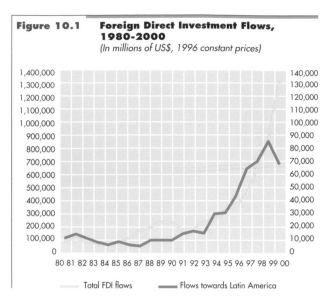

Figure 10.1 Foreign Direct Investment Flows, 1980-2000
(In millions of US$, 1996 constant prices)

Total FDI flows — Flows towards Latin America

Source: IMF, *International Financial Statistics.*

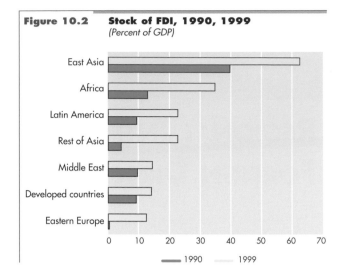

Figure 10.2 Stock of FDI, 1990, 1999
(Percent of GDP)

1990   1999

Source: IDB calculations based on IMF, *International Financial Statistics* and World Bank, *World Development Indicators.*

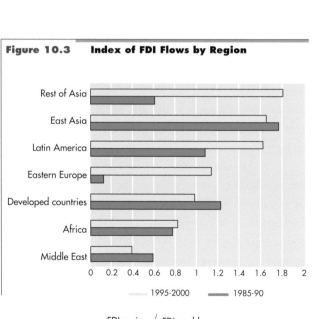

Figure 10.3 Index of FDI Flows by Region

1995-2000 — 1985-90

Note: $Index\ region_i = [\frac{FDI\ region_i\ /\ FDI\ world}{GDP\ region_i\ /\ GDP\ world}]$

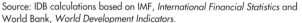

Source: IDB calculations based on IMF, *International Financial Statistics* and World Bank, *World Development Indicators.*

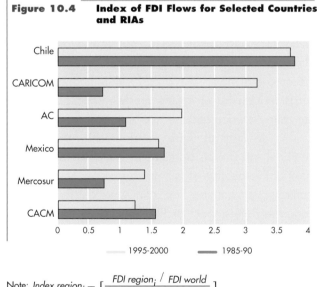

Figure 10.4 Index of FDI Flows for Selected Countries and RIAs

1995-2000 — 1985-90

Note: $Index\ region_i = [\frac{FDI\ region_i\ /\ FDI\ world}{GDP\ region_i\ /\ GDP\ world}]$

Source: IDB calculations based on IMF, *International Financial Statistics* and World Bank, *World Development Indicators.*

A different way to compare the evolution of FDI in Latin America with that of other regions is by using an index of inward FDI developed by UNCTAD, in which a region's share in world FDI flows is divided by its share in world GDP (Figure 10.3). A value of 1 in this index indicates that the country attracts FDI in exact proportion to its GDP. The value of the index for Latin America increased substantially, from 1.08 dur-

ing the second half of the 1980s to 1.62 in the late 1990s. In other words, Latin America now receives 60 percent more FDI than what would be warranted by its share in world GDP. In fact, the region is now near the top of the rankings according to this index, closely following East Asia and the rest of Asia, which is dominated by China.

Figure 10.4 shows the same index for inward FDI for a number of RIAs, and for some countries in Latin America. Chile was included by itself in the figure because its integration strategy has not followed a sub-regional pattern. Mexico, apart from NAFTA, has a similar integration strategy and, had it been included within NAFTA, its index would have reflected mainly the evolution of FDI in the United States, by far the largest member of the group. Table 10.1 presents the evolution of the index for each of the individual countries as well. The results shows that the index increased for each of the RIAs considered, except for the Central American Common Market (CACM), which shows a small decline. Particularly noteworthy is the Caribbean Community (CARICOM), where the index increased dramatically. This group's share in FDI inflows is now three times larger than its share of GDP. The Andean Community (AC) and Mercosur are the other two groups with large increases in the index. Mexico, and especially Chile, while showing small declines in the index, are still among the countries that receive the most FDI in relation to GDP.

Figure 10.5 shows the evolution of the composition of FDI by sector. For the world as a whole, there has been a shift in FDI from natural resources to services, which now account for half of total FDI stocks, while the share of manufacturing has remained fairly constant at about 40 percent. Not surprisingly, FDI in developed countries follows a similar pattern, since those nations represent a very large share of the total stocks.

In Latin America, however, the pattern has been very different. First, the share of FDI in natural resources has increased from 9.6 to 12 percent. This can be explained by deregulation and privatization in mining, oil and gas, coupled with the discovery of new reserves. Second, the share of manufacturing has been cut in half. A likely explanation for this is the end of import-substitution industrialization. As we will see later in this chapter, one of the reasons for multinational activity is that it allows firms to "jump" trade barriers, and serve through domestic production a market that is too costly to serve through trade. As tariff barriers decline, this motivation for firms to engage in multinational activity becomes weaker. Third, the increase in the share of services in Latin America has been particularly large compared with other regions. While around the world the increase in services has been

Table 10.1 | FDI Inflows to Latin America
(Percent of GDP)

	1985-90	1995-2000
Mercosur	0.73	1.37
Argentina	1.18	1.77
Brazil	0.59	1.25
Paraguay	0.40	1.06
Uruguay	0.45	0.45
CACM	1.55	1.22
Costa Rica	2.27	1.77
El Salvador	0.58	1.00
Guatemala	2.03	0.57
Honduras	1.47	1.38
Nicaragua	0.00	4.01
AC	1.08	1.96
Bolivia	0.71	4.57
Colombia	2.70	1.61
Ecuador	1.31	1.79
Peru	0.17	2.21
Venezuela	0.28	2.00
CARICOM	0.71	3.16
Antigua & Barbuda	15.12	2.65
Bahamas	-0.35	na
Barbados	0.79	0.37
Belize	4.36	1.69
Dominica	9.77	6.05
Grenada	7.50	5.09
Guyana	0.22	1.66
Jamaica	0.99	2.38
St. Lucia	11.35	4.21
St. Kitts & Nevis	22.80	7.28
St. Vincent	5.85	10.43
Suriname	-13.55	na
Trinidad & Tobago	0.97	4.28
Chile	3.76	3.69
Mexico	1.68	1.59

Source: IDB calculations based on IMF, *International Financial Statistics* and World Bank, *World Development Indicators*.

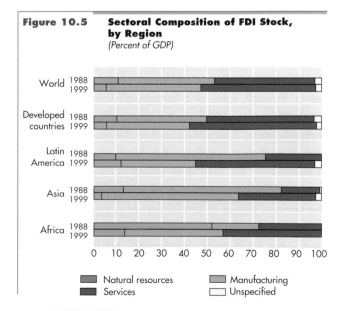

Figure 10.5 Sectoral Composition of FDI Stock, by Region
(Percent of GDP)

Source: UNCTAD (2001).

Box 10.1   FDI in Mercosur in the 1990s[1]

Mercosur as a whole received more than $200 billion of foreign direct investment inflows between 1990 and 2000, of which 98 percent went to Argentina and Brazil. FDI came mostly from extra-regional sources, especially in the larger countries, where intra-regional FDI amounted to just around 1 percent of the total. In contrast, intra-regional FDI accounted for 20 to 25 percent of FDI inflows to Uruguay and 40 percent to Paraguay.

What has been the role of Mercosur in attracting extra-regional FDI inflows? At first glance, it would seem that Mercosur did contribute in this regard. While Mercosur partners received 1.4 percent of world FDI inflows between 1984-89, this figure increased to 2.1, 3.7 and 6 percent in 1990-93, 1994-96 and 1997-99, respectively. However, it is difficult to disentangle the role of Mercosur from the other changes that took place simultaneously, such as the adoption of structural reform programs and a more favorable macroeconomic climate than in the 1980s. An examination of the sectoral pattern of FDI inflows and of the objectives and strategies of multinational corporations (MNCs) that invested in the region in the 1990s may shed light on this issue.

Services were the main destination sector for FDI, accounting for 80 percent of FDI inflows to Brazil, and around half of total inflows in the other three countries. Mercosur probably had little to do with attracting this purely market-seeking FDI, which was concentrated in public utilities (linked to privatization in Argentina and Brazil), banking, and retail and wholesale trade. For the most part, these investments led to stand-alone affiliates that replicate, at smaller scales, most of the functions of the respective headquarters, without closely integrating with the rest of the corporation units.

FDI aimed at exporting labor-intensive goods has been marginal in all Mercosur countries, especially Brazil and Argentina. Instead, export-oriented, resource-seeking investments, although marginal in Brazil, have been the main form of vertical FDI in the region, accounting for 35 percent of flows to Argentina (in the mining and oil sectors), and 20 to 25 percent of sales of MNCs in Paraguay and Uruguay.[2] With the possible exception of FDI in agriculture in Paraguay, Mercosur has probably had little impact on the location of these resource-seeking MNCs, since their exports are mainly directed to countries outside the regional integration agreement.

The manufacturing sector has attracted mostly horizontal market-seeking investments. In Argentina and Brazil, as a general rule, these investments have been directed toward the domestic rather than the extended market. Although a substantial share of exports from manufacturing MNCs has gone to Mercosur—60 percent for Argentina, 30 percent for Brazil—these exports represent

a very small portion of these firms' sales.[3] In contrast, in Uruguay and Paraguay, exports to Mercosur comprise a much larger share of manufacturing MNC sales. Thus, intra-regional exports are more relevant in MNC strategies in the case of the smaller member countries. This would suggest that membership in Mercosur has been more important as a locational advantage for FDI in Paraguay and Uruguay than in Argentina and Brazil. However, especially in Uruguay, there is also evidence of MNCs divesting in the country in order to supply the market from Argentina or Brazil, a possibility favored by the dismantling of trade barriers among Mercosur member countries. There is also some evidence of investment diversion from Argentina to Brazil, especially after the 1999 devaluation of the real, in a context where significant incentives were offered by national and subnational governments in Brazil, mainly in the automotive sector.

Mercosur has perhaps been most relevant in sectors where efficiency-seeking strategies have been used. This is notably the case of the automotive sector, where U.S. and European MNCs, on the basis of their own global and regional strategies, and fostered by specific policies in Mercosur, have tended to specialize their affiliates, creating a horizontal regional division of labor in which Argentine affiliates produce low-volume vehicles while Brazil specializes in high-volume models.

What has been the impact of Mercosur on intra-regional FDI? While both Argentina and Brazil have become more significant as source countries (approximately tripling their annual outflows of FDI between the first and the second half of the 1990s), the bulk of these outflows went to extra-regional host countries.[4] Available estimates covering 1990-96 indicate that Mercosur accounted for only 17 percent and 10 percent of outward FDI in Argentina and Brazil, respectively (see Chudnovsky, Kosacoff and López, 1999). However, these figures correspond to a period when Mercosur was not yet in full force, and there is some evidence that the intra-regional share may have increased considerably in the late 1990s.

---

[1] This box was written by Daniel Chudnovsky and Andrés López.

[2] For Argentina, the figure excludes FDI in agriculture, which has been significant, but for which data are not available.

[3] Even in sectors where MNC exports are relatively high (higher than the host country's average), exports to Mercosur by MNCs in manufacturing in Argentina and Brazil are only 10 percent and 4 percent of total sales, respectively (Chudnovsky and López, 2001).

[4] FDI outflows from Argentina jumped from an annual average of $500 million to $1.9 billion between 1989-94 and 1995-2000, while in Brazil the respective figures were $600 million and $1.7 billion.

Box 10.2   Has NAFTA Increased FDI in Mexico?[1]

Since the formation of the North American Free Trade Agreement (NAFTA) in 1994, Mexico has had an impressive increase in FDI inflows. From an annual average of $4.6 billion over 1989-93, FDI increased to $9.9 billion in 1996, $14.2 billion in 2000, and $24.7 billion in 2001 (Dussel Peters, 2002). Only China and Brazil outshine Mexico as targets of FDI among the emerging markets (UNCTAD, 2000). Whether the bulk of FDI inflows following NAFTA have come from Mexico's NAFTA partners, the United States and Canada, or from the rest of the world, is a subject of contention. Different databases suggest different stories. According to Dussel Peters, for example, the United States and Canada appear to be the main engines behind the increase in these inflows, with their share rising from 50 percent in 1994 to 79 percent in 2000 (the maquiladora sector excluded). However, a comparison of data on total inflows from the Banco de México, and data on U.S. outflows to Mexico from the U.S. Bureau of Economic Analysis, suggests that the share of FDI inflows corresponding to the United States remained fairly stable throughout the period.

The bulk of FDI in Mexico has flowed to the manufacturing sector—particularly the automotive, electronics and electrical equipment industries—which captured more than 60 percent of the total over 1994-2000. However, the importance of FDI in financial services has become more pronounced with foreign acquisitions of Mexican banks and insurance companies. In 2000-2001, FDI in financial services reached $18 billion, or 48.2 percent of total FDI flows to Mexico.[2]

Does NAFTA explain foreign investors' growing interest in Mexico? There are at least four reasons to believe so: (1) Mexico's preferential access to the North American market may have attracted both extra- and intra-regional FDI to exploit the country's comparative advantage in labor-intensive processes; (2) NAFTA's rules of origin may have induced input suppliers to move to Mexico from outside the NAFTA region; (3) NAFTA's investment provisions and dispute settlement mechanism likely enhanced Mexico's credibility as a favorable investment location; and (4) NAFTA in general has fostered Mexico's economic prospects by locking in and extending the country's unilateral economic reforms launched in the 1980s.

However, NAFTA's impact on the upswing of FDI in Mexico is difficult to separate out from other competing explanations, such as the country's liberal foreign investment law of 1993 that opened nearly all economic sectors to foreign capital. Furthermore, the growth of FDI in Mexico is part of a global trend of increased FDI

to emerging markets. Indeed, while FDI to Mexico increased significantly in the 1990s, the country's share of total FDI flows to developing countries, or even to all of Latin America and the Caribbean, actually declined, as did its share in FDI outflows from the United States, from 3.8 percent in 1990-93 to 2.9 percent in 1994-2000. In the case of manufacturing, on the other hand, Mexico did increase its share in U.S. outflows (Dussel Peters 2002).

These factors notwithstanding, NAFTA can be considered key to solidifying Mexico's economic reforms, as well as to ensuring continuous FDI inflows, even in the wake of the 1995 peso crisis. Indeed, had NAFTA not been formed, it is estimated that FDI flows from Canada and the United States to Mexico would have been 42 percent lower between 1994 and the end of 1999 (Waldkirch, 2001). NAFTA's impact can also be discerned from qualitative changes in firm behavior: it has made North America a single spatial unit, resulting in locational reshuffling and integration of the three countries' industries into regional production networks, particularly in the automotive sector (Eden, 2002).

What of extra-regional FDI? The impact of NAFTA on extra-regional investment remains contested. While some argue that NAFTA served mainly to boost intra-regional FDI (Waldkirch, 2001), others maintain that the agreement was instrumental in inducing extra-regional investors to move to Mexico in order to enjoy preferential access to the North American market (Blomström and Kokko, 1997). Still others speculate that extra-regional investors may have redirected part of their FDI from the United States and Canada to Mexico following the start-up of NAFTA (World Bank, 2000).

In sum, notwithstanding the fact that NAFTA coincided with other factors accounting for the growth of FDI in Mexico, it can be regarded as important in shaping firms' regional strategies as well as in fostering Mexico's investment climate and thus helping sustain FDI inflows. Furthermore, plausible causal variables inherently related to NAFTA—such as sector-specific rules of origin—may be too subtle to be captured by an analysis of aggregate FDI inflows, and await a more careful examination of firm- and industry-level data.

---

[1] This box was written by Kati Suominen.

[2] Unless otherwise noted, these figures are taken from Dussel Peters, Paliza and Loria Diaz (2002).

ies, however well informed, cannot provide definitive answers.[19]

Another way to proceed, which provides a nice complement to the case studies, is to try to control for some of those circumstances within a large set of countries, all of which are sources or hosts of FDI, and most of which are parties to RIAs. There are enough RIAs in existence, and enough bilateral FDI data, to try to sort out quantitatively the effects of an RIA from the effects of other circumstances. What follows are the results of our own study (Levy Yeyati, Stein and Daude, 2002). As far as we know, this is the first systematic empirical evaluation of the effects of regional integration on FDI for a large sample of countries.

EMPIRICAL EVALUATION

Before turning to the evidence, it may be useful to discuss briefly the different channels through which RIAs may affect FDI. To organize the discussion consistent with the case study evidence focusing on the different effects of FDI from insiders and outsiders, we consider what could be expected to happen when both the source and host are party to a particular RIA, and then compare that to what would happen were only one or the other party to the agreement.

Channels of Influence

Effects on FDI from insiders. If the source and host countries become members of the same RIA, the data may evidence a tariff-jumping effect or an international vertical integration effect, depending on the kind of FDI that predominates. If FDI is horizontal, with tariff jumping as its motive, the reduction in trade barriers implicit in the RIA will probably lead to a reduction in FDI, as trade and foreign investment are alternative ways to serve the domestic market. If FDI is vertical, with integration of stages of production as its motive, the effect of the RIA will probably be to increase FDI, as transaction costs to engage in vertical integration across international borders are reduced. The net effect should depend, among other things, on how high the trade barriers were in the first place. Regardless of its impact on total FDI, an RIA can have the effect of changing the composition of FDI from horizontal to vertical. As sug-

gested previously, FDI among developed countries is in part associated with the production of differentiated varieties, and so fits neither the horizontal nor the vertical models. To the extent that this third type of FDI depends on the possibility of trading differentiated goods, an RIA should facilitate multinational activity of this type.

Whatever the motive for FDI, if an RIA includes investment provisions to liberalize capital flows, harmonize legal norms, and set up institutions to handle cross-border disputes, it should be expected through this channel to increase FDI flows between its members.[20]

Effects on FDI from outsiders. The entrance of a country into an RIA may make it a more enticing host of FDI from an extra-regional source through an *extended market effect*, particularly if the FDI is horizontal. When Brazil entered Mercosur, for example, it may have been perceived as a more attractive host for FDI from outside sources. Foreign investors may find it more worthwhile to "jump" the common external tariff and set up plants in Brazil to supply the entire Mercosur region, whereas before they supplied each of the countries individually through exports. On the other hand, the extended market may encourage vertical FDI just as well as horizontal: an RIA reduces the costs incurred by extra-regional sources of FDI in locating different stages of production in several of the countries within the region. In fact, this effect can also be present for the case of FDI from source countries within the same RIA. Thus, whatever the motive for FDI, the extended market effect of a host country's entry into an RIA should result in more FDI for the RIA as a whole.[21, 22]

---

[19] The problem is one of too many variables that may matter, and too few observations from which to make inferences.

[20] See Slemrod (1990) for an empirical study of the effects of investment provisions to FDI for the United States.

[21] This effect may be particularly large in the case of Southern countries forming North-South RIAs. These countries may become particularly attractive to outside sources, since they combine some "southern" locational advantages (for example, low wages) with access to a developed market. Production of some Volkswagen automobiles in Mexico is a case in point.

[22] In the case of free trade areas, rules of origin provide an additional reason for RIAs to foster extra-regional FDI, as firms in the region may shift from extra-regional suppliers to intra-regional suppliers of intermediate inputs in order to comply with the origin rules, providing incentives for the foreign suppliers to establish production within the region (see Chapter 3).

Yet within the RIA there may be winners and losers. Notwithstanding the increased FDI brought to the region as a whole, there may be a redistributive effect of FDI within the region. Before the RIA is launched, for instance, a multinational corporation might have horizontal FDI in each of the countries in the region. When barriers to trade within the region are eliminated, the firm may choose to concentrate production in a single plant in a single country and supply the rest of the countries through trade.

The size of the individual economies may be an important variable in determining whether they are winners or losers from the redistributive effect. In the preceding example, Brazil was chosen deliberately. Plant-level fixed costs may induce the firm to locate its plant in the larger market, or perhaps the most centrally located market, in order to minimize the cost of supplying the whole region. The biggest losers, meanwhile, could be medium-sized countries: large countries are more likely to be FDI winners, and small countries are more likely to be supplied by trade rather than FDI with or without the RIA.[23] Beyond market size and location, countries that offer a more attractive overall package for foreign investors due to the quality of their institutions, the quality of their labor force, the development of their infrastructure, or their tax treatment of multinationals will be more likely to be winners in this redistributive game.

Effects of RIA by source country. When a source country enters into an RIA, the data may evidence a diversion or dilution effect. If membership in a regional integration agreement makes each member a more attractive host for FDI—as it does in the vertical model—then the RIA will make non-members appear relatively less attractive. We call this effect FDI diversion, an analogy to Viner's (1950) classic trade diversion concept: FDI from a source to non-partners may decline as the source enters an RIA.[24, 25]

Members of an RIA may experience a similar effect when the agreement is enlarged. Take, for instance, the potential effects of the FTAA on FDI flows from the U.S. to Mexico. To the extent that U.S. investment in Mexico is intended to exploit some locational advantages of Mexico, then as the preferential access of Mexico to the U.S. becomes *diluted* by the FTAA, part of the FDI may be relocated to members of the larger agreement that have similar advantages.[26]

Empirical Evidence

In order to look at the impact of RIAs on FDI, we use data on bilateral FDI stocks from the OECD's *International Direct Investment Statistics.* The dataset covers FDI from 20 source countries, all of them from the OECD, to 60 host countries, from 1982 through 1998. One shortcoming of these data is that they do not cover FDI between developing countries. Yet, it is the most complete source available for bilateral FDI, which is a key ingredient to study the effects of integration on foreign investment.

As in several chapters of this volume, the empirical approach is based on the gravity model (see Box 3.1, Chapter 3), which has been used widely in the literature to examine the determinants of bilateral trade, and has more recently been used to study the determinants of FDI.[27] In its simplest formulation, the model presumes that bilateral trade flows (in our case, bilateral FDI stocks) are related positively to the product of the GDPs of both economies and negatively to the distance between them.

In studying the impact of RIAs on FDI, one approach would be to work with cross-section regressions, thus exploiting the variation across countries to see whether RIAs matter for FDI. The question, in this case, would be whether countries that share RIAs with the source country receive more FDI than countries that

---

[23] As an example, the auto industry in Uruguay was virtually undeveloped even during the years of import-substitution industrialization.

[24] As in Viner's trade diversion, the formation of an RIA may divert FDI from the most efficient location to a partner. For example, following NAFTA, a U.S. firm may locate in Mexico the production of an intermediate input it might have otherwise located in Costa Rica, in the absence of the preferential access enjoyed by Mexico. In Mexico, this "trade diversion" effect will be combined with all other effects of common membership with the source country. What we call trade diversion is the loss suffered by Costa Rica, as well as other countries, as a result of the creation of NAFTA.

[25] Another example of investment diversion is found in the European Union. See Baldwin, Forslid and Haaland (1999).

[26] Dilution is in a way different from diversion. Going back to the example of NAFTA and U.S. FDI in Mexico and Costa Rica, dilution is more the result of leveling the playing field, at least for a certain group of countries. In this case, with the FTAA, Costa Rica and Mexico will now be playing under the same rules, and FDI will go to the most efficient location within the region.

[27] See Eaton and Tamura (1994), Frankel and Wei (1997), Wei (1997, 2000), Blonigen and Davis (2000), Stein and Daude (2001), and Levy Yeyati, Panizza and Stein (2001).

do not. There are a number of problems with this approach. First, it is possible that FDI is affected by other characteristics of the countries, which are difficult to account for. Second, countries may form RIAs because they already have large stocks of FDI, in which case there will be problems of endogeneity. In other words, trade agreements would not be causing FDI; rather, FDI would be causing RIAs. Finally, while the cross-section evidence may provide useful information, it does not answer directly the policy question that one would want to address: what is the impact of changes in RIAs on the countries that form them?

Our empirical evaluation deals with these issues by using data that combine the cross-section and time series dimensions (i.e., panel data), and by concentrating on the effects of changes in RIAs on the bilateral FDI of each country pair.[28] The fact that we are following each country pair over time helps us control for all the characteristics of the country pairs that are invariant over time, such as distance, whether the two countries share a common border or a common language, the similarity of their factor proportions, etc. It also helps account for other variables that may be relevant for FDI location but which may be difficult to observe. In addition, the data allow us to focus on the right policy question, that is, on the effects of changes in the RIA status of country pairs, leaving out the cross-sectional dimension.[29] We also include source and host nominal GDP to control for size, and year dummies to control for the spectacular increase in FDI over time. Finally, we include a number of variables associated with the effects of regional integration.

The first of our regional integration variables is *Same FTA*, a dummy variable that indicates whether the source and the host countries belong to the same free trade area.[30] This variable captures a combination of channels: tariff-jumping, international vertical integration, and the potential effect of investment provisions on FDI. A second integration variable we use is *Extended market host*, which captures the size of the extended market of the host country.[31] For example, for the case of Brazil in the years before Mercosur, *Extended market host* takes the value of Brazil's GDP at the time; for the years after Mercosur, it takes the value of the four Mercosur countries combined. Following the previous discussion, as well as the existing empirical evidence, we expect an increase in the size of the

extended market to have positive effects on FDI for the RIA as a whole. Finally, a third integration variable is *Extended market source*, which captures the FDI diversion/dilution effects. We expect its coefficient to have a negative sign, suggesting that FDI to a host country diminishes when firms in the source country have other free trade agreement partners in which to locate their investments.

Appendix Table 10.1 presents the results of our regressions.[32] The main results are shown in Figure 10.6, which corresponds to column 1 in Appendix Table 10.1. The first bar in the figure shows the impact of the same free trade agreement variable. The impact is very large: forming an agreement with a source country increases the stock of FDI from that country by 116 percent.[33] The positive effect reveals that the possible FDI loss due to the tariff-jumping argument is more than offset by other effects that operate in the opposite direction.

The second bar captures the impact of the host extended market effect. Doubling the size of the extended market increases FDI from all sources by nearly 6 percent. Thus, by enlarging its home market through a free trade agreement, the host increases its attractiveness as a location for FDI. While this effect appears to be small, it is important to keep in mind that sometimes the increase in the size of the extended mar-

---

[28] We do this by including in the regressions country-pair fixed-effects, that is, dummy variables corresponding to each of the country pairs.

[29] To a certain extent, the inclusion of the country pair dummies addresses potential endogeneity problems, which would arise if countries select their RIA partners on the basis of the multinational activity between them.

[30] The dummy is also 1 if countries are in the same customs unions or single market. However, we did not include as free trade agreements country pairs that have preferential trade agreements in which trade barriers among members are reduced but not eliminated. The source for this variable is Frankel, Stein and Wei (1997).

[31] It is defined as the log of the joint GDP of all the countries to which the host has tariff-free access due to common membership in a free trade agreement (we include the host's own GDP as well).

[32] The dependent variable is the log (1 + FDI). The log specification is the one typically used in the gravity model literature. The reason we add 1 to FDI is to avoid throwing away all the observations with no FDI, which provide useful information. For a discussion of the methodological issues associated with the treatment of the observations with 0 FDI, see Levy Yeyati, Stein and Daude (2002).

[33] The coefficient for the same free trade agreement in Appendix Table 10.1 is 0.7682. Since FDI is in logs, it is necessary to transform this coefficient, by computing exp(0.7682)-1=1.155.

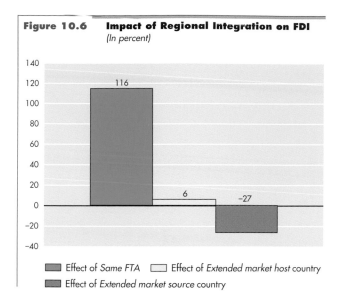

Figure 10.6   Impact of Regional Integration on FDI
(In percent)

Note: All the coefficients are significant at the 1% level.
Source: Levy Yeyati, Stein and Daude (2002).

ket is very large: for instance, when Mexico entered NAFTA its extended market increased by a factor of 18. Finally, the doubling of the extended market of the source leads to an expected decline in the FDI stock originating from that country of nearly 27 percent. Columns 2 and 3 in Appendix Table 10.1 show that these results do not change much when we account for other variables that may explain FDI location, such as the stock of privatization to date (in order to control for the fact that most FDI linked to privatization is in non-tradables) or the rate of inflation (in order to control for macroeconomic conditions).

An interesting exercise that gives us a notion of the magnitude of these effects is to compare the impact that the creation of the FTAA would have for FDI from the United States to Mexico and Argentina, according to the results presented above.[34] Since it does not have a free trade agreement with the United States, Argentina would benefit from the direct effect of sharing an agreement with the source, increasing U.S.-originated FDI stock by 116 percent. In addition, the Argentine economy would become more attractive to FDI because of the extension of its market from Mercosur to the FTAA.[35] The 900 percent increase of its market would lead to an increase of U.S.-originated FDI stock of 53 percent.[36] On the other hand, the source extended market effect would partially offset these

increases. The FTAA would represent an increase of around 16 percent in the extended market of the United States, with an associated decline of U.S.-originated FDI of 4.3 percent due to the dilution effect.[37] In sum, the overall effect of the creation of the FTAA would be a significant increase of nearly 165 percent in the United States' direct investment position in Argentina.

The result for Mexico would be quite different. Since Mexico and the United States are already members of NAFTA, the FTAA would have no direct effect on U.S.-originated FDI. There would be an indirect effect, however, due to the extension of Mexico's market. The extension of Mexico's market from its existing free trade agreements to the FTAA would be a scant 13 percent, corresponding to an increase of U.S.-originated FDI of only 0.75 percent.[38] Netting the source extended market effect (−4.3 percent), we arrive at an overall decline of U.S. FDI stocks in Mexico of 3.5 percent. While this small loss may be partially compensated by additional FDI from other sources (which also would increase by three-quarters of a percent), the fact that the United States is by far the biggest FDI player in Mexico may still mean that this country could lose FDI as a result of the FTAA.

The numbers in this simple exercise can illustrate potential asymmetries in the impact of the FTAA for different countries, but they must be taken with a great deal of caution. The estimates that we use represent the average impact of our regional integration variables over the whole sample. However, the impact may differ according to the characteristics of the countries in question. For example, FDI in countries that are highly protected may be mostly horizontal, a type of FDI that substitutes for trade, in which case the impact

---

[34] The exercise is meant as an illustration of potential effects, and does not pretend to measure the specific effects of the FTAA on Argentina and Mexico with a high degree of precision.

[35] Note that given our methodology, the results would also be similar for any of the Mercosur countries, since the extended market variables change in the same way for all of them.

[36] $0.058*921 = 53.418$.

[37] $-0.267*16.06 = -4.3$.

[38] The extension of the market for Mexico is smaller than that for the United States, since Mexico has a host of other free trade agreement partners in the region.

of *Same FTA* may be higher in more open economies. Similarly, the impact of extending the size of the host market may depend on the initial size of the market, or on the relative attractiveness of the economies that make up the extended host market. In what follows, we will perform some additional exercises in order to look, in a preliminary way, at potential asymmetries of the effect of regional integration on FDI.

Two factors that may affect the impact of common membership in a regional integration agreement on FDI are the openness of the host country, and the similarity of factor proportions between the host and the source. These variables may matter because they help determine whether the bilateral stock of FDI is mostly vertical or horizontal. All else being equal, closed economies are expected to have a larger share of horizontal FDI, which according to the theory should decrease with regional integration. Economies that are similar in their factor endowments are not expected to have vertical FDI. This would suggest that FDI between similar countries should not benefit as much from integration. However, if a large part of FDI among developed countries is, as suggested above, of the differentiated good type, then the effects of similarity of factor endowments may be ambiguous.

So the question is not just whether belonging to the same free trade agreement has an impact on bilateral FDI between the source and the host country. We want to know whether the impact of the same agreement changes with the degree of openness of the host country, and with the similarity in factor endowments between the source and the host. The results are reported in columns 4 and 5 of Appendix Table 10.1.[39] The simplest way to present these results here is by means of Figure 10.7a, which shows that the impact of *Same FTA* increases with openness.[40] In Figure 10.7b, we can see that its impact decreases as factor endowments (we used the absolute difference in capital per worker) become more dissimilar.[41] In this last case, our results suggest that a host country that is very different from the source country with which it integrates may actually experience a fall in FDI from this source. These results have to be taken with caution, however, since they are drawn from the countries that have RIA links with source countries. In our sample, then, these results are drawn only from the experience of developed countries and Mexico.

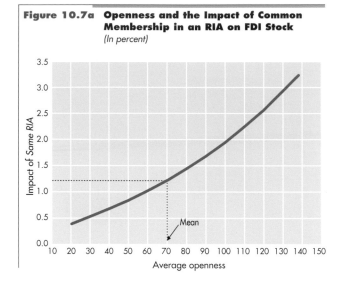

Figure 10.7a   Openness and the Impact of Common Membership in an RIA on FDI Stock
(In percent)

Note: The extension of the line corresponds to the range of the sample regarding the degree of openness of the countries included.

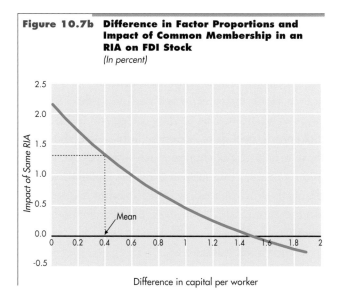

Figure 10.7b   Difference in Factor Proportions and Impact of Common Membership in an RIA on FDI Stock
(In percent)

Note: The extension of the line corresponds to the range of the sample regarding the difference in capital per worker of the countries included.
Source: Levi Yeyati, Stein and Daude (2002).

---

[39] Our regressions looked at these issues by adding to our baseline regression an interaction term multiplying *Same FTA* by openness, or by similarity of factor endowments. This allows us to look at the impact of common membership in the agreement at different values of these variables.

[40] We used average openness for the host country during the sample period (see Appendix 10.1 for details). The impact of openness is weaker if, instead of interacting openness with *Same FTA*, we use a dummy variable for openness, which classifies as open those countries for which trade over GDP is above the sample mean.

[41] Differences in land per capita, or the level of skill of the labor force, yield qualitatively similar results, although results are weaker when land per capita is used.

As with our *Same FTA* variable, the effect of RIAs through the extension of the size of the market may depend on country characteristics as well. Extending the size of the market will bring more FDI for the RIA as a whole, but the effects may be unevenly distributed. A firm that had production facilities in each of the countries in an RIA may want to concentrate production in a single facility once internal trade barriers are eliminated, and serve the whole extended market from that location. The choice for that location may depend on country size (particularly if trade costs are not completely eliminated) and, more generally, on the overall attractiveness of the host country. Preliminary results (not shown in the appendix) suggest that most of the benefits from the extension of the market are concentrated either on the largest country in the RIA, or on the one that seems to offer the most attractive overall package. This last finding suggests that market enlargement has a stronger positive effect on FDI in an FDI-friendly environment.[42]

FDI POLICY IN INTEGRATING COUNTRIES

The evidence discussed in this chapter suggests that RIAs can have important effects on foreign direct investment to members and non-members alike, although those FDI gains are unlikely to be distributed evenly. The results indicate that the gains may be smaller for countries that are less developed, closed to international trade, and altogether unattractive to foreign investors.

The discussion throughout this chapter has equated gains in FDI with gains in general welfare. The national "winners" from RIAs are presented as those whose FDI inflows increase, and the national "losers" are those whose FDI inflows might decline. However, the question of whether FDI generates positive welfare effects for the host countries has been a subject of great debate. While most authors believe that FDI tends to be beneficial, there are some who believe that foreign investment is at best a mixed blessing, bringing with it a measure of harm that may outweigh the good.

Our presumption that FDI is good is based on the idea that it may generate positive spillovers for the rest of the economy through a variety of channels. If the foreign firm is technologically more advanced than most domestic companies, the interaction of its techni-

cians, engineers and managers with domestic firms may result in knowledge spillovers. Positive spillovers may also arise if the foreign firm trains workers who may eventually be hired by domestic firms. A related source of positive spillovers, studied by Rodríguez-Clare (1996), is the potential for the development of new inputs, encouraged by the demand created by the foreign firm, which may then become available to domestic producers. Aitken, Hanson and Harrison (1997) point out that multinationals that export their goods to foreign markets may induce domestic firms to follow suit, thus acting as catalysts for domestic firms to become exporters. Borensztein, De Gregorio and Lee (1998) find evidence that FDI has a positive effect on growth, provided the level of human capital in the host country is sufficiently high. Thus, in order to benefit from the advanced technology introduced by foreign firms, the host country has to have the capacity to absorb it.[43]

However, FDI may also generate negative spillovers. Domestic firms may be displaced by the foreign firm, or may find that the cost of factors of production increases as a result of the foreign investment. While most of the earlier empirical literature on the subject supported the presence of positive externalities, recent work based on firm-level data has found some evidence of negative externalities. Aitken and Harrison (1999) find that growth of total factor productivity in Venezuela was lower for domestic firms in sectors where FDI was greater. The authors focus on within-industry spillovers, however. Kugler (2000) and Chapter 11 in this volume find evidence of important positive inter-industry spillovers for Colombia and Mexico.[44]

---

[42] To examine this last issue, we constructed an index of attractiveness for host countries by looking at the extent to which they receive FDI, after controlling for size, and for the formation of RIAs, and for geographical characteristics. Once we control for these characteristics, whether a country receives little or much FDI may depend on factors such as the quality of institutions, the education of the labor force, the quality of their infrastructure, their tax treatment of multinationals, and their factor proportions—in other words, on their overall attractiveness as a destination for foreign investment.

[43] For a more complete discussion of FDI spillovers, see Blomström and Kokko (1998) and Hanson (2000).

[44] Kugler (2000) argues that the lack of intra-industry spillovers may be due to the fact that foreign affiliates will appropriate as many of the benefits as possible of their imported technology, thus preventing spillovers from leaking to their competitors. On the other hand, they may want to upgrade the technological capabilities of a supplier, which explains the existence of inter-industry spillovers.

Beyond the possibility of negative spillovers, other authors have identified other potential sources of welfare losses for host countries as a result of FDI. Some have focused on national security concerns, when FDI occurs in sectors related to the defense industry, particularly if it involves a technology that the government would prefer to keep secret.[45] Others have noted that, if ownership of capital in a country is mostly in foreign hands, policies that increase domestic production but at the same time redistribute income from labor to capital will mostly benefit foreigners, while most domestic citizens will lose.[46] But both sets of circumstances are relatively uncommon. The few instances in which national security is an issue can be addressed by simply limiting FDI in those particular cases; and a policy tilted towards capital at the workers' expense, combined with an overwhelming concentration of foreign ownership, is unlikely in a democracy where most voters are workers and none are foreigners.

A different problem may be related to the fact that compared to domestic firms, affiliates of multinational companies tend to import more of their inputs, and thus contribute to generating balance of payments deficits.[47] Yet even this problem may be uncommon. Just as foreign affiliates tend to import more of their inputs, they also export more of their outputs, and as discussed above, this may even induce domestic firms to mimic their behavior and export more as well.[48]

This discussion of the potential benefits and costs of FDI suggests that not all FDI carries similar benefits. In particular, FDI may be more beneficial if it targets more advanced industries (so that potential technological spillovers are larger); if it establishes strong forward and backward linkages with domestic firms (which may thereby absorb the spillovers); if it exports part of the production (relaxing balance of payments concerns, and inducing domestic firms to follow suit); and if domestic firms have the capacity to absorb those spillovers. The key question is, what kind of policies can countries adopt to ensure that the resulting FDI inflows are beneficial? In addition, how does regional integration affect the desirability and effectiveness of those policies? And what does all this suggest regarding the type of provisions that should be included in an RIA investment chapter?

Some of the policies that countries have used to try to get the most out of FDI involve technology transfer and performance requirements. Domestic affiliates of foreign-owned firms may be required to train domestic workers to certain standards, locate R&D activities in the country, use a minimum content of local inputs, export a certain proportion of their output, or employ certain technologies. Such policies clearly aim to relieve balance of payments pressures and promote spillovers, and there are reasons why they may be effective. If FDI is horizontal, the purpose of the investment is to serve the domestic market. If the multinational firm has not served the market according to the stipulated requirements, it would not be able to serve it at all—a powerful inducement to accept the requirements, provided they are not too onerous. For that reason, although RIAs commonly include investment chapters that bind members to the principle of national treatment (as did the Canada-U.S. free trade agreement), the members may negotiate exceptions to the principle to allow some performance requirements (as they did subsequently in NAFTA).[49] Yet the evidence suggests that performance requirements have been ineffective. Blomström, Kokko and Zejan (2000, Chapter 13) offer strong evidence that the requirements actually reduce multinational employment of technology, and weaker evidence that they increase capital imports as well. In addition, some of these requirements, such as local content or trade balancing requirements, are either prohibited or being phased out under current WTO rules.

Whether or not performance requirements are beneficial under some circumstances, they are least likely to be so in circumstances of regional integration. RIAs tend to promote vertical over horizontal FDI; they

---

[45] Graham and Krugman (1995, Chapter 6) offer several examples. An illustrative one is the prevention of the attempted takeover in the early 1990s of a U.S. aerospace industry supplier, Mamco Manufacturing Company, by the China National Aerotechnology Import and Export Corporation.

[46] The commonly cited reference for this possibility is Bhagwati and Brecher (1980).

[47] See Graham and Krugman (1995, p. 70).

[48] Horizontal FDI, which may rely on imported capital and intermediate inputs but produces for the domestic market, may contribute to balance of payments deficits, depending on whether it substitutes imports or crowds out domestic production. Export-oriented vertical FDI, on the other hand, probably does not.

[49] See Graham and Krugman (1995, p. 136).

also tend to extend the market for horizontal FDI from individual countries to that of the RIA, thus making FDI more footloose within the region. While a horizontal multinational firm may accept performance requirements if it is necessary to serve a particular country's output market, enlargement of the market with an RIA allows the firm to choose as its host whichever member country has the fewest requirements. A vertical multinational, even more, may simply choose a country outside the region for a particular stage of production.[50] Performance requirements, in other words, may be best suited for a state of the world that RIAs are designed deliberately to dismantle. The implication for regional integration policy is that, where it comes to an RIA's investment chapter, unadulterated national treatment may work better than any alternative to help a country avoid becoming an FDI loser.[51]

If performance requirements are not helpful in attracting FDI to integrating countries, two other polar strategies may attract it. The first, which has been compared to a "beauty contest" (by Oman, 2000), involves improving the quality of institutions, educating the labor force and developing the country's infrastructure. The second entails aggressive use of fiscal and financial incentives to attract foreign investors. This is obviously a false dichotomy, as countries tend to do a little of both. Yet it provides a useful way of organizing the discussion.

Beauty Contest

One important advantage of what has been called the "beauty contest" strategy is that, beyond its effects on FDI, it can generate more obvious benefits for the whole society. Improvements in infrastructure, education or the quality of the institutional environment will certainly benefit domestic citizens and firms, regardless of their impact on FDI. Beyond these general benefits, there is evidence suggesting that improving the quality of institutions can have a large impact on FDI.[52]

The evidence regarding the impact of education and infrastructure on the location of FDI is weaker.[53] This, however, does not mean that countries should not pursue these policies. While they may not contribute to the total amount of FDI a country receives, such policies can affect the benefits host countries derive from FDI. Education, for example, can affect

these benefits through two different channels. First, an educated labor force may influence the type of FDI a country receives, shifting it toward more advanced industries, which may generate larger spillovers. Second, for a given type of investment, better education increases the capacity of the labor force and of domestic firms to absorb spillovers. In addition, foreign firms that are attracted by an educated labor force become a strong constituency in favor of further improvements in education. This is clearly the case of Intel in Costa Rica, where enrollment in engineering schools has doubled in a matter of only a couple of years. In contrast, foreign firms that are attracted by cheap labor will probably lobby for the government to ensure its continuous availability—a scenario far less appealing as a development strategy.

Competition in Incentives

To the extent that FDI produces positive spillovers, it makes sense for governments to offer incentives to potential investors to lure them into their territory.[54] Provided there are economies of scale, eliminating trade barriers will induce firms to produce in just one location within a bloc and serve the extended market from this location. Competition between countries for FDI may become intense. Yet the competition in incentives leads to allocative efficiency: the efficient number of investments end up being made, and they are

---

[50] Coordinated adoption of performance requirements may solve the problem of location within the extended market, but it does not stop vertical FDI from seeking more convenient locations.

[51] The FTAA draft as of the Spring of 2002 includes in its investment chapter an article on performance requirements that would proscribe them. But the text is thoroughly bracketed and includes several bracketed exceptions. The question is under negotiation. See http://www.ftaa-alca.org/ftaadraft/eng/draft_e.asp

[52] Stein and Daude (2001) show that a 1 standard deviation improvement in an index of institutional quality developed by Kaufmann, Kraay and Zoido-Lobatón. (1999) results in an increase in bilateral FDI of 130 percent. According to their study, reducing excessive regulation, enforcing property rights, improving the quality of the bureaucracy and reducing corruption seem to be some of the most promising policies in terms of attracting foreign investors.

[53] See Stein and Daude (2001).

[54] That is, it makes sense as long as the government is considered a social planner seeking to maximize the country's welfare. A potential problem with incentive-based competition, however, is that negotiations with potential entrants are rarely transparent and open to public scrutiny, so they could lead to arbitrariness and corruption.

Slemrod, J. 1990. Tax Effects on FDI in the United States: Evidence from a Cross-Country Comparison. In A. Razin and J. Slemrod (eds.), *Taxation in the Global Economy.* Chicago: University of Chicago Press.

Stein, Ernesto, and Christian Daude. 2001. Institutions, Integration, and the Location of Foreign Direct Investment. Inter-American Development Bank Research Department, Washington, DC. Mimeo.

UNCTAD. 2000. *World Investment Report 2000: Cross-Border Mergers and Acquisitions and Development.* New York: United Nations.

———. 2001. *World Investment Report 2001: Promoting Linkage.* New York and Geneva: United Nations.

Venables, A. 1998. The Assessment: Trade and Location. *Oxford Review of Economic Policy* 14(2) Summer: 1-6.

Viner, J. 1950. *The Customs Union Issue.* New York: Carnegie Endowment for International Peace.

Waldkirch, A. 2001. *The "New Regionalism" and Foreign Direct Investment: The Case of Mexico.* Working Paper, Oregon State University.

Wei, S. J. 1997. *Why Is Corruption So Much More Taxing than Tax? Arbitrariness Kills.* NBER Working Paper no. 6255. National Bureau of Economic Research, Cambridge, MA.

———. 2000. How Taxing Is Corruption to International Investors? *Review of Economics and Statistics* 82(1): 1-11.

World Bank. 2000. *Trade Blocks.* Oxford: Oxford University Press.

Chapter 11

REGIONAL INTEGRATION AND PRODUCTIVITY

One of the key rationales for what has been called the "new regionalism" is to increase productivity. While economists since Adam Smith and his pin factory have known that productivity enhancement is not an end in itself, it is arguably the principal source of economic growth and rising standards of living. As such, it takes on particular importance to regions such as Latin America and the Caribbean, where long-term sustainable growth has long been an elusive goal. Growth in the region has trailed that of East Asia since the 1960s, and in the past two decades has fallen below the overall developing country average (IDB, 2001).

Growth accounting exercises that isolate the contributions of inputs (e.g., capital, education and labor) and total factor productivity to the growth process suggest that Latin America has been not only slow in accumulating inputs, but also particularly weak in raising productivity. The World Bank (1991) estimates that the region's average productivity growth over 1967-87 was zero, whereas the averages for East Asia and the developing countries as a whole were, respectively, 1.9 and 0.6 percent. The IDB (2001) estimates that productivity in Latin America declined in the 1980s and 1990s despite gains achieved elsewhere, particularly in the developed world.

Against this backdrop, it seems clear that by promising productivity gains, the move to regional integration has touched a raw nerve in the region. Why and how these gains are supposed to be delivered in Latin America, and what empirical evidence is available to date to support those positions, is the focus of this chapter. It gives particular attention to the two largest economies in the region, Brazil and Mexico, and to the performance of their manufacturing sectors. Given the size, geography and relative sophistication of their economies, these two nations might not be wholly representative points of comparison for all Latin American countries, but their experiences are nonetheless important because they involve two alternative modes of integration in the region: North-South and South-South agreements. Mexico pursued North-South integration through NAFTA, whereas Brazil signed South-South agreements, joining Mercosur. These divergent strategies provide a valuable policy experiment in terms of assessing implications for productivity growth.

WHY REGIONAL INTEGRATION MATTERS FOR PRODUCTIVITY

Regional integration is, perhaps above all, about promoting trade and investment among countries (see Chapter 2). One can argue, then, that the nature of the costs and benefits involved is, to a great extent, the same as that of a process of unilateral, non-preferential integration into the world economy. This is particularly true for the "channels" that might impact productivity. Yet, there are some important specificities related to the preferential nature of integration that cannot be overlooked. For analytical purposes, it is worth looking first at the more general (non-preferential) case of integration and then move on to the specifics of the regional schemes. Hereafter, the term "integration" is used in the sense of the general process

---

Box 11.1   Externalities and Linkages

Economists define externalities as actions by firms (or individuals) that affect other firms (or individuals), but are not reflected in their costs and benefits. Externalities can be transmitted by market transactions or bypass the market altogether. The former is called pecuniary externalities and can be found, for example, when the investment made by an automobile company generates enough demand for the development of an auto parts industry. Among those that bypass the market, the so-called technology externalities (Scitovsky, 1963) stand

out. A good example is the hiring of highly trained workers of a foreign firm by its local competitor.

Thanks to the work of Hirschman (1958), externalities (pecuniary or not) transmitted across the production chain also became known as linkages. They are said to be "backward" when producers generate positive externalities to suppliers, and "forward" when suppliers generate positive externalities to producers. In the automobile company example given above, the firm's demand for auto parts is seen as part of its backward linkages.

---

technology transfer, spillovers are more likely to be "vertical" (among their clients and suppliers) than "horizontal" (among their competitors) (Kugler, 2000).

Finally, the rationale behind the linkage effects is similar to the input availability channel discussed in the "new growth" theories, but the transmission mechanism is more complex. The argument relies on the concept of pecuniary externalities (see Box 11.1). FDI is believed to generate positive pecuniary externalities to local firms by improving the local supply (quality and variety) of intermediate goods (Markusen and Venables, 1999). This happens both directly through investment in these industries (forward linkages), or indirectly through investment in final (consumer) goods, which could create enough demand and technology spillovers for the establishment of intermediate industries (backward linkages).

What Does Regional Integration Specifically Bring to Productivity?

The preferential character of regional integration adds some specificity to the way trade and FDI channels operate. This is particularly important for trade-related linkages, where there are two major issues worth considering: comparative advantage and the scale effects. On the FDI side, the changes are mainly related to the level and type of flows, and since the impact on productivity is at best indirect, these changes are discussed elsewhere in this report (Chapter 10).

Comparative advantage. When integration is regional, the traditional comparative advantage gains from trade are no longer assured. To understand why, one has to come to terms with the concepts of trade creation and diversion discussed in Chapter 3. Trade creation generates exactly the same gains experienced by a country that opens up unilaterally. So there is nothing specific about it. Trade diversion, though, reduces productivity and is very specific to regional agreements, since it can only arise because of preferences given to partner countries. This productivity loss arises because the importer country is not buying from the most efficient suppliers and the exporter country is moving away from its comparative advantage. True, this loss might be compensated, as discussed below, by scale gains generated by these very same preferences. As far as comparative advantage is concerned, though, the impact of trade diversion is negative, and, accordingly, the overall productivity impact of regional integration is ambiguous, depending on the balance between trade creation and diversion. Venables (1999) gives more nuances to the trade diversion story by arguing that this type of loss is more likely in South-South (e.g., Andean Community) agreements than in North-South (e.g., NAFTA) ones because, inter alia, the North concentrates the most efficient producers of the goods most likely to be imported by the South (see Chapter 3).

Scale. In contrast to comparative advantage effects, the specificities of regional integration regarding scale are not so clear-cut. What is readily evident is that the potential gains from scale are much higher in the context of non-preferential worldwide integration than in a regional setting. The former offers the world, the latter only a region of this world. This, though, is just one part of the story. The other part lies in the uncertainty of these scale gains. There is always the threat of increasing returns industries being dislocated by imports, the more so for a developing country whose domestic market is limited and whose firms, as a consequence, face size disadvantages. These scale losses might also have long-term negative implications for productivity growth. The smaller the markets, the lower the financial viability of R&D activities. What a firm can learn depends not only on the volume of output produced at each point in time (so-called static economies), but also on the cumulative output across time (so-called dynamic economies, along the lines of the learning-by-doing story examined earlier).

One can argue, then, that regional integration involving a smaller number of partners lowers the risk of damaging dislocations, while at the same time boosting the (static and dynamic) scale advantages of the member countries vis-à-vis the rest of the world either through trade creation or diversion (Devlin and Ffrench-Davis, 1999).[2] This might be particularly relevant for South-South integration, where the difference in market size among member countries tends to be smaller and the size disadvantages with respect to the rest of the world more pressing. The flip side of South-South agreements, though, is that small differences in size might be especially damaging for the smaller and poorer members. In the absence of institutional safeguards, the combination of scale disadvantages and agglomeration economies (i.e., the advantages that arise when firms locate close to each other) might concentrate the more productive industries in the larger partners (Venables, 1999). In North-South agreements, this risk would be mitigated by the differences in input costs such as that of labor, which tends to favor the smaller and poorer countries. Moreover, one can also argue that Southern countries have more to "learn" in North-South agreements (i.e., the potential knowledge spillovers through trade and FDI would be higher), given that the stock of knowledge is concentrated in the North.

The Evidence on Regional Integration

Looking first at the macro, economy-wide level, the results for the 1990s—the decade when virtually all of Latin America embraced integration—are not very encouraging. True, there has been no effort to establish any causality between integration and productivity. Yet, the examples that exist suggest that for most countries, what few integration-related gains that occurred were not strong enough to offset other negative influences such as the region's extreme macroeconomic volatility.

The IDB (2001) found that Latin America's total factor productivity (TFP) (see Box 11.2) fell by 0.6 percent a year in the 1990s, with only six of 22 countries showing TFP growth.[3] The report attributes these results mainly to the region's poor educational levels (low absorptive capacity) and fragile public institutions (poor incentives to develop and assimilate new technologies). Baier, Dwyer Jr. and Tamura's (2002) results are even more disappointing, with TFP in the region dropping by approximately 2.9 percent a year. Fajnzylber and Lederman (1999) somehow buck the trend, reporting 1.1 percent TFP growth for Latin America during 1990-95. However, their analysis does not cover the whole decade and they do not take into account changes in human capital (basically education), which can drastically reduce the TFP "residual."

Looking at the sectoral level and more specifically at manufacturing—the most protected sector during the import substitution years—the picture is not so gloomy. Figure 11.1 shows that labor productivity in the region's largest countries grew substantially during the 1990s, particularly in Argentina, Brazil and Mexico. These three countries outperformed the United States (though not Korea) by a large margin, suggesting a reduction in the productivity gap vis-à-vis the country considered to have the best practices in technology. Although impressive, this evidence has some important pitfalls. First, since labor productivity does not take into account all the inputs used in production,

---

[2] One could also argue that regionalism, by formally guaranteeing market access among member countries, reduces the uncertainty that might restrict the scale (or enlarged market) gains (see Chapter 3).

[3] They were Chile, Argentina, Uruguay, the Dominican Republic, Peru and Barbados.

Box 11.2   How to Measure Productivity?

Productivity looks at first sight to be a very simple concept: the ratio of output to input. Yet it is not that simple, since this concept admits different measurements. The most intuitive and widely used is what is called labor productivity, i.e., output divided by the number of workers. It does not take a high level of sophistication to see that this is only a partial measure—all the other inputs used in production, such as machinery and raw material, are not accounted for. This can lead to misinterpretations, such as labor productivity growth being read as improvements in technology, when it is not more than the result of an increase in the number of machines (capital stock) per worker.

Given this drawback, economists came up with the notion of total factor productivity (TFP), which is defined as the ratio of output to all inputs combined. Most TFP analysis focuses on how it changes over time and uses the "production function" approach pioneered by Solow (1956). In this approach, TFP growth is measured by the residual growth rate not explained by inputs. For example, assume that a firm's output has grown 3 percent a year in the last five years. Its capital stock also

grew at about the same rate, whereas the number of employees grew at only 1 percent per year. Assuming that this firm uses only these two inputs and that their share of total output is, respectively, one-third and two-thirds, input contribution to output growth would be 1.7 percent a year (one-third x 1 percent plus two-thirds x 3 percent). So, the TFP contribution would be 1.3 percent per year, which is the difference between output (3 percent) and input growth (1.7 percent).

This so-called Solow residual is supposed to measure the impact of technical and organizational innovations that happen within firms (industries or countries). In practice, though, due to difficulties in measuring the flow of inputs, particularly capital stock, and in estimating the firms' technology (production function), this residual ends up capturing other unwanted contributions. This problem prompted one economist to argue that this residual is a "measure of our ignorance" (Abramovitz, 1956). Despite the difficulties, TFP is the profession's best available tool to measure productivity changes.

Figure 11.1   Labor Productivity in Manufacturing in Selected Latin American Countries, Korea and the United States
(Index)

Korea   Argentina   Colombia   Chile
Brazil   Mexico   USA

Source: Country Statistical Offices.

it gives only a partial view of what actually happened in terms of technology. Second, this data only cover a handful of countries in the region. Finally, as with the

macro-evidence, the evidence tells little about the causal relationship between integration, regional or otherwise, and productivity.

Studies based on firm-level data have made progress in addressing the first and the last of these problems (Tybout, forthcoming). The number of countries studied, though, is still limited. For instance, studies on Mexico, Brazil and Chile report positive rates of TFP growth in manufacturing. For Mexico, Tybout and Westbrook (1995), covering the first period of trade liberalization (1986-90), put TFP annual growth at 1.8 percent. Calculations in this chapter (see next section) put the same figure for the NAFTA period (1993-99) at 1.1 percent. Muendler (2002) estimates 0.8 percent of TFP annual growth for Brazil over 1992-98, which covers most of the country's trade liberalization period, while this chapter finds annual increases of 5.2 percent for the second half of the 1990s. Finally, Pavcnik (2000) estimates 2.8 percent in TFP annual growth for Chile following the country's radical trade reforms (1979-86). To give some perspective to this story, similar plant-level studies on East Asia point to 3 percent or higher TFP growth after liberalization. Aw, Chen and Roberts (2001) speak of 3.2 percent annual TFP growth in Taiwan in the 1981-91 period.

On the issue of how much of this TFP growth can be ascribed to trade liberalization, most of these studies concentrate on the trade channel and more specifically on the import discipline, scale and turnover hypotheses. Pavcnik (2000), Fernandes (2001), Tybout and Westbrook (1995) and Muendler (2002) find evidence of a strong import discipline effect in, respectively, Chile (1979-86), Colombia (1977-1991), Mexico (1986-90) and Brazil (1986-98). There is little evidence of important turnover or scale-related gains. Nonetheless, Pavcnik's (2000) estimates suggest that import discipline would have been dwarfed by the turnover effect, and Muendler (2002) finds that the elimination of trade barriers increases the likelihood that low-efficiency firms will shut down, which in the long run would have a positive impact on aggregate productivity.

Evidence is more limited on the other trade effects, particularly those that are believed to impact not only the level but also the rate of productivity growth. On the availability of world-class inputs and related technology acquisition effects, Muendler (2002) finds a positive but relatively unimportant impact on productivity in Brazil. Yet, Alvarez and Robertson (2000), working with plant-level data from Chile and Mexico, detect a significant and positive relationship between importing intermediate inputs and innovation in the latter country.[4]

Evidence based on country and sectoral level data also point to a positive input effect. Blyde (2002) finds that technological spillovers diffused through imported machinery have a positive impact on productivity. Estimates by Schiff, Wan and Olarreaga (2002) point to North-South and South-South technological spillovers, diffused through imports. North-South spillovers would be higher and would affect mainly R&D intensive industries, whereas South-South spillovers would be relevant mostly to other types of industries.

The acquisition of knowledge through exports is also the subject of a few studies, although the evidence is mixed. Clerides, Lach and Tybout (1998) found no evidence of learning-by-exporting on plant

level data for Colombia (1981-91) and Mexico (1984-90). Results from Alvarez and Robertson (2000), however, point to a strong link between exporting and investment in innovation in both Mexico (1993-95) and Chile (1993-95). The World Bank (2000), based on plant-level data for Mexico over 1990-1998, found suggestive signs of learning-by-exporting.

Finally, the (scarce) evidence on the FDI channel tends to support the prevalence of vertical (inter-industry) over horizontal (intra-industry) spillovers and to highlight the importance of countries' absorptive capacity.[5] Aitken and Harrison (1999) find that foreign equity participation raises plant productivity in Venezuela (1976-89), but also that horizontal spillovers are negative. Likewise, Kugler (2000) reports limited horizontal spillovers for Colombian manufacturing plants over 1974-98, but finds evidence of "widespread inter-industry spillovers from FDI." Results from Kugler (2000) as well as Kokko, Tansini and Zejan (1996) support the relevance of absorptive capacity. The former shows that the absorptive capacity of local firms lagged behind that of foreign firms, which, in turn, would explain the prevalence of vertical (generic knowledge) over horizontal (specific knowledge) spillovers in Colombia. The latter find evidence that horizontal spillovers among Uruguayan plants (1988) were virtually non-existent, except for a small group of firms whose technological gap vis-à-vis foreign plants was relatively small.

INTEGRATION AND PRODUCTIVITY IN BRAZIL AND MEXICO

Whether through the trade or FDI channels, the evidence on how integration might affect productivity seems to make up only part of a story that, while generally consistent with what the theorists say, still lacks some main chapters. When it comes to the more reliable microeconomic, plant-level analysis, coverage of

---

[4] They were unable to test the link between imported inputs and innovation in Chile due to data limitations.

[5] For a general review that includes studies from other regions, see Blomström, Kokko and Zejan (2000).

the countries in the region is still very limited, just as is discussion about the long-term growth effects of integration on productivity. One of the key missing chapters of this story seems to be the specific effects of regional integration.

The dearth of evidence on regional integration is understandable, since most of the efforts to study it are relatively new. To deal properly with this issue, one must confront two challenges: first, to distinguish between the competing forces that affect a country's productivity; and, second, to differentiate between preferential and non-preferential integration. The discussion that follows provides some initial evidence of how integration in the Americas has affected productivity, with a focus on Brazil and Mexico during the 1990s.

Changes in Trade and Investment Policies

Both Brazil and Mexico moved towards integration after at least half a century of import-substitution policies. These policies—an arsenal of tariffs, quotas, import licenses, multiple exchange rates, FDI regulations and soft loans—were effective in promoting growth and in pushing their economies through a substantial structural change. Yet, by the late 1970s there were clear signs that the model was no longer sustainable. Productivity after an initial period of high growth set into a downward trend and by the early 1980s was clearly stagnated (see Bacha and Bonelli, 2001, on Brazil, and World Bank, 1998, on Mexico). This slowdown, compounded by macroeconomic mismanagement, eventually lead to the collapse of the old regime amid the debt crisis of the 1980s. The countries' response to that technological and economic stagnation was integration into the world markets.

Mexico moved first and faster, and by the early 1990s had already made substantial progress. Tariffs on a most favored nation (MFN) basis fell from 28.5 percent in 1985 (the first year of trade liberalization) to 11.4 percent in 1993, while only 192 tariff lines were subject to import licenses—in contrast to 1982, when all imports were subject to them.[6] In manufacturing, tariffs fell from around 30 percent in 1985 to 15.5 percent in 1993, although in general they were less subject to import licensing requirements. From 1994 on, as a result of NAFTA, these tariffs declined

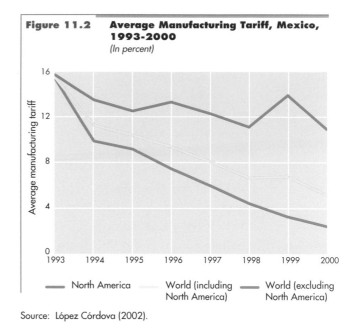

Figure 11.2   Average Manufacturing Tariff, Mexico, 1993-2000
(In percent)

Source: López Córdova (2002).

even further and more rapidly. While in 1993 only around 15 percent of imports from the United States were subject to tariffs under 10 percent, in 1994 that figure reached 60 percent. By the year 2000, less than 1 percent of manufacturing imports faced duties of 10 percent or higher. As a result, Mexico's average tariff on manufacturing imports from the world was only 5 percent in 2000 (Figure 11.2). Some industries such as textiles and apparel saw MFN tariffs increase during the 1990s. The share of Mexico's trade subject to MFN tariffs has declined, however, since the country has established a network of free trade agreements in the Americas and with European nations. Trade liberalization was accompanied by FDI deregulation, also deepened by NAFTA, which led to the removal of most sectoral restrictions and approval and performance requirements.[7]

Brazil, by contrast, took longer to open up. The removal of nontariff barriers and a drastic drop in tariffs had to wait until 1990. The average for MFN tariffs fell from 52 percent in 1987 to 9.9 percent in 1994 and edged up to 12.9 percent by 2000, reflect-

[6] See Ten Kate (1992) and López Córdova (2001).

[7] See Dussel Peters, Paliza and Diaz (2002).

Figure 11.3   *Average MFN and Mercosur Tariff, Brazil, 1987-2000*
(In percent)

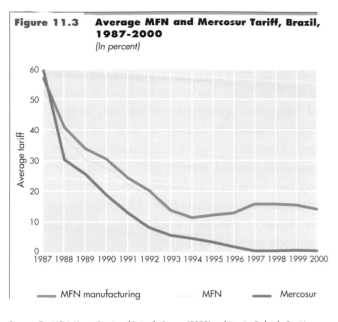

MFN manufacturing   MFN   Mercosur

Source: For MFN, Kume, Piani and Bráz de Souza. (2000) and Receita Federal. For Mercosur, Estevadeordal, Goto and Saez (2000) and Receita Federal.

ing Brazil's response to the 1995 Mexican crisis.[8] Tariffs on manufacturing followed a similar trend, with the average dropping from 57 percent in 1987 to 11 percent in 1994 and rising marginally to 13.9 percent by 2000. As in Mexico, trade liberalization was deepened by a regional trade agreement, Mercosur, and was associated with deregulation on FDI. The former brought the intra-regional average tariff from 59.5 percent in 1987 (one year after the first Brazil-Argentina agreement) to close to zero in 2000 (Figure 11.3), and the latter extended national treatment to foreign firms except for a few sectors (such as investments in communications services).

These policy changes had a profound impact on trade and investment flows in both countries. In Mexico, both imports and exports boomed. Total imports grew on average by 16.3 percent a year during 1985-2000, followed closely by exports, which reached an average growth of 14.2 percent a year. Manufacturing exports and intra-regional (NAFTA) trade were the key factors behind the export take-off. The share of manufactured goods in total exports rose from 27 percent in 1985 to 83 percent in 2000, whereas NAFTA's share of total Mexican trade went from 78 to 83 percent (and the share of total exports from 80 to 91 percent) during the same period.[9] There was also rapid growth in FDI, with average flows

increasing from $2.6 billion over 1980-88 to $5.7 billion over 1989-93. During the initial NAFTA period (1994-2000), FDI flows received another boost, reaching an average of $14.5 billion (see Chapter 10).[10]

In Brazil, the trade boom was mainly restricted to imports, which increased on average by 13.8 percent a year in the post-liberalization period from 1990-2000. Exports also grew, but at the much more modest rate of 5.8 percent. The changes in the export composition were also modest, with manufacturing exports increasing their share of total exports from 54 to 58 percent over the same period. Exports to Mercosur, though, proved to be more dynamic, increasing at 16.8 percent a year, which raised the regional agreement's share of total exports from 5.6 percent in 1990 to 14 percent in 2000 (and from 6 to 20 percent in the case of manufacturing exports). The share of Mercosur in Brazil's total trade followed a similar trend, jumping from 7 to 14 percent over the same period.[11] FDI flows also responded to the new regime, but only after inflation was controlled in the second half of the 1990s.[12] Average flows, which were close to $1.3 billion over 1980-94, climbed to $19.3 billion over 1995-2000.

Figure 11.4 presents a good picture of what all these changes in trade flows meant for manufacturing in the two economies. There are three issues worth noting. First, the two countries were in distinctly different positions when they moved into trade liberalization. In the first year of Mexico's trade reforms, 1985, the import penetration ratio in manufacturing was 9.3 percent (Weiss, 1999, not shown in the figure), whereas in Brazil, in an equivalent year (1989), the same figure was 4.9 percent. In other words, Brazil went much further down the import-substitution road. Second, import penetration increased substantially in both countries, but the "openness gap" remained consider-

[8] See Kume, Piani and Bráz de Souza (2000).

[9] Mexican trade data is from Banco de México (www.banxico. org.mx). Unless otherwise stated, figure includes maquiladora (in-bond assembly) trade.

[10] Due to methodological changes, pre- and post-NAFTA figures are not strictly comparable. See Dussel Peters, Paliza and Diaz (2002).

[11] Brazilian trade data is from Secex (www.mdic.gov.br).

[12] See Pinheiro, Giambiagi and Moreira (2001).

Figure 11.6a   Brazil: Annual Total Factor Productivity Growth, 1996-99
(In percent)

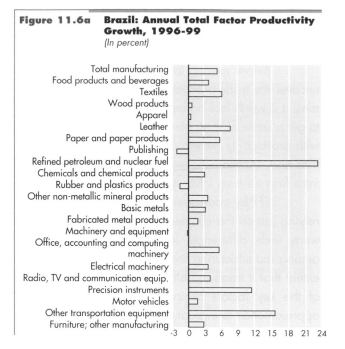

Figure 11.6b   Mexico: Annual Total Factor Productivity Growth, 1996-99
(In percent)

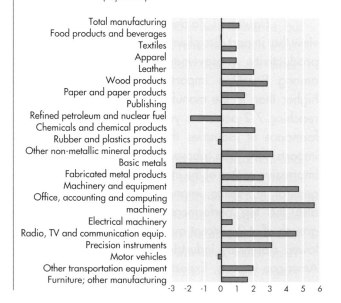

Source: López Córdova and Moreira (2002).

However, whereas in Brazil exporting industries grew below the manufacturing average, particularly those exporting to Mercosur, this was not the case in Mexico, where regional and international exporting industries performed at or above average.

The lower relative growth rate of exporting industries in both countries could be explained by the possibility that, in order to participate in foreign markets successfully, producers must show a degree of efficiency, leaving less room for additional productivity improvements. The relatively better performance of exporting industries in Mexico, though, might reflect the post-NAFTA export boom, something that Brazil could not replicate with Mercosur. But, perhaps, the more telling contrast in Figures 11.7a and b is the poor performance in both countries of industries with few trade links.

Intra-firm versus reallocation gains. Another way of looking behind the aggregate figures is to decompose annual changes in TFP into three effects: intra-firm gains (i.e., variations in productivity that occurred inside the firms resulting from technological and managerial innovations); intra-industry reallocation or turnover, reflecting changes in market share between low and high productivity firms within the same industry; and inter-industry reallocation, measuring changes in TFP brought about by shifts in the composition of manufacturing output (e.g., the share of the car industry rises whereas that of textiles falls). The details of this decomposition are in Appendix 11.1.

The results in Figures 11.8a and b show that reallocation effects in both countries, particularly across industries, were a major force behind productivity growth. In Brazil, reallocation accounted for 51 percent of total productivity growth, with reallocation across industries explaining 63 percent of total reallocation gains. In Mexico, the importance of these effects was even more pronounced and was the overwhelming factor behind TFP growth. As in Brazil, shifts in the composition of manufacturing output accounted for the lion's share of the reallocation gains. Although one cannot attribute these changes directly to trade on the basis of this evidence alone, it does clearly suggest, first, that trade might have played a role in the replacement of low productivity firms by higher productivity ones. Second, as indicated by the inter-industry reallocations gains—particularly important in industries

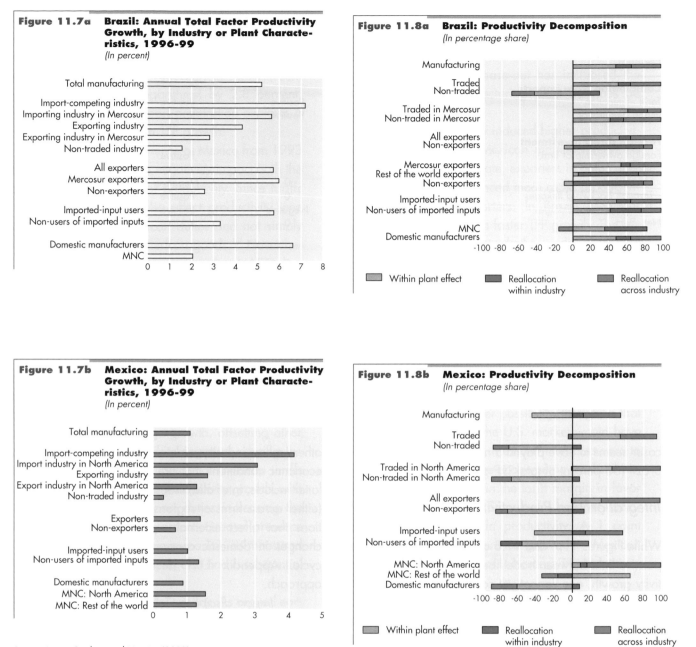

Figure 11.7a Brazil: Annual Total Factor Productivity Growth, by Industry or Plant Characteristics, 1996-99
(In percent)

Figure 11.8a Brazil: Productivity Decomposition
(In percentage share)

Figure 11.7b Mexico: Annual Total Factor Productivity Growth, by Industry or Plant Characteristics, 1996-99
(In percent)

Figure 11.8b Mexico: Productivity Decomposition
(In percentage share)

Source: López Córdova and Moreira (2002).

Source: López Córdova and Moreira (2002).

more exposed to trade (traded industries)—the dislocation of increasing return or knowledge producing industries by imports might not have been significant, or, at least, not significant enough to offset comparative advantage and scale gains.

When industries are grouped by trade orientation, what stands out is that in both countries, traded industries accounted for almost all TFP growth and intra-firm gains. This exercise also hints at the relative importance of the regional agreements for both countries. Although it is extremely difficult to disentangle regional from extra-regional effects, NAFTA seems to have played a major role for Mexico, explaining virtually all TFP and intra-firm improvements, whereas Mer-

cerned. Tariff reductions as part of the agreement appear to have had a sizable positive impact on productivity growth, which added to the already substantial gains reaped during the period of non-preferential liberalization. As the theory suggests, the differences in labor costs between NAFTA partners appear to have kept the threat of damaging dislocations in increasing returns and knowledge-intensive sectors at bay.

On the other hand, there is not enough evidence to argue that Brazil's more cautious approach to trade, which involved Mercosur, was misguided. The fact that the preferential and non-preferential liberalizations were carried out simultaneously makes it very difficult to disentangle regional and nonregional effects. What one can argue without erring too much on the side of speculation is that the lion's share of Brazil's productivity gains during this period came from the non-preferential liberalization, given that Mercosur at its peak did not account for more than 17 percent of Brazil's total trade. And this comes as no surprise in view of the relative size and resources of Brazil's partners in the regional agreement. The little evidence uncovered in this regard points to learning-by-exporting gains on Mercosur trade, but these gains do not appear to have been any different from those from exports to the rest of the world. Considering the limits

of Mercosur gains, the importance of the import-discipline effect and the fact that productivity growth only took off in the second half of the 1990s, it is tempting to believe that Brazil would have had a better performance if it had pursued a more aggressive approach towards integration, that is, one that would not have excluded Mercosur, but that would have gone beyond it, in search of more sizable trade gains.

Leaving strategic and counterfactual considerations aside, the bottom line seems to be that both Brazil and Mexico reaped important productivity gains from integration. It is perhaps too soon to tell how much of these gains were "level or growth effects" or whether or not the "integration shock" will produce the same sort of rapid, sustainable and long-term productivity growth seen in East Asia. That will depend very much on the long-term effects of import discipline on the countries' rate of innovation. In any case, one could not realistically expect that integration would do the entire job. When it comes to a stable macroeconomic environment and investment in education, technological capabilities and institutions—all key ingredients of productivity growth—both countries (not to mention the entire region) still lag behind their counterparts in East Asia.

APPENDIX 11.1
EMPIRICAL METHODOLOGY

This appendix summarizes findings on the impact of integration in Brazil and Mexico on total factor productivity in manufacturing.[1] The underlying analysis relies on firm- or plant-level data, which pose challenges but allow for better estimates of productivity.

Methodology: The analysis applies an algorithm by Olley and Pakes (1996) to account for simultaneity and sample selection issues in estimating parameters of a Cobb-Douglas production function with labor (skilled and unskilled), material and capital inputs, and output as the dependent variable. Different production functions were estimated for 8 manufacturing industries (industries 31–38 in the International Standard Industrial Classification, revision 2). Productivity was defined as output unexplained by the inputs.

Aggregate productivity growth in Figures 11.6 and 11.7 was calculated as the output-weighted average of firm-level productivity growth, excluding the lower and upper 1 percent tails of the distribution of TFP to remove outlying observations. Figure 11.8 extends the productivity decomposition of Griliches and Regev (1995) by distinguishing between intra- and inter-industry reallocation of resources. That decomposition requires aggregating across firms in industries with different production functions, so TFP estimates were normalized as in Pavcnik (2000) by subtracting the productivity level of a "reference firm" in the initial year (1996 for Brazil, 1993 for Mexico). Thus, implicit TFP growth rates in Figure 11.8 are not readily comparable to those in Figures 11.6 and 11.7.

With the productivity estimates in hand, one may explain a firm's efficiency as a function of trade policy variables (e.g., tariffs), foreign capital participation and FDI, exports, imported input use, as well as other controls needed to prevent omitted variable biases. Thus, one may estimate equations of the form:

$$Productivity_{ijt} = \beta_1 Trade_{ijt} + \beta_2 FDI_{ijt} + controls + \varepsilon_{ijt}$$

where the dependent variable, Productivity in plant i, belonging to industry j, during year t, is measured either in log-levels or in log-differences. The availability of panel data allows tracking each plant over time and controlling for unobserved plant characteristics via fixed-effect panel techniques.

Since trade policy is potentially endogenous—for example, less productive industries may receive more protection from policymakers—one needs to find appropriate instrumental variables to obtain consistent estimates of the coefficient β_1 in the previous regression equation. In the Mexican case, the analysis uses the NAFTA tariffs as instruments for the actual Mexican tariffs on world trade, as well as for U.S. tariffs on Mexican goods. NAFTA tariff phase-out negotiations finished in August 1992. Moreover, according to NAFTA Annex 302.2, paragraph 2, the base rates for determining import duties after applying the staging category agreed upon "generally reflect the rate of duty in effect on July 1, 1991." Thus, we can safely consider that they are exogenous (not influenced by plant-level TFP levels during the 1993-99 period). Moreover, they are highly correlated with actual tariffs.

To address the potential endogeneity between import penetration and productivity, we used a gravity equation approach to estimate trade flows based on geographical variables. This estimate was used as an instrumental variable in the regression analysis.

Data: The data come from annual industrial surveys in Brazil (Pesquisa Industrial Anual) and Mexico (Encuesta Industrial Anual) on approximately 11,000 manufacturing firms (in Brazil) and 6,500 plants (in Mexico). These data were complemented with trade, tariff and other information from official sources in Brazil, Mexico and the United States.

To measure intra- and inter-industry spillovers from FDI, the analysis uses information on the percent of equity owned by foreigners (1996 for Brazil, 1993 for Mexico). We assume that the structure of ownership remained unchanged through 1999. A firm is considered to be "foreign" if foreigners owned more than 50 percent of equity. The proportion of industry output produced by foreign plants in each industry was taken as the measure for foreign capital participation. To account for the possibility of spillovers from industries upstream or downstream in the production process, we consider average foreign capital participation in industries with backward or forward linkages based on input-output information for each country.

---

[1] See López Córdova & Moreira (2002) and López Córdova (2002).

Appendix Table 11.1 | Total Factor Productivity and Integration in Brazil: Regression Results

Independent variables	Dependent variable: TFP (log)			Dependent variable: Change in TFP (log)						
	Reg 1	Reg 2	Reg 3	Reg 4	Reg 5	Reg 6	Reg 7	Reg 8	Reg 9	Reg 10
Exporting activity										
World exporter (dummy)					0.0024 (0.0087)					
Mercosur exporter (dummy)						0.0082 (0.0088)				
Exports/sales							0.0009 (0.0004)**			
Mercosur exports/sales								0.0008 (0.0010)		
Imported intermediate goods										
Imported-input/material costs		-0.0009 (0.0002)***							-0.0004 (0.0002)	
Imports/material costs			0.0006 (0.0001)***							0.0003 (0.0001)***
FDI spillovers										
Intra-industry (%)	-0.1358 (0.1000)	-0.1391 (0.0999)	-0.1349 (0.0999)	0.1131 (0.1009)	0.1131 (0.1009)	0.1122 (0.1009)	0.1134 (0.1008)	0.1129 (0.1009)	0.1116 (0.1009)	0.1133 (0.1008)
From forward linkages	-0.4939 (0.1854)***	-0.4809 (0.1853)***	-0.5067 (0.1852)***	-0.4022 (0.1870)**	-0.4021 (0.1870)**	-0.4021 (0.1870)**	-0.4032 (0.1870)**	-0.4039 (0.1870)**	-0.3966 (0.1870)**	-0.4076 (0.1870)**
From backward linkages	0.9778 (0.2707)***	0.9671 (0.2707)***	0.9915 (0.2705)***	0.4310 (0.2732)	0.4312 (0.2732)	0.4285 (0.2732)	0.4443 (0.2732)	0.4300 (0.2732)	0.4266 (0.2732)	0.4393 (0.2732)
Number of observations	29,103	29,103	29,100	29,103	29,103	29,103	29,103	29,103	29,103	29,100
Number of firms	10,859	10,859	10,858	10,859	10,859	10,859	10,859	10,859	10,859	10,858
Within R^2	0.0103	0.0110	0.0115	0.5892	0.5892	0.5892	0.5893	0.5892	0.5892	0.5893
F statistic for null hypothesis (Sum FDI spillovers = 0)	1.89	1.88	1.91	0.31	0.31	0.29	0.37	0.30	0.31	0.32

Notes: All regressions were estimated using fixed effects on a panel of firms. All regressions include the following controls: size, industry output (excluding the plant's own output), capacity utilization, industrial and geographic concentration indices, U.S. consumption, log of exchange rate times, U.S. PPI in the industry, and year dummies. Regressions 4 to 10 also include log TFP in year t. Standard errors in parentheses.
* Significant at the 10% level.
** Significant at the 5% level.
*** Significant at the 1% level.

Appendix Table 11.2 | Total Factor Productivity and Integration in Mexico: Regression Results

Independent variables	Dependent variable: TFP (log)				Dependent variable: Change in TFP (log)					
	Reg 1	Reg 2	Reg 3	Reg 4	Reg 5	Reg 6	Reg 7	Reg 8	Reg 9	Reg 10
Competition from imports										
Mexican tariff on total imports (%)	-0.0050 (0.0023)**	-0.0087 (0.0022)***	-0.0084 (0.0022)***	-0.0087 (0.0022)***	-0.0122 (0.0021)***	-0.0119 (0.0021)***	-0.0118 (0.0021)***	-0.0120 (0.0021)***	-0.0110 (0.0020)***	-0.0119 (0.0021)***
Imports/industry output			0.0216 (0.0060)***				0.0186 (0.0058)***			
Exporting activity										
Exporter (dummy)								-0.0083 (0.0049)*		
Exports/sales									-0.0182 (0.0145)	
U.S. tariff (Mexico-rest of the world)	-0.0046 (0.0021)**	-0.0052 (0.0020)**	-0.0053 (0.0020)***	-0.0053 (0.0020)***	-0.0029 (0.0020)	-0.0028 (0.0020)	-0.0028 (0.0020)	-0.0029 (0.0020)	-0.0010 (0.0019)	-0.0026 (0.0020)
Imported intermediate goods										
Imported inputs/total non-labor costs				0.0463 (0.0155)***						-0.0422 (0.0149)***
FDI spillovers										
Intra-industry (%)		-0.1509 (0.0570)***	-0.1458 (0.0570)**	-0.1519 (0.0570)***		-0.0310 (0.0548)	-0.0269 (0.0548)	-0.0324 (0.0548)	-0.0256 (0.0515)	-0.0304 (0.0548)
From forward linkages		1.1427 (0.1740)***	1.0755 (0.1746)***	1.1387 (0.1740)***		0.7169 (0.1677)***	0.6602 (0.1683)***	0.7140 (0.1677)***	0.6845 (0.1593)***	0.7194 (0.1676)***
From backward linkages		0.3964 (0.0788)***	0.4120 (0.0789)***	0.3989 (0.0788)***		0.2815 (0.0759)***	0.2954 (0.0759)***	0.2845 (0.0759)***	0.2319 (0.0722)***	0.2798 (0.0758)***
Observations	26,703	26,683	26,683	26,683	26,703	26,683	26,683	26,683	25,903	26,683
Number of plants	5,302	5,302	5,302	5,302	5,302	5,302	5,302	5,302	5,191	5,302
Within R²	0.0142	0.0144	0.0164	0.0145	0.3638	0.3653	0.3662	0.3650	0.3595	0.3656
Chi² statistic for null hypothesis (Sum FDI spillovers = 0)		49.56	46.31	49.39		25.89	23.87	25.82	24.33	25.982

Notes: All regressions were estimated using two-stage least squares on a panel with fixed effects. Instruments are NAFTA-negotiated tariffs to control for potential endogeneity of tariffs in Mexico and the United States. All regressions include the following controls: age, age squared, size, industry output (excluding the plant's own output), capacity utilization, industrial and geographic concentration indices, U.S. consumption, log of exchange rate times, U.S. PPI in the industry, and year dummies. Regressions 5 to 10 also include log TFP in year t. "Mexican tariff" is the ISIC (rev 3) 4-digit industry tariff on world imports, weighted by trade. "U.S. tariff" is the difference between effective tariffs on Mexican imports and on imports from the rest of the world in the industry. FDI variables refer to the fraction of output produced by foreign plants; linkages were calculated using Mexican input-output data as weights. Standard errors in parentheses.
* Significant at the 10% level.
** Significant at the 5% level.
*** Significant at the 1% level.

REFERENCES

Abramovitz, Moses. 1956. Resource and Output Trends in the United States since 1870. *American Economic Review* 46(2) May: 5-23.

Aitken, Brian, and Ann E. Harrison. 1999. Do Domestic Firms Benefit from Foreign Direct Investment? Evidence from Venezuela. *American Economic Review* 89(3): 605-18.

Alvarez, Roberto, and Raymond Robertson. 2000. Exposure to Foreign Markets and Firm-Level Innovation: Evidence from Chile and Mexico. Mimeo.

Aw, Bee Yan, Xiaomin Chen, and Mark J. Roberts. 2001. Firm-level Evidence on Productivity Differentials and Turnover in Taiwanese Manufacturing. *Journal of Development Economics* 66: 51-86.

Bacha, E., and Regis Bonelli. 2001. Crescimento e produtividade no Brasil: o que nos diz o registro de longo prazo. Seminários Dimac no. 52. IPEA, Rio de Janeiro.

Baier, Scott L., Gerald P. Dwyer Jr., and Robert Tamura. 2002. *How Important Are Capital and Total Factor Productivity for Economic Growth.* Working Paper Series 2002-2, Federal Reserve Bank of Atlanta.

Bernard, Andrew, and J. Bradford Jensen. 2001. *Exporting and Productivity.* NBER Working Paper 7135. April.

Blomström, Magnus, and Ari Kokko. 1998. Multinational Corporations and Spillovers. *Journal of Economic Surveys* 12: 247-277.

Blomström, Magnus, A. Kokko, and M. Zejan. 2000. *Foreign Direct Investment. Firm and Host Country Strategies.* London: Macmillan.

Blyde, Juan S. 2002. Integration and Technology Diffusion: The Role of Imports of Capital Goods and Foreign Direct Investment. Inter-American Development Bank, Washington, DC. January.

Clerides, Sofronis, Saul Lach, and James Tybout. 1998. Is Learning by Exporting Important? Micro Dynamics Evidence from Colombia, Mexico and Morocco. *Quarterly Journal of Economics* 113(3): 903-47.

Devlin, R., and Ricardo Ffrench-Davis. 1999. Towards an Evaluation of Regional Integration in Latin America in the 1990s. *World Economy* 22: 261-90.

Dussel Peters, Enrique, L. M. G. Paliza, and Eduardo Loria Diaz. 2002. Visión macroeconómica de los impactos de la integración regional en la inversión inter e intrarregionales. El caso de la inversión extranjera directa en México. RedINT, Inter-American Development Bank.

Estevadeordal, Antoni, Juchini Goto, and Raul Saez. 2000. *The New Regionalism in the Americas: The Case of Mercosur.* Intal-ITD Working Paper no. 5, Inter-American Development Bank, Washington, DC.

Ethier, Wilfred. 1982. National and International Returns to Scale in the Modern Theory of International Trade. *American Economic Review* 72: 950-59.

Fajnzylber, Pablo, and Daniel Lederman. 1999. *Economic Reforms and Total Factor Productivity Growth in Latin America and the Caribbean, 1950-95: An Empirical Note.* Policy Research Working Paper 2114, World Bank, Washington DC.

Fernandes, Ana. 2001. Trade Policy, Trade Volumes and Plant Level Productivity in Colombian Manufacturing Industries. Department of Economics, Yale University, New Haven, CT.

Goh, Ai-Ting. 2000. Opportunity Cost, Trade Policies and the Efficiency of Firms. *Journal of Development Economics* 62: 363-83.

Griliches, Zvi, and Haim Regev. 1995. Firm Productivity in Israeli Industry 1979-1988. *Journal of Econometrics* 65: 175-203.

Grossman, Gene, and Elhanan Helpman. 1991. *Innovation and Growth in the Global Economy.* Cambridge, MA: MIT Press.

———. 1994. *Technology and Trade.* NBER Working Paper 4926. November.

Helpman, Elhanan, and Paul Krugman. 1985. *Market Structure and Foreign Trade.* Cambridge, MA: MIT Press.

———. 1989. *Trade Policy and Market Structure.* Cambridge, MA: MIT Press.

Hirschman, A. O. 1958. *The Strategy of Economic Development.* New Haven: Yale University Press.

Inter-American Development Bank (IDB). 2001. *Competitiveness: The Business of Growth. Economic and Social Progress in Latin America.* Washington, DC: Inter-American Development Bank.

Keller, Wolfang. 2001. *International Technology of Diffusion.* Center for Economic Policy Research Discussion Paper no. 3133.

Kokko, Ari, Ruben Tansini, and Mario C. Zejan. 1996. Local Technological Capability and Productivity Spillovers from FDI in the Uruguayan Manufacturing Sector. *Journal of Development Studies* 32(4) April: 602-11.

Kugler, Maurice. 2000. *The Diffusion of Externalities from Foreign Direct Investment: Theory Ahead of Measurement.* University of Southampton Discussion Papers.

Kume, Honório, Guida Piani, and Carlos F. Bráz de Souza. 2000. A Política Brasileira de Importação no Período 1987-98: Descrição e Avaliação. IPEA, Rio de Janeiro. Mimeo.

Leamer, Edward. 1996. *In Search of Stolper Samuelson Effects on U.S. Wages.* NBER Working Paper 5427. January.

López Córdova, Ernesto. 2001. Las negociaciones de acceso a los mercados en los tratados de libre comercio de México con Bolivia y Costa Rica. In A. Estevadeordal and C. Robert (eds.), *Las Américas sin barreras: Negociaciones comerciales de acceso a mercados.* Washington, DC: Inter-American Development Bank.

———. 2002. NAFTA and Mexico's Manufacturing Productivity: An Empirical Investigation using Micro-level Data. Inter-American Development Bank, Washington, DC. Unpublished.

López Córdova, Ernesto, and Mauricio Mesquita Moreira. 2002. Regional Integration and Productivity: The Experiences of Brazil and Mexico. Inter-American Development Bank, Washington, DC. Unpublished.

Lucas, Robert E., Jr. 1988. On the Mechanics of Economic Development. *Journal of Monetary Economics* 22(1): 3-42.

Mankiw, N. Gregory. 1995. *The Growth of Nations.* Brookings Papers on Economic Activity 1: 275-310.

Markusen, James, and Keith Maskus. Forthcoming. General Equilibrium Approaches to the Multinational Firm: A Review of Theory and Evidence. In James Harrigan (ed.), *Handbook of International Economics,* vol. 38. Basil-Blackwell.

Markusen, James, and Anthony Venables. 1999. Foreign Direct Investment as a Catalyst for Industrial Development. *European Economic Review* 43(2): 355-56.

Melitz, Marc J. 2002. The Impact of Trade on Intra-Industry Reallocations and Aggregate Industry Productivity.Department of Economics, Harvard University, Cambridge, MA.

Muendler, Marc-Andreas. 2002. Trade, Technology and Productivity: A Study of Brazilian Manufacturers, 1986-1998. University of California, Berkeley, CA. Mimeo.

Olley, G. Steven, and Ariel Pakes. 1996. The Dynamics of Productivity in the Telecommunications Equipment Industry. *Econometrica* 64(6) November: 1263-97.

Pavcnik, Nina. 2000. Trade Liberalization, Exit and Productivity Improvements: Evidence from Chilean Plants. Department of Economics, Dartmouth College, Hanover, NH.

Pinheiro, Armando, Fabio Giambiagi, and Mauricio Mesquita Moreira. 2001. *Brazil in the 1990s: A Successful Transition?* BNDES Discussion Paper 91, Rio de Janeiro.

Roberts, M. J., and James Tybout (eds.).1996. *Industrial Evolution in Developing Countries.* New York: Oxford University Press.

Rodrik, D. 1992. Closing the Productivity Gap: Does Trade Liberalization Really Help? In G. K. Helleiner (ed.), *Trade Policy Industrialization and Development.* Toronto and Helsinki: Wider, UNU.

Saggi, K. 2000. *Trade, Foreign Direct Investment and International Technology Transfer. A Survey.* Policy Research Working Paper 2349, World Bank, Washington, DC.

Schiff, Maurice, Yanling Wan, and Marcelo Olarreaga. 2002. North-South and South Trade-Related R&D Spillovers: An Industry-Level Analysis. World Bank. March.

Scitovsky, T. 1963. Two Concepts of External Economies. In A. N. Agarwala and S. P. Singh (eds.), *The Economics of Underdevelopment.* New York: Oxford University Press.

Solow, Robert M. 1956. A Contribution to the Theory of Economic Growth. *Quarterly Journal of Economics* 70(1): 65-94.

Ten Kate, Adriaan. 1992. Trade Liberalization and Economic Stabilization in Mexico: Lessons of Experience. *World Development* 20(5): 659-72.

Tybout, James. 2000. Manufacturing Firms in Developing Countries: How Well Do They Do and Why? *Journal of Economic Literature* 38(1): 11-44.

——. Forthcoming. Plant and Firm-Level Evidence on New Trade Theories. In James Harrigan (ed.), *Handbook of International Economics,* vol. 38. Basil-Blackwell.

Tybout, James, and M. Daniel Westbrook. 1995. Trade Liberalization and the Dimensions of Efficiency Change in Mexican Manufacturing Industries. *Journal of International Economics* 39: 53-78.

UNCTAD. 2001. *World Investment Report 2001.* Geneva: UNCTAD.

Venables, Anthony. 1999. *Integration Agreements: A Force for Convergence or Divergence? Proceedings of World Bank ABCDE Conference.* Policy Research Working Paper Series no. 2260, Washington, DC.

Weiss, John. 1999. Trade Reform and Manufacturing Performance in Mexico: From Import Substitution to Dramatic Export Growth. *Journal of Latin American Studies* 31: 151-66.

Westphal, Larry. 2001. Technology Strategies for Economic Development in a Fast Changing Global Economy. Department of Economics, Swarthmore College, Swarthmore, PA.

World Bank. 1991. *World Development Report.* Washington, DC: World Bank.

——. 1998. Mexico. Enhancing Factor Productivity Growth. Country Economic Memorandum. Report 17392-ME, Washington, DC.

——. 2000. Mexico. Export Dynamics and Productivity. Analysis of Mexican Manufacturing in the 1990s. Report 19864-ME, Washington, DC.

Young, Alvin. 1991. Learning by Doing and the Dynamic Effects of International Trade. *Quarterly Journal of Economics* 106(2): 396-406.

——. 1995. The Tyranny of Numbers: Confronting the Statistical Realities of the East Asia Growth Experience. *Quarterly Journal of Economics* 110: 641-80.

Chapter 12

REGIONAL INTEGRATION AND WAGE INEQUALITY

There is little disagreement among most economists that countries benefit from trade liberalization. Yet, whether unilateral, multilateral (through the World Trade Organization) or through regional integration agreements (RIAs), trade liberalization has been one of the most controversial economic issues of our time. It is the focus of everyone from politicians to union leaders and anti-globalization forces because, while there are overall welfare gains from liberalization, these gains are not evenly distributed. What's more, in addition to some groups actually hurt by trade liberalization, there are others who have the perception at the very least that it has led to increased inequality, that is—that the burden of trade liberalization falls mainly on the poor.

Latin America has come a long way in terms of liberalization, reducing barriers to trade and eliminating restrictions to capital flows. While much of the liberalization occurred at the unilateral level, during the 1990s most countries deepened trade links at the subregional level as well (see Chapter 2), entering into a variety of South-South and North-South RIAs within the Americas. Several countries are currently negotiating trade arrangements with the European Union, and the hemisphere as a whole is moving toward the Free Trade Area of the Americas (FTAA).

South-South and North-North integration may have very different effects on wage inequality. In the context of the wave of trade liberalization sweeping Latin America—and all the perceptions and controversies surrounding it—this chapter will examine its impact on wage inequality in the region, with a focus on how wage inequality is affected by different forms of regional integration. The effects on poverty are examined as well (see Box 12.1), although the link between trade and poverty is less direct than that between trade and wage inequality, since in the former, factors such as labor force participation decisions among household members and the price of the consumption basket intervene.

The chapter first explores trends in relative wages across skill groups, then moves on to examine the theory behind how trade and labor markets are related. We begin with the neoclassical Heckscher-Ohlin model in which countries differ in the relative endowment of factors. In its strictest form, this model offers relatively straightforward predictions of how trade and wages—especially wage inequality—should be related. This model is perhaps most relevant for countries with large differences in relative endowments (North-South trade). Relaxing some assumptions allows for considering the effects of North-North and South-South trade, in which trading partners are generally more similar in terms of relative factor endowments. After describing the model and its implications, we focus on the assumptions of the model and try to gauge how they contrast with reality, including Latin America's relative endowments and tariff structures prior to liberalization, labor market imperfections (which give rise to unemployment), and the flows of capital.

The chapter then reviews empirical studies of how trade liberalization in Latin America has affected labor markets. While our interest is on the effects of different types of integration, the bulk of the literature

Box 12.1   Poverty and Trade Liberalization

The relationship between trade liberalization and poverty is far from straightforward, encompassing various channels of influence. One might think that higher wage inequality automatically implies higher poverty levels, but this is not necessarily the case. Consider four interceding transmission mechanisms.

• *Level of wages.* Productivity may have risen for less-skilled workers, but at a lower rate than for the higher skilled. A rise in the wage level for low-skilled workers should lower the poverty rate, regardless of how much higher the wages of high-skilled counterparts have risen. (See Chapter 11 for more details on the debate over the effect of trade on productivity.)

• *Distribution of the newly unemployed among households.* The distribution of wages is calculated at the unit of individual earners, whereas poverty rates are based on the average income per capita of household members. The level and distribution of wages observed among earners may stay the same, but if unemployment associated with the adjustment to new labor demand is concentrated among families that were previously close to the poverty line, poverty will increase.

• *Distribution of new jobs among households.* Trade may alter the demand for labor and bring new workers with new wages into the labor market. Suppose the wages stayed the same for all workers who had been in the labor market prior to liberalization, but that new opportunities attracted low-skilled women into the labor market. Under this scenario, the incomes among the poorest households would likely rise. Although the per capita incomes of the poor may be higher, wage inequality as measured by the wages of all earners would increase with the addition of very low wages to the distribution.

• *Price of consumption basket.* Since poverty is defined in relation to the ability to purchase a constant basket of consumption goods, any change in the real price of the goods basket will change the poverty rate. If trade causes the purchasing power adjusted price level for the basket to fall, the poverty line falls, which reduces the number of families living below the threshold.

The many different channels of influence make tracing the effects of trade on poverty extremely difficult. Further complicating the task are other determinants of poverty that are unrelated to trade but are changing over time and have important implications for the poverty rate. The most important factor is changing demographics. As the dependency ratio falls over time, income is divided among fewer family members, leaving more households above the poverty line. The decline in fertility rates and household size are unlikely to be linked to trade liberalization, but have powerful implications for the poverty rate.

One major debate is centered on how to interpret declines in poverty rates occurring simultaneously with trade liberalization. Within Latin America, Székely

focuses more generally on trade liberalization. We will try to extract implications from this existing literature for the issue at hand: the link between different types of integration and wage inequality. Several results emerge from the empirical studies. First, there is no clear consensus about the long-run effects of trade liberalization on wage inequality. Isolating the effects of a change in one set of factors may be straightforward in a laboratory setting but far more complicated in a world with simultaneously changing policies and economic conditions. Some Latin American countries experienced an increase in wage inequality following trade liberalization, but emerging evidence suggests that this pattern may reverse in the long run. Second, while the direct links between trade and wage inequal-

ity are disputed, trade liberalization was generally associated with rising productivity and changes in firm behavior that contributed to increased demand for skill, and therefore rising wage inequality. Firms initially reduced employment and made investments that helped the remaining workers become more productive. This reallocation of labor and investment generates some optimism for long-run growth. Third, some studies suggest that the direct effect of trade via changes in goods prices and factor supplies may be small relative to the role played by changes in technology or increases in foreign direct investment associated with integration.

(2001) documents the meager reduction in poverty over the 1990s: the poverty rate fell on average by only 4 percentage points, from a level of 43 percent to 39 percent, based on calculations for 11 countries.[1]

Using international data, Dollar and Kraay (2000) examine the trend in the incomes of the poorest quintile and suggest that in periods of economic growth, these incomes generally rise at the same rate as the incomes of the rich. In addition, they find that countries with a higher share of trade per GDP experience more economic growth. Rodrik (2001) and Rodrik and Rodríguez (1999) question the supposition that recent declines in poverty are linked to trade liberalization. From their perspective, stating that declines in poverty caused trade liberalization makes as little sense as saying that trade liberalization caused declines in poverty, since the correlations in the two trends are unlikely to be causally related and instead are likely to be reflecting other factors.

It is extremely difficult to properly control for the various determinants of poverty when attempting to identify the effects of trade liberalization. Most studies do not present a convincing link to liberalization, often relying on the problematic "before and after" approach. An ambitious set of studies by Gonzaga, Filho and Terra (2001) attempts to link the effect of trade liberalization to changes in poverty by specifically examining the pathways of change at the microeconomic level.[2] The studies examine changes in the wages of earners and

changes in employment, unemployment and job informality for the Dominican Republic, Paraguay, Jamaica, Brazil and Chile. The studies find inconsistent effects of whether poverty increases or decreases with liberalization, but in all cases the magnitude of the effects of trade liberalization on poverty are small.

While rising inequality does not necessarily imply higher poverty rates, it can be shown theoretically that in the presence of asymmetries of information and capital market imperfection, high income inequality can lower the accumulation of human capital and the prospects for long-term growth. Furthermore, the higher the level of income inequality, the lower the reduction in poverty for a given level of growth (see Ravallion, 1997. Given that wage inequality is the primary determinant of income inequality, the distributional effects of liberalization on wages are important to consider.

---

[1] Székely's measure of poverty is the share of individuals with per capita household incomes under $2 a day.

[2] The studies consider the effects of trade liberalization and financial liberalization on the full distribution of per capita income. For the countries mentioned, a computable general equilibrium model is used to explicitly model the effects of liberalization, and then is combined with microsimulations to trace the pathways at the household level. The effects of capital account liberalization are also found to be small.

DIFFERENCES IN WAGES ACROSS SKILL LEVELS

In terms of the ratio of "skilled" to "unskilled" wages in Latin America, it is best to begin with words of caution: skill is in the eye of the beholder. That is to say, there is no agreed upon definition of "skill" in the literature. Some studies compare the wages of production workers to non-production workers; others compare wages across education levels. To examine relative wages across skill groups, we compare wages of workers who have completed different levels of schooling. We examine the difference in wages for a group whose wages are most likely to reflect changes in the demand for skill: urban males between the ages of 30 and 50 who worked at least five hours in the reference week. By

using specific measures of completed schooling for this group, which has persistently high employment rates over the period, we are more likely to pick up changes in prices, and not compositional changes.

Figure 12.1a shows that on average, the hourly wage for workers with completed tertiary schooling is approximately 100 percent higher than for workers who have completed secondary schooling.[1] According to this measure of the skills gap, the skill premium rose slightly over the 1990s. The figure is based on the differences in the 12 countries shown in

---

[1] The definition of the exact years of completing the different schooling levels per country are shown in the notes for Table 12.1.

One concern with the first two measures of skill is that they are both potentially affected by the increased supply of workers with secondary schooling. In other words, these measures may be capturing more about the supply of secondary schooling than a change in the demand for skill. For the last measure, we consider the gap between workers with tertiary and primary schooling, since it is not affected by the supply of secondary schooling. Figure 12.1c shows no generalized trend in this third and preferred measure of the skill gap. It is important to consider the disaggregated trends, which are presented in Figure 12.2 for the 12 countries. While the tertiary to primary wage gap has been falling in Panama, Honduras, Argentina and, more recently, in Colombia, it has been rising in Mexico, Uruguay, Chile, Peru, Costa Rica, Bolivia and Venezuela. The gap for Brazil changed little over the decade. Both Mexico and Costa Rica had rapid increases in the gap in the early 1990s with reversals occurring in the latter part of the decade.

It is difficult to read any widespread trends in the skill premium from the full set of figures, but perhaps that in itself is noteworthy. Increases in skill gaps are observed in many cases, but as a whole, these figures contrast somewhat with the widespread view that less skilled workers in the region are consistently falling farther and farther behind their more skilled counterparts. Although there is evidence of a rise in the return to very highly skilled labor in numerous countries, the pattern of tertiary to primary wages found for Panama, Honduras and Argentina conflict with perceptions.[5] How can we reconcile the results with the widespread notion among trade economists as well as anti-globalizers that liberalization is associated with rising gaps in wages across skill groups? First, early studies for Mexico and Costa Rica correctly noted the rapid increase in the skills gap in the early 1990s, but few countries have since mirrored such large increases. Second, by applying the typical measure of tertiary to secondary schooling, the skills gap may in some countries be contaminated by large changes in the supply of secondary schooling, instead of reflecting changes in the demand for skill. Brazil, Costa Rica and Peru show much more moderated change in the tertiary to primary gap than in the tertiary to secondary gap. Third, even estimates of the skill-premium from regressions indicate that the typical approach of comparing two points over time

may be inaccurate for capturing the trend. Finally, it is important to note that the information in Figures 12.1 and 12.2 is not explicitly linked to trade. It may be that while liberalization does increase the demand for skill and bring pressure for wage inequality to increase, in some countries these pressures may have been offset by other changes in the labor market.

THEORETICAL PREDICTIONS: HOW DOES TRADE LIBERALIZATION AFFECT LABOR MARKETS?

Stolper-Samuelson Theorem

The study of the relationship between trade liberalization and labor markets has a long history in economics. One of the first formal treatments of the relationship between trade liberalization and wage inequality was by Wolfgang Stolper and Paul Samuelson (1941). They based their analysis on the neoclassical Heckscher-Ohlin trade model, which predicts that comparative advantage emerges from differences in relative factor endowments. These differences are most stark between Northern and Southern countries, suggesting that this model may be most relevant for North-South integration. Countries that are relatively abundant in low-skilled labor (generally assumed to be the countries in the South) will be able to produce goods that intensively use low-skilled labor more cheaply than countries with relatively more high-skilled labor. This difference in costs will determine the pattern of trade as countries export the goods they produce at least cost.

Trade theory predicts that such voluntary trade will create net gains for all trading partners, but these gains may not be equally distributed throughout the population. Stolper and Samuelson show that, following trade liberalization, some groups gain, others lose, but the gains to the winners would be enough to compensate the losers. To understand the empirical relevance of these predictions, it is helpful to explain the mechanics behind the theory.

---

[5] Regression results are similar, but sensitive to the specification used to characterize experience and education.

Figure 12.2   Percent Difference In Hourly Wages (Complete Tertiary vs. Complete Primary) Urban Males Ages 30-50, 1985 to 2000

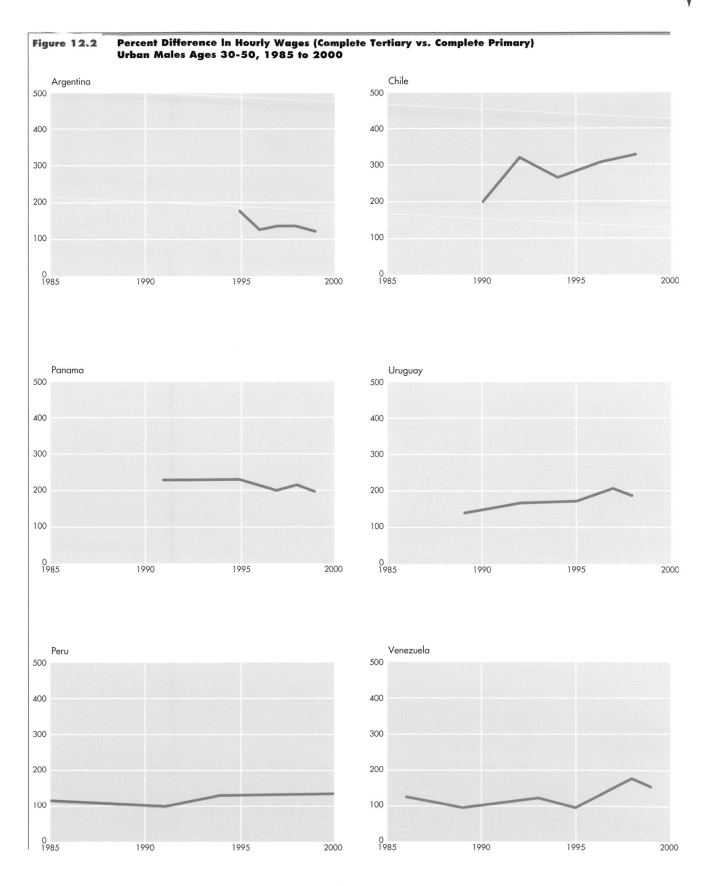

Figure 12.2 (cont.)

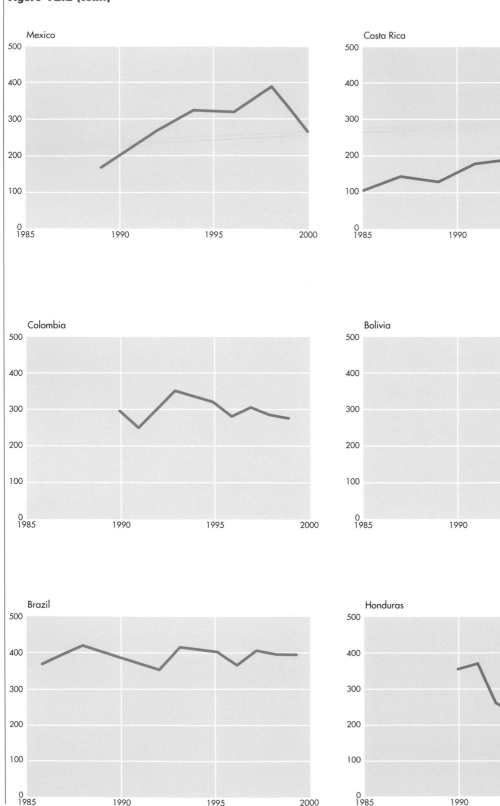

Notes: Countries are sorted from highest to lowest average education.
Source: IDB calculations based on household surveys.

A reduction in tariffs will reduce the relative price of imported goods. These price changes will be greatest between countries that are the most different. Since less skill-abundant countries would be importing more skill-intensive goods, they would experience falling prices for skill-intensive goods after trade liberalization. The fall in the price of the skill-intensive goods (and the corresponding increase in the relative price of the less skill-intensive good) would change the demand for skill. The increase in the relative price of the less skill-intensive good would increase the demand for less-skilled workers, relative to skilled workers, and therefore the wages of the less skilled workers would increase and the wages of the skilled workers would fall. Since less skilled workers have lower wages to begin with, this kind of trade liberalization should reduce wage inequality.

While the theory applies to trade liberalization in general, it can be loosely extended to examine the effects of preferential agreements to lower tariffs across countries or regions. For example, if Brazil signs a preferential agreement with Canada, a parallel reduction in tariffs between the two countries implies that the relative price of skilled goods would fall in Brazil and rise in Canada. It is then likely that Canada would import more low skill-intensive products from Brazil, while Brazil would import more of Canada's high skill-intensive exports. This implies that in Brazil, the relative demand for the relatively abundant factor, low-skilled labor, would increase, leading to a reduction of wage inequality. As the relative demand for the high-skilled workers rises in Canada, wage inequality would increase there. A different partner or set of partners is likely to have different implications for the changes in wages. For example, a preferential agreement signed with China could have very different implications for Brazil, since in comparison to China, Brazil is abundant in skilled labor. As tariffs fell, the demand for unskilled labor would likely fall in Brazil, while the demand for skilled labor would likely increase. As the wages of the less skilled rose in comparison with the wages of the more skilled, wage inequality would rise in Brazil. Regardless of the changes in relative wages, the gains from trade in the form of lower prices and higher income per capita should be larger, given wider differences in the factor endowments of the trading countries.

The key to this story is that changes in trade policy affect wages through changes in the relative prices of goods. However, the precise theoretical relationship between output prices and relative wages, known as the Stolper-Samuelson (SS) theorem, only holds under very restrictive assumptions.

In particular, the model assumes that there are two goods made with two factors of production (labor and capital, or low-skilled and high-skilled labor). In addition, the model assumes that markets are perfect, that factors can costlessly move between industries, that factors cannot move across countries, and that returns to scale and technology are constant and the same for all countries. The numerous restrictions embodied in the theory create a large number of ways in which the model may deviate from reality. These deviations affect our expectations of how trade liberalization will affect inequality.

Pattern of Protection

One example lies in the pattern of protection. The Stolper-Samuelson theorem predicts that the change in tariffs will affect relative wages through a change in prices. Yet, how tariff reductions affect prices depends on the pattern of tariffs prior to liberalization, particularly on differences in tariff levels between skill-intensive and less skill-intensive goods. Since a country's scarce factor stands to lose from trade liberalization, a reasonable expectation based on the theory is that countries use tariffs to protect their scarce factor. If this were the case, the Stolper-Samuelson predictions would apply. But country realities may differ from these expectations. For instance, prior to joining the GATT in 1986, Mexico protected its less skilled workers by placing higher tariffs on those goods that intensively used less skilled workers.[6] Similarly, for Argentina, the Mercosur tariff is higher and provides more protection in the industries that are intensive in low-skilled workers (Porto, 2001). Under these conditions, trade liberalization that reduces protection in the low-skilled manufacturing sector to a greater extent than in other sectors may increase the gap in wages between skill groups, a

---

[6] Hanson and Harrison (1999), Revenga (1997) and Robertson (2002) describe these patterns for Mexico.

result that would appear to contradict the predictions of Stolper-Samuelson. There are at least two possible explanations for this apparent contradiction. First, less skilled workers may have more of an influence in trade policy in that they are relatively more successful in securing tariffs to protect their wages.[7] If the pattern of tariff protection is more strongly linked to the political process than to the concept of comparative advantage, it is not necessarily expected that trade liberalization will increase the relative wages of the abundant factor. Another possibility is that Latin American countries are not relatively abundant in less skilled workers, in which case the pattern of protection would be consistent with expectations.

Abundance of Which Factor?

The question of whether Latin American countries are abundant in less skilled workers depends critically on what countries fall into the relevant comparison group. Should a country's relative supply of labor be compared with the countries it trades with, or with the rest of the world? While Latin American countries are relatively endowed with less skilled labor when compared to the developed countries, they are probably not abundant in less skilled labor relative to the rest of the world, especially with respect to Asia and Africa.[8] Thus, while over 70 percent of Mexico's imports and exports are with the United States, China's growing international market presence may have important effects on wages in Mexico. In the context of bilateral and regional agreements, wage changes should be linked to differences in factor endowments across partners, but the presence of other trading associates external to the agreement may moderate the gains from trade. In our example of a preferential agreement between Canada and Brazil, the relative wage of the less skilled in Brazil may rise to a lesser extent after the agreement if Canada has been trading with China.

Similarly, there may be large differences in the definition of "skill" across countries. Workers considered skilled in one country may be unskilled in another, complicating direct comparisons. While a worker with 10 years of education would be considered skilled in Mexico, he or she may not be considered skilled in the United States. Furthermore, the rankings of factor abundance also depend on what factors are consid-

ered. If a third factor of production is introduced, such as natural resources or land, the standard Stolper-Samuelson result does not necessarily hold.[9]

Factor Content

The Stolper-Samuelson theorem predicts that the change in relative prices drives the change in relative wages. Several analysts have suggested that changes in imports and exports, rather than changes in relative prices, can be compared with changes in wages to determine how liberalization affects inequality. The justification for using imports and exports, aside from being intuitive measures of trade, is that imports increase the effective supply of the factors used to produce them. For example, importing labor-intensive goods would increase the effective supply of labor in the country importing those goods. The effects on labor markets can therefore be determined by the factor content of traded goods. Trade economists tend to be skeptical of this approach because imports may increase for reasons other than trade liberalization (such as an economic boom), but some studies have shown that this approach is appropriate under certain conditions.[10] The results of this debate notwithstanding, imports and exports remain popular measures of integration, as the empirical results illustrate.

Adjustment Costs/Unemployment

The neoclassical model generally assumes that markets adjust easily, so that, in the purest form, there is no unemployment. Understanding market imperfections and adjustment costs that give rise to unemployment

---

[7] Marktanner (2000) finds that it may be more politically efficient to use trade policy to address distributional concerns, which may explain the use of tariffs in ways contrary to the Stolper-Samuelson predictions.

[8] Wood (1997) and Spilimbergo, Londoño and Székely (1999) make this point by comparing the relative endowments of several factors.

[9] Fischer (2001) shows that when a country is land abundant (relative to labor), trade liberalization may increase income inequality in the long run. He finds this effect for land-abundant Chile, while the opposite happened in labor-abundant Taiwan. See also Leamer et al. (1999).

[10] For more on this debate, see Freeman (1995), Panagariya (2000) and Deardorff (2000).

can also help us understand how trade liberalization will affect employment and unemployment. When barriers to trade fall, resources move in response to the change in relative prices. If adjustment costs are significant, and therefore adjustment is slow, unemployment may result.[11] Several studies examine adjustment costs in Latin American countries. The persistence of inter-industry wage differentials and labor market adjustment costs suggests that labor markets may not adjust instantly, leading to worker dislocation.

The degree of market inflexibility in Latin America has also been the subject of debate. Heckman and Pagés (2000) show that mandatory hiring and firing provisions are more stringent in Latin America than in industrial countries. However, while the results of their 2000 study suggested a negative effect on employment, their recent work with better regulatory measures and a larger data set suggests otherwise. It is likely that the presence of large informal labor markets reduces the effect of mandatory regulations in Latin America. In terms of costs, Robertson and Dutkowsky (2002) use industry-level data and find that measured labor market adjustment costs in Mexico are about one-tenth the size of comparably-measured adjustment costs in the United States and the United Kingdom. The size of the adjustment costs affects the relative adjustment of wages and employment. When labor market adjustment costs are high, negative shocks may affect wages more than employment.

Trade among Similar Countries

Differences in relative factor endowments give rise to trade in the Heckscher-Ohlin model, but most world trade is between the developed countries of the North that have relatively similar factor endowments. In the early 1980s, this phenomenon inspired a "new" trade theory based on intra-industry trade (two-way trade in similar products) and monopolistic competition. In these models, countries with similar endowments specialize in varieties of products and exchange different varieties to satisfy consumers' love of variety. Trade liberalization between similar countries tends to favor intra-industry trade, as has been well established for developed countries. Guell and Richards (1998) find that regional agreements between Latin American countries have increased intra-industry trade there as well.

Relatively little theoretical work has been done relating intra-industry trade with wage inequality. That is not surprising, given that the models are based on a representative agent methodology that does not lend itself to an analysis of relative wages. One might expect smaller changes in wages if South-South trade is based on smaller differences in comparative advantage. Current research, however, suggests that intra-industry trade may also contribute to rising inequality. Dinopoulos, Syropoulos and Xu (1999) find that increasing intra-industry trade can increase the demand for skill and therefore increase wage inequality.

Other Implications of Integration

Integration generally involves much more than reducing trade barriers. Recent measures to promote integration include provisions to facilitate capital flows and increase the flow of technology. Each of these can have significant implications for the effects of integration on labor markets.

One constraint on growth and employment is the lack of capital. Integration agreements that promote FDI can therefore increase labor demand. The implications for wage inequality depend on the kind of workers that are generally employed by foreign capital. Conventional wisdom suggests that plants with foreign capital tend to use more advanced technology and hire relatively more skilled workers. In fact, it is also possible that capital movements from developed to developing countries can raise the demand for skill in both countries, thus increasing inequality in both countries (Feenstra and Hanson, 1996). For example, if capital that generally employs workers with a high school education moves from the United States to Mexico, this will reduce the demand for high school workers in the United States (where they are low skilled workers) and increase the demand for these workers in Mexico (where they are high skilled).

Acemoglu (1999) shows that if trade is associated with changes in technology that are more likely

---

[11] Hungerford (1995) finds that trade shocks have only a small effect on the probability of layoffs in the United States. Kletzer (1998), on the other hand, finds evidence of significant job displacement in some U.S. industries.

to be used by high skilled workers, wage inequality will increase in both the high-skill abundant and low-skill abundant trading partners. This process is often referred to as skill-biased technological change. Greater integration may reduce the costs of technology and therefore motivate innovation. Technology has received much attention as a factor raising the demand for skills in the developed countries.[12] Most technology in Latin America is imported. Thus, trade liberalization may reduce the costs of importing technology. If this technology complements skills, the lower cost of technology will increase the demand for skill. Notice that if trade leads to the adoption of new technology, and technology is complementary with skill, trade will at the same time increase productivity and increase inequality. Thus, increases in wage inequality are not necessarily welfare reducing; the level of wages for the high skilled may have merely increased at a greater rate than the wages for the low skilled (for example, poverty rates can fall while the skill gap increases).

REVIEW OF EMPIRICAL FINDINGS

Does Trade Liberalization Increase Inequality?

In between the passionate anti-globalization view that trade liberalization increases inequality and poverty, and the equally strong convictions of trade theorists that liberalization increases living standards, lies the simple fact that, despite a great deal of careful empirical work, the debate over the effect of trade liberalization on wages in developing countries remains unresolved. A definitive answer may be elusive in a changing world: societies are not laboratories where tariffs can be lowered while everything else is kept constant in order to see what happens. Other reforms press ahead simultaneously, and societies change constantly in terms of related variables ranging from the female labor supply to family structure and macroeconomic conditions.

However, while the empirical evidence on the short-run effects of trade liberalization on wage inequality in Latin America is not entirely clear, the results seem to suggest that the reduction of tariffs in Latin America was followed at least initially by an increase in wage inequality. In the longer run, wage inequality may fall depending on further liberalization of the initial trade reforms. Wage inequality in Chile rose from 1970 to 1990, when inequality began to fall.[13] The cause for the reversal is not clear. Mexico experienced a similar reversal that may be easier to explain. Various studies find that wage inequality rose in Mexico following its accession to the GATT, but fell following Mexico's entrance into NAFTA (Figure 12.3).[14] This is consistent with the idea that the *type* of integration matters (North-South vs. South-South). The GATT liberalization for Mexico occurred with respect to the world, while the NAFTA liberalization was with the North, which may help explain the different patterns in subsequent wage inequality. Mexico is not necessarily abundant in less-skilled workers in comparison to world trading partners such as China, but it is less skilled in comparison with the United States and Canada. It is also possible that the changes in wages in the initial years after GATT were dominated by the dismantling of the extra protection for less-skilled workers, given Mexico's pattern of protection before GATT.

Interestingly, GATT and NAFTA liberalization also had different effects on another dimension of inequality—the geographical distribution of employment in manufacturing (see Box 12.2).

Coinciding trends of rising wage inequality and trade liberalization, even when they do occur, do not necessarily imply that one causes the other. Likewise, liberalization can contribute to a change in the demand for skill that is offset by other changes in the economy. Formal studies of the link between inequality and liberalization in Latin America vary somewhat based on the theoretical method motivating the approach. In particular, studies can be grouped into those that examine the link between tariffs, prices of goods, and wages (price studies); studies that examine the effects of changes in trade volumes on inequality; and studies that look at other channels.[15]

---

[12] Two of many studies in developed countries that compare trade and technology are by Haskel and Slaughter (1999, 2001).

[13] See Bravo and Marinovic (2001).

[14] See Airola and Juhn (2001), Acosta and Montes Rojas (2001), and Robertson (2001). The trends in the secondary to primary wage gap for Mexico shown in Table 12.1 are similar to the trends in Figure 12.3.

[15] For a thorough review of the literature, see Robertson (2002).

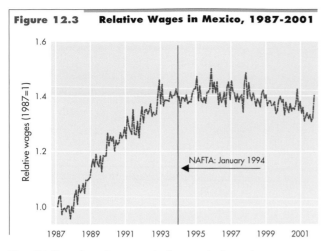

Figure 12.3   Relative Wages in Mexico, 1987-2001

Note: This figure shows the wage ratio of nonproduction workers to production workers, weighted by industry employment. The data are from Mexico's Monthly Industrial Survey conducted by INEGI. The ratio is normalized so that the value of January, 1987 is equal to one.
Source: Robertson (2001).

Price Studies

Price studies link changes in relative prices to changes in relative wages. Although the link from prices to wages is the closest to the Stolper-Samuelson theory, relatively few Latin American studies take this approach. Beyer, Rojas and Vergara (1999) compare changes in relative prices and wages in Chile and find that the rise in the relative price of skill-intensive goods helps explain the increase in inequality. This is consistent with the standard theory if Chile is relatively abundant in skilled labor.[16] For Mexico, Hanson and Harrison (1999) examine firm-level data and industry-level prices during 1984-90 and find little evidence of a relationship between changes in output prices and changes in wage inequality. Alternatively, they identify changes within industries, such as foreign investment and export orientation, as significant contributors to rising wage inequality. Robertson (2001) finds that movements in relative prices were both consistent with Mexico's tariff liberalization and the rise in inequality between 1986 and 1994. He finds that the relative price of skill-intensive goods fell after 1994, which may help explain the fall in wage inequality after NAFTA. Another possible explanation is that the effects of liberalization have different short- and long-run effects.

For Brazil, Gonzaga, Filho and Terra (2001) compare tariff changes, price changes and wage inequality, concluding that wage inequality fell follow-

ing trade reforms in 1988, and that trade liberalization may help explain the fall in wage inequality. However, while wage inequality fell in Brazil, one of the countries with the lowest levels of schooling in the region, inequality rose in Chile, which has high levels of education. Meanwhile in Mexico, wage inequality rose during the GATT years and fell after NAFTA (Figure 12.3). This evidence, taken together, may be consistent with observations that while Mexico is not abundant in low-skilled labor with respect to the world, it is abundant in low-skilled labor with respect to Canada and the United States.

Supply and Demand Studies

A supply and demand approach has been commonly used to compare the factors that may affect the relative demand for skill, although the links to theory are much weaker. Many of the studies ignore the factor content of trade and focus on the quantity of trade. These studies generally find that increased trade flows are associated with increased wage inequality.

In Argentina, Galiani and Sanguinetti (2000) find that trade flows increased wage inequality following liberalization. Rising inequality in Argentina and falling inequality in its largest Mercosur partner, Brazil, is consistent with standard trade theory in the sense that Brazil can be considered abundant in low skill and Argentina abundant in high skill. In Brazil, 50 percent of persons ages 20 to 60 have completed less than six years of schooling, while in Argentina the respective figure is 8 percent.

In terms of magnitude, Galiani and Sanguinetti (2000) find that trade explains a small portion of the increase in inequality. In another study on Argentina, Acosta and Montes Rojas (2001) find that while trade did contribute to the rising demand for skill, technology probably played a more important role. Thus, both studies reach similar conclusions as found in U.S. studies: the direct effect of trade was small and technology was probably more important.

In Costa Rica and Colombia, Robbins and Gindling (1999) and Robbins (1996) find that trade increased wage inequality. They use household surveys

---

[16] The average years of schooling in Chile for the population age 25 and older is 9.6. In the United States, the average is 13.

**Box 12.2 Integration and the
Economic Geography of Mexico**

The gains from trade may be distributed unevenly not only across wage classes, but across regions. In Mexico, the regional effects of trade policies can be viewed from the vantage point of two milestones: Mexico's entry into the GATT in 1986 and formation of the North American Free Trade Agreement (NAFTA) in 1994.

In 1985, Mexico's trade-weighted tariff on manufactured goods stood at 28.5 percent, and 92.2 percent of such goods required import licenses. By 1998, the trade-weighted tariff had fallen to 6.6 percent and the licenses were nearly eliminated. Over the same years, the ratio of Mexico's exports to GDP rose from 15.4 percent to 30.8 percent, and the share of its exports sold to the United States rose from 60.4 percent to 87.9 percent. In short, through these trade policy changes, Mexico has become more integrated with the rest of the world and, in particular, with the U.S. As a result, it has also experienced extensive changes in the distribution of employment among municipalities.

In 1998, of Mexico's 2,443 municipalities, the 16 that constitute the Federal District contained 12 percent of the nation's manufacturing employment. If the municipalities of the surrounding state of Mexico are added, the statistic doubles to 24 percent. Yet, if Mexico City's preeminence is striking, so too was its erosion during the preceding 10 years of integration. Table 1 ranks leading cities by changes in their percent shares of national manufacturing employment from 1988 to 1998. Of the negative changes, one was in Monterrey, one in Guadalajara, and the rest in *delegaciones* of the Federal District. Over the decade, Mexico saw a deconcentration, if not an exodus, of manufacturing from its mega-city and its burgeoning cousins.

Among the greatest positive changes were those in border cities such as Tijuana, Ciudad Juárez and Mexicali. Collectively, they grew from being home to 5.6 percent of Mexico's manufacturing workforce in 1988 to 10 percent in 1998. This marked an increase of 275,000 workers in three municipalities that together now rival the industrial preeminence of the Federal District. But much of the story is told below the top ten. Figure 1a shows the changes in municipal shares from 1988 to 1993, and Figure 1b shows the changes from 1993 to 1998. Positive changes are represented by red peaks, negative changes by blue depressions. Although other factors have also influenced the outcomes, comparing the figures shows whether the two different trade policies—non-preferential opening under the GATT and preferential opening under NAFTA—have had different consequences.

The figures show many similarities: Tijuana, Ciudad Juárez and Reynosa on the U.S. border stood out as growth centers in both periods. Their growth was led by radio, television, communications and medical equipment assembly and apparel manufacture, almost

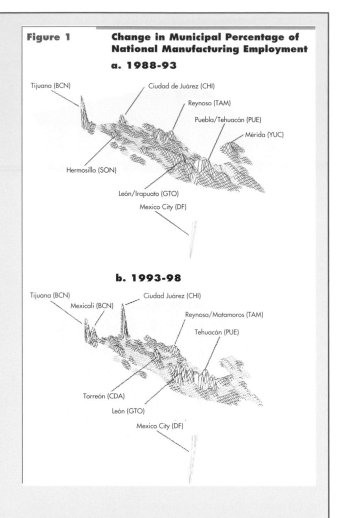

Figure 1 **Change in Municipal Percentage of National Manufacturing Employment**
a. 1988-93
b. 1993-98

all destined for export to the U.S. Tehuacán, in the state of Puebla, and León, in Guanajuato, although less than 250 miles from Mexico City, also flourished as apparel export manufacturing centers in the 1990s.

But the figures also show notable differences. Mérida and several other municipalities in Quintana Roo, Campeche and Chiapas, near ports or the southern border, grew in the non-preferential opening period but not in the preferential opening period. Conversely, Mexicali, on the U.S. border, and Torreón, near it, grew substantially in the preferential period but not in the non-preferential period. On balance, there is some evidence of regional repercussions of Mexico's change from non-preferential to preferential trade liberalization.

The dominant features of the figures—the peaks centered on Tijuana, Ciudad Juárez, León and Tehuacán, and the crevasse underlying Mexico City—represent a dramatic reversal of fortune. There was some perceived advantage to the mega-city's agglomeration, after all, that continued to fuel its growth in both absolute and relative terms until the mid-1980s. Part of the advantage was undoubtedly the centralization in Mexico City of power, political influence and public spending; part stemmed from externalities, manifested

Table 1   **Cities Ranked by Share Change in National Manufacturing Employment, 1988-98**

Positive changes

		Employment, 1988 (number of persons)	Employment, 1998 (number of persons)	Share in national manufacturing,1998 (%)	Change in share
1	Tijuana (BCN)	41,872	153,530	3.76	2.15
2	Ciudad Juárez (CHI)	108,172	240,782	5.90	1.74
3	Apodaca (NLN)	8,303	37,214	0.91	0.59
4	Zapopan (JAL)	24,989	63,337	1.55	0.59
5	Mexicali (BCN)	24,562	61,375	1.50	0.56
6	Guadalupe (NLN)	13,289	41,414	1.02	0.50
7	Reynosa (TAM)	24,141	55,080	1.35	0.42
8	León (GTO)	55,508	103,397	2.53	0.40
9	Tehuacán (PUE)	8,981	28,471	0.70	0.35
10	Hermosillo (SON)	11,294	31,795	0.78	0.34

Negative changes

1	Azcapotzalco (D-F)	87,493	74,588	1.83	-1.71
2	Tlalnepantla (MEX)	80,502	73,606	1.80	-1.45
3	Naucalpan (MEX)	80,202	78,697	1.93	-1.32
4	Monterrey (NLN)	92,001	103,457	2.53	-1.19
5	Guadalajara (JAL)	102,453	126,737	3.10	-1.04
6	Cuauhtémoc (D-F)	60,838	62,710	1.54	-0.93
7	Gustavo Madero (D-F)	47,944	43,718	1.07	-0.87
8	Miguel Hidalgo (D-F)	55,061	58,143	1.42	-0.80
9	Iztapalapa (D-F)	68,293	79,502	1.95	-0.82
10	Benito Juárez (D-F)	36,386	31,122	0.76	-0.71

in technological spillovers and labor training; and part lay in the simple fact that people had already chosen to locate there. Manufacturing industries were unlikely to stray far from their principal output market, particularly given the large transport costs they would incur in supplying that market from outside the Valle de México.

The GATT liberalization and NAFTA combined with other causes to unravel these advantages. Political decentralization supporting state and municipal self-government militated against the first advantage; negative externalities in the form of congestion costs, including pollution and the consequent limitations to auto circulation and factory emissions, began to balance against the second; and Mexico's opening, combined with its physical geography and transport infrastructure, undermined the third. As Mexico exports a larger part of its output, more of manufacturing firms' output markets lie in the United States rather than Mexico City. The capital's distance from the border, coupled with the lack of multi-lane and restricted access divided highways over parts of the distance, gives more advantages to establishing manufacturing plants in the north and fewer advantages to Mexico City. What is more, the north's advantages are compounded cumulatively as its share of manufacturing industry grows: other northern plants and migrant employees are among the new plants' suppliers and consumers, so by locating in the North they are all locating alongside a growing portion of their markets.

Integration has thus diminished regional

inequalities in Mexico—with an important caveat. It has "chosen" regions that might not have figured as largely as others in policymakers' development plans, particularly post-NAFTA. To illustrate, in Figure 1b, a path of red is discernible running south from Ciudad Juárez past Torreón, surrounded by a sea of blue. The red is situated exactly on one of the principal highways from Mexico's interior to the northern border; the blue contains the small towns and *ejidos* far from it. In the immediate post-GATT period, in addition to well-situated areas like those on the highway, many of the more numerous and poorly situated areas also experienced relative growth. This cannot be said as accurately of the post-NAFTA period. From 1988-93, 68 percent of municipalities recorded positive changes in their shares of national manufacturing employment, but over 1993-98, that fell to 51 percent.

Will the trend of manufacturing deconcentration in Mexico City, and its growing concentration at the border and a handful of particular areas inland, continue? Perhaps not. The limitations to agglomeration already confronted by Mexico City now begin to emerge in the border cities, as labor and congestion costs there rise. Meanwhile, improvements in national transport infrastructure should reduce the cost difference between serving the U.S. market from the border and from more distant locations. Trade liberalization and integration will continue to influence shifts in Mexico's economic geography, but their epicenters may change.

to control for changes in the supply of education (and several other institutional factors) and find that much of the increase in wage inequality that followed trade liberalization in both countries was due to a rising demand for skill.

A few studies examine changes in trade policy instead of changes in trade quantity. Although they do not analyze the effect of changes in the prices of goods, these studies are closely related to the policy decision to lower tariffs. A recent study takes the novel approach of linking indices of policy reforms to a series of household surveys from 18 countries covering the 1990s. Behrman, Birdsall and Székely (2001) compare the contributions of trade liberalization, privatization, financial market reforms and technology using data from 18 Latin American countries. They find that trade liberalization had no significant effect on wage inequality, but technology and financial market reforms (including capital account liberalization and tax changes) had a significant impact on changes in wage inequality.[17]

Robbins (1996) relates changes in wages to changes in tariffs in Costa Rica and does not find evidence that trade liberalization increased the demand for skills in ways consistent with the Stolper-Samuelson theorem. Instead, he argues that technological changes were behind the increase in wage inequality.

Concern continues to be raised about the impact of trade liberalization on women's wages and employment opportunities. The "before and after" studies that claim to measure the effects of trade liberalization are even more problematic for women than for men, since the secular changes in female labor force participation may have larger effects on the distribution of female wages than changes in trade liberalization. The effects of trade liberalization on women's labor market outcomes remain an important area for future research.

FDI and Technology

Chapter 10 suggests that regional integration agreements are associated with an increase in foreign direct investment both from member countries and outside sources. Foreign investment flows have played a very important role in the economies of Latin America.[18] Foreign investment may affect employment either directly (through new hires and expansions over time) or indirectly (through linkages with local firms) (Lall,

1995). Regarding the direct channel, Feenstra and Hanson (1996, 1997) develop and test a model in which foreign capital represents a transfer of jobs that are considered less skilled in the developed countries but are skilled in the developing countries. Examining Mexico's maquiladoras, they find support for their hypothesis that foreign capital increased wage inequality in Mexico.

Foreign capital can also bring in new technologies whose complementarity with skills may increase the demand for skill.[19] Thus, integration that increases capital and technology flows may increase inequality. This effect may be especially important in Latin American countries that develop much less of their own technology. Alvarez and Robertson (2001) find that domestic firms that partner with foreign capital are more likely to innovate than firms without foreign capital. Foreign capital tends to use the most advanced production techniques (Buitelaar, Padilla and Urrutia, 1999). These effects are complementary with trade liberalization that makes importing machine tools, especially computer-controlled machine tools, much less expensive for Latin America (Alcorta, 2000). These imports may have contributed to rising productivity. If workers need more skills to work with these technologies, the demand for these skills, and thus inequality, increases.

Another channel through which integration may affect relative wages and poverty is through technology. In the United States and developed countries, trade and technology are often posited as alternative explanations for changes in the wage structure.[20] The fact that the South in general, and Latin America in particular, generally do not develop technology to the same extent as the North suggests that increased integration between the North and the South may facilitate

---

[17] Trade liberalization is measured as the mean of the average level and average dispersion of tariffs, per Lora (1997).

[18] Some of the many studies that discuss capital flows into Latin American countries are Agosin, Fuentes and Letelier (1994); Agosin and Ffrench-Davis (1997); and Gil Diaz (1999).

[19] Blonigen and Slaughter (1999) find that, for the United States, FDI increases the demand for less skilled workers.

[20] Acemoglu (1998, 1999) shows some of the patterns of skill and suggests that in the United States, the increase in the supply of skilled workers has induced the development of skill-complementary technology. These technologies affect the relative demand for skill (Autor, Katz and Krueger, 1998).

technology flows southward. Since living standards depend on productivity, these flows may hold the promise of reducing poverty as well.

There are several ways that technology may change as a result of trade liberalization. First, exporting may create the incentives to implement more advanced technologies to meet the demands of world consumers or reduce inefficiency afforded to them by protection.[21] Several studies have found that exporting firms are more productive, and that exporting is linked to incentives to invest in new technology (see Chapter 11).[22] These new technologies may have increased the demand for skill (Macario, 2000). Importing intermediate inputs as well as machinery may also create effects analogous to technological change. Finally, reducing barriers to trade may make it easier to acquire foreign technologies. If countries have more flows of goods, services and communication between them, the cost of diffusing technology falls. Firms are more able to learn from other countries and apply that accumulated knowledge at home. Acosta and Montes Rojas (2001), using household-level data for Mexico and Argentina, compare the roles of trade and technology and find that technology may have had larger effects on inequality than trade flows.

POLICY IMPLICATIONS

The most ambitious integration initiative pending for the region is the Free Trade Area of the Americas (FTAA). Under the assumption that the South is relatively abundant in less skilled workers, North-South integration should reduce wage inequality there. On the other hand, if integration facilitates the flow of capital and technology, this integration may increase the demand for skill and increase wage inequality (at least in the short run). The existing empirical literature offers only little clarity. There seems to be some consensus that wage inequality increased in Latin America following trade liberalization, and most studies agree that this increase in inequality was correlated with an increase in the demand for skill, especially in the short run.

While there are several factors that may explain the response of inequality to integration, all of the factors seem to generate similar policy implications. Regardless of whether further integration is North-

South or South-South, economic integration causes a reallocation of resources between industries. Trade opening is expected to bring long-run gains in the form of increases in productivity and growth, but the process of integrating markets means that economies are more susceptible to swings in world prices. Given the fact that some adjustment is certain, programs to facilitate the process for workers and families are important.

Training and Job Search Programs

Worker training and job search programs that smooth transitions to new types of employment will particularly help workers become more productive sooner. The availability of effective programs prior to further rounds of liberalization will also make workers less anxious about prospects for integration. New skills taught to displaced workers should reflect the new profile of demands in the economy, regardless of whether those news demands derive from generalized technological change or tariff reductions. Currently, most training institutes are designed based on the pre-1980s framework of import-substitution, in which the state could highlight a few industries and provide training for a determined set of skills. Although flush with funds from earmarked taxes, many institutes have not been linked to the changing demands for skill.

One promising innovation is the regulatory approach to training being used in Chile. The National Training and Employment Service (SENCE) does not provide the training directly, but rather uses an income tax rebate for businesses that contract or directly provide a program to their employees. The program must meet SENCE's criteria for relevance and quality for the firm to be eligible for the rebate. Since the firms are self-financing a portion of the training costs, they have the incentive to select programs that suit their demands. The same type of rebate is available to firms offering

---

[21] Currie and Harrison (1997) find evidence that firms increased productivity following trade liberalization in Morocco.

[22] See Aw and Hwang (1995), Bernard and Jensen (1997), and Alvarez and Robertson (2001). Dijkstra (2000) argues that the link between trade liberalization and technological change seems weak. Technological change may have been correlated with other factors, such as industrial policy and exchange rate movements that encouraged restructuring in the manufacturing sector.

apprenticeships to potential employees drawn from workers displaced from their old jobs.

The challenge for institutes that provide their own courses, such as the National Training Institute (INA) in Costa Rica, is to identify and provide training that provides skills that are well aligned with the demands of businesses.

Displaced workers with high levels of education may have strong prospects for being re-hired without job training, and may benefit quickly from job search programs. But it is important for job search assistance to be well integrated with the training programs. A new program in El Salvador run by the non-governmental organization FEDISAL lists training course openings in the national job registry. Programs combine counseling along with listings of job openings. The model is innovative in that private, non-governmental and governmental institutions are collaborating to better link services with changing demands. Walk-in facilities that offer computerized searches of national job registries are becoming more common, but these services are not necessarily accessible in all geographic areas (Mazza, 2001).

Unemployment Insurance and Workfare Programs

Traditionally, unemployment insurance in the region came in the form of a generous severance payment available when formal sector workers were involuntarily separated from their jobs. Heckman and Pagés (2002) suggest that unemployment insurance slows the reallocation of workers to new positions, since employers have the incentive to maintain inefficient staff to avoid paying the stiff penalty. Unemployment insurance as is implemented by developed countries, with smaller monthly payments, is often criticized for discouraging labor supply. A new hybrid unemployment insurance in Chile directs a share of wages and the employer's contribution to individual accounts. Workers first draw down their personal accounts before they are eligible to receive government payments. Since the worker's contributions roll over to retirement accounts if they are not used, the worker has the incentive to conserve the account. These schemes are also portable from job to job, an attractive feature in dynamic economies.

Employment programs in which participants receive a minimum wage in exchange for work have advantages over standard unemployment insurance, since the unemployment transfers are typically only available for formal sector workers and provide a disincentive to work. Workfare programs are more expensive to administer than cash transfers, but do not discourage labor supply. If the wage is not set artificially high, the program is effectively "self-targeted" in that jobs tend not to be captured by high-skilled workers who have better prospects elsewhere. Another feature of a low-level wage is that participants have the incentive to self-graduate to "regular" jobs with better wages. Unfortunately, too often the allocation of positions is subject to discretionality based on political objectives, diminishing the effectiveness of the program.

The ensuing benefits to society of trade liberalization—higher productivity and growth and lower prices—are diffuse, whereas the costs of economic transformation are concentrated and visible. Perceived losses by workers in specific industries create strong interest groups opposed to the dismantling of protection. Targeting re-training programs to specific industries or geographic areas with expected losses can reduce political opposition to integration. Generous severance packages may reduce opposition in the short run, but do not necessarily leave the dislocated workers with good prospective earning streams. Some workers may have interests in running their own businesses but lack the capital and expertise. Providing credit and training to small and medium-sized enterprises is important for directing displaced labor towards more efficient production. Promoting exports, ties to foreign markets, and new technologies may help increase worker productivity in ways that are necessary for long-run improvements in living standards.

Safety Nets

Targeting employment and training programs to workers in sectors affected by liberalization may be desirable, but most social welfare policies should not be linked to the process or policies of liberalization. Social safety nets should be available to those in poverty, regardless of the direct cause of that poverty. In the context of reducing poverty and raising living standards, social safety nets must consider the welfare and capacities of all family members, not only those who have lost jobs. Still, the added vulnerability of families to external shocks, such as precipitous drops in coffee prices, indicates that the social safety nets need to be flexible enough to expand during crises.

Promotion of Competitiveness in Rural Economic Activities

Worldwide trade liberalization in agriculture is critical for making trade work for the poor. Poverty tends to be concentrated in rural, agricultural areas throughout the region. Continued subsidies in the agriculture sectors in the developed world keep the international price of commodities artificially low, which effectively blocks off a path out of poverty for the approximately 20 percent of families in the region whose main livelihood comes from agriculture.[23] In the highly indebted poor countries (HIPC) of the region, approximately 30 percent of households depend primarily on the agricultural sector as their main source of household income.[24] Low prices are not the only problem. There is a lack of technology and production alternatives, particularly in tropical countries where agriculture has been protected. Regional integration in infrastructure, such as transportation, is critical for generating opportunities in agriculture. There have also been difficulties in getting agricultural products from Latin America to foreign markets because firms have not met export standards, which are not uniform among importing countries. Some unification of the standards would facilitate exports. Countries can also provide assistance to small and medium-sized firms to help them meet the standards required for their agricultural products. Both technical assistance and credit for investing in new technologies can facilitate commodity exports by small and medium-sized producers.

Education

The education of the next generation of workers should be a priority. A labor force with a high level of general skills will be best placed to take advantage of or weather the adjustments from changes in international prices and advancements in technology. Targeted human development programs such as Bolsa-Escola in Brazil, Oportunidades in Mexico, and PRAF in Hon-

duras are succeeding in raising the schooling attainment of school age children by providing cash transfers to families conditional on their children remaining in school. Other programs such as Nuevas Oportunidades in Costa Rica change the supply of schooling. The program offers flexible schedules that enable dropouts, both children and adults, to complete primary and secondary schooling at their own pace. Students attend a minimum number of formal course hours with teachers operating in non-standard facilities such as churches or municipal buildings, and complete the lion's share of coursework according to their own schedules. PRAF also includes components to improve the quality of education.

Often a basic set of skills is necessary before job specific training is effective. If the relative demand for skill increases, the increasing returns to skill provide an additional incentive to stay in school longer. But this is not possible if the quality and quantity of educational opportunities are lacking. To meet the rising demand for skill that seems to follow liberalization, public investment in broad-based education becomes increasingly important. While the temptation exists to retain protection for highly mobilized or vulnerable groups, delaying the dismantling of protection creates new generations of potential workers with misaligned skills.

---

[23] Some workers in the labor-intensive sector of non-traditional agriculture benefit from trade barriers.

[24] Based on sector of activity of the household head. The estimates are 31 percent in Honduras, 34 percent in Bolivia and 35 percent in Nicaragua.

REFERENCES

Acemoglu, Daron. 1998. Why Do New Technologies Complement Skills? Directed Technical Change and Wage Inequality. *Quarterly Journal of Economics* 113(4) November.

———. 1999. *Patterns of Skill Premia*. NBER Working Paper no. 7018.

Acosta, Pablo, and Gabriel Montes Rojas. 2001. Trade Reform, Technological Change and Inequality: The Case of Mexico and Argentina in the '90s. University of Illinois at Urbana-Champaign. September.

Agosin, Manuel, and Ricardo Ffrench-Davis. 1997. Managing Capital Inflows in Chile. *Estudios de Economía* 24 (December): 297-326.

Agosin, M., R. Fuentes, and L. Letelier. 1994. Los capitales extranjeros en las economías latinoamericanas: Chile. In José Antonio Ocampo (ed.) *Los capitales extranjeros en las economías latinoamericanas.* FEDESARROLLO and the Inter-American Development Bank.

Airola, Jim, and Chinhui Juhn. 2001. Income and Consumption Inequality in Post-reform Mexico. Paper presented at the 2001 Latin American and Caribbean Economic Society Meetings. October.

Alarcon, Diana, and Terry McKinley. 1997. The Rising Contribution of Labor Income to Inequality in Mexico. *North American Journal of Economics and Finance* 8(2): 201-12.

Alcorta, Ludovico. 2000. New Economic Policies and the Diffusion of Machine Tools in Latin America. *World Development* 28(9) September: 1657-72.

Alvarez, Roberto, and Raymond Robertson. 2001. Exposure to Foreign Markets and Firm-level Innovation: Evidence from Chile and Mexico. Macalester College. Mimeo.

Autor, David H., Lawrence F. Katz, and Alan B. Krueger. 1998. Computing Inequality: Have Computers Changed the Labor Market? *Quarterly Journal of Economics* 113(4) November: 1169-213.

Aw, B. Y., and A. R. Hwang. 1995. Productivity and the Export Market: A Firm-level Analysis. *Journal of Development Economics* 47: 313-32.

Behrman, Jere, Nancy Birdsall, and Miguel Székely. 2001. Economic Policy and Wage Differentials in Latin America. University of Pennsylvania. November.

Bell, Linda. 1997. The Impact of Minimum Wages in Mexico and Colombia. *Journal of Labor Economics* 15(3): S102-35.

Bernard, Andrew, and J. Bradford Jenson. 1997. Exporters, Skill Upgrading, and the Wage Gap. *Journal of International Economics* 42(1-2) February: 3-31.

Beyer, Harald, Patricio Rojas, and Rodrigo Vergara. 1999. Trade Liberalization and Wage Inequality. *Journal of Development Economics* 59(1) June: 103-23.

Blonigen, B., and M. Slaughter. 1999. *Foreign-Affiliate Activity and U.S. Skill Upgrading.* NBER Working Paper no. W7040.

Bravo, David, and Alejandra Marinovic. 2001. Wage Inequality in Chile: 40 Years of Evidence. Paper presented at the XVII Latin American Meeting of the Econometric Society, University of Chile.

Buitelaar, Rudolf M., Ramon Padilla, and Ruth Urrutia. 1999. The In-Bond Assembly Industry and Technical Change. *CEPAL Review* 0(67) April: 137-56.

Currie, Janet, and Ann E. Harrison. 1997. Sharing the Costs: The Impact of Trade Reform on Capital and Labor in Morocco. *Journal of Labor Economics* 15(3) July: S44-71.

Deardorff, Alan V. 2000. Factor Prices and the Factor Content of Trade Revisited: What's the Use? *Journal of International Economics* 50(1) February: 73-90.

Dijkstra, A. Geske. 2000. Trade Liberalization and the Industrial Development in Latin America. *World Development* 28(9) September: 1567-82.

Dinopoulos, Elias, Constantinos Syropoulos, and Bin Xu. 1999. Intra-Industry Trade and Wage Income Inequality. University of Florida. Mimeo.

Dollar, David. 1992. Outward-Oriented Developing Economies Really Do Grow More Rapidly: Evidence from 95 LDCs, 1976-1985. *Economic Development and Cultural Change* 40(3) April: 523-44.

Dollar, David, and Aart Kraay. 2000. Growth Is Good for the Poor. Development Research Group. World Bank, Washington, DC. March. Mimeo.

Duryea, Suzanne, Olga Jaramillo, and Carmen Pagés. 2002. *Latin American Labor Markets in the 1990s: Deciphering the Decade.* Inter-American Development Bank Research Department Working Paper.

Feenstra, R. C., and G. H. Hanson. 1996. Foreign Investment, Outsourcing, and Relative Wages. In R. C. Feenstra, G. M. Grossman and D. A. Irwin (eds.), *Political Economy of Trade Policy: Essays in Honor of Jagdish Bhagwati.* Cambridge, MA: MIT Press.

——. 1997. Foreign Direct Investment and Relative Wages: Evidence from Mexico's Maquiladoras. *Journal of International Economics* 42: 371-93.

Feliciano, Zadia M. 2001. Workers and Trade Liberalization: The Impact of Trade Reforms in Mexico on Wages and Employment. *Industrial and Labor Relations Review* 55(1) October: 95-115.

Fischer, Ronald D. 2001. The Evolution of Inequality after Trade Liberalization. *Journal of Development Economics* 66(2) December: 555-79.

Freeman, Richard. 1995. Are Your Wages Set in Beijing? *Journal of Economic Perspectives* 9(3) Summer: 15-32.

Galiani, Sebastian, and Pablo Sanguinetti. 2000. Wage Inequality and Trade Liberalization: Evidence from Argentina. Universidad Torcuato Di Tella. July.

Ganuza, Enrique, Ricardo Paes de Barros, Lance Taylor, and Rob Vos (eds.). 2001. Liberalización, desigualdad y pobreza: América Latina y el Caribe en los 90. PNUD, CEPAL. June.

Gil Diaz, Francisco. 1999. Capital Flows to Latin America. In Martin Feldstein (ed.), *International Capital Flows.* National Bureau of Economic Research Conference Report series. Chicago and London: University of Chicago Press.

Gonzaga, Gustavo, Naercio Filho, and Cristina Terra. 2001. Wage Inequality in Brazil: The Role of Trade Liberalization. PUC-Rio. September.

González, Diana Alarcon, and Terry McKinley. 1997. Paradox of Narrowing Wage Differentials and Widening Wage Inequality in Mexico. *Development and Change* 28(3) July: 505-30.

Guell, Robert C., and Donald G. Richards. 1998. Regional Integration and Intra-industry Trade in Latin America, 1980-90. *International Review of Applied Economics* 12(2) May: 283-300.

Hanson, Gordon, and Ann Harrison. 1999. Trade, Technology, and Wage Inequality. *Industrial and Labor Relations Review* 52(2) January: 271-88.

——. 1999. Who Gains from Trade Reform? Some Remaining Puzzles. *Journal of Development Economics* 59(1) June: 125-54.

Haskel, Jonathan, and Matthew J. Slaughter. 1999. *Does the Sector Bias of Skill-Biased Technical Change Explain Changing Skill Differentials?* NBER Working Paper no. 6565.

——. 2001. Trade, Technology and U.K. Wage Inequality. *Economic Journal* 111(468) January: 163-87.

Heckman, James, and Carmen Pagés. 2002. Law and Employment: Lessons from Latin America and the Caribbean. May.

Hungerford, Thomas L. 1995. International Trade, Comparative Advantage and the Incidence of Layoff Unemployment Spells. *Review of Economics and Statistics* 77(3) August: 511-21.

Kletzer, Lori. 1998. Trade and Job Loss in US Manufacturing 1975-1994. NBER. February.

Krugman, Paul, and Raul Livas Elizondo. 1996. Trade Policy and the Third World Metropolis. *Journal of Development Economics* 49: 137-51.

Lall, Sanjaya. 1995. Employment and Foreign Investment: Policy Options for Developing Countries. *International Labour Review* 134(4-5): 521-40.

Leamer, Edward E. 1998. In Search of Stolper-Samuelson Linkages between Trade and Lower Wages. In S. Collins (ed.), *Imports, Exports, and the American Worker.* Washington, DC: Brookings Institute Press.

Leamer, Edward E., Hugo Maul, Sergio Rodríguez, and Peter K. Schott. 1999. Does Natural Resource Abundance Increase Latin American Income Inequality? *Journal of Development Economics* 59(1) June: 3-42.

Lora, Eduardo. 1997. *A Decade of Structural Reform in Latin America: What Has Been Reformed and How to Measure It.* Inter-American Development Bank Research Department Working Paper 348. June.

Macario, Carla. 2000. The Behavior of Manufacturing Firms under the New Economic Model. *World Development* 28(9) September: 1597-610.

Marktanner, Marcus. 2000. Why Do Politicians in Developed Nations Prefer Foreign Trade Policy to Income Redistribution to Counteract Income Inequality Resulting from Globalization? *Global Business and Economics Review* 2(2) December: 235-45.

Mazza, Jacqueline. 2001. Labor Intermediation Services: A Review for Latin American and Caribbean Countries. Sustainable Development Department, Inter-American Development Bank. Mimeo.

Panagariya, Arvind. 2000. Evaluating the Factor-Content Approach to Measuring the Effect of Trade on Wage Inequality. *Journal of International Economics* 50(1) February: 91-116.

Paus, Eva, and Michael D. Robinson. Real Wage Performance under Greater Trade Openness: Lessons from Latin America and Asia. *Journal of Developing Areas* 33(2) Winter: 269-88.

Porto, Guido. 2001. The Distributional Effects of Mercosur Using Survey Data to Assess Trade Policy. Princeton University. Mimeo.

Ravallion, Martin. 1997. *Can High-Inequality Developing Countries Escape Absolute Poverty?* World Bank Policy Research Department Working Paper no. 1775, Washington, DC. June.

Revenga, Ana. 1997. Employment and Wage Effects of Trade Liberalization: The Case of Mexican Manufacturing. *Journal of Labor Economics* 15(3) July: S20-43.

Robbins, Donald. 1996. Stolper-Samuelson (Lost) in the Tropics? Trade Liberalization and Wages in Colombia: 1976-1994. Harvard University.

Robbins, Donald, and T. H. Gindling. 1999. Trade Liberalization and the Relative Wages for More-Skilled Workers in Costa Rica. *Review of Development Economics* 3(2) June: 140-54.

Roberts, Mark J., and James R. Tybout. 1997. The Decision to Export in Colombia: An Empirical Model of Entry with Sunk Costs. *American Economic Review* 87(4) September: 545-64.

Robertson, Raymond. 2001. Relative Prices and Wage Inequality: Evidence from Mexico. Macalester College. Mimeo.

————. 2002. Trade Liberalization and Wage Inequality: A Review of the Latin American Experience. Inter-American Development Bank Research Department, Washington, DC. Mimeo.

Robertson, Raymond, and Donald H. Dutkowsky. 2002. Labor Adjustment Costs in a Destination Country: The Case of Mexico. *Journal of Development Economics* 67(1) February: 29-54.

Rodrik, Dani. 2001. The Global Governance of Trade as if Development Really Mattered. Trade and Sustainable Human Development Project, United Nations Development Programme. Mimeo.

Rodrik, Dani, and Francisco Rodríguez. 1999. *Trade Policy and Economic Growth: A Skeptic's Guide to the Cross-National Evidence.* NBER Working Paper no. 7081. April.

Slaughter, Matthew. 2000. What Are the Results of Product-Price Studies and What Can We Learn from Their Differences? In Robert C. Feenstra (ed.), *The Impact of International Trade on Wages,* National Bureau of Economic Research Conference.

Spilimbergo, Antonio, Juan Luis Londoño, and Miguel Székely. 1999. Income Distribution, Factor Endowments, and Trade Openness. *Journal of Development Economics* 59(1) June: 77-101.

Stolper, W., and P. Samuelson. 1941. Protection and Real Wages. *Review of Economic Studies* 9 (November): 58-73.

Székely, Miguel. 2001. The 1990s in Latin America: Another Decade of Persistent Inequality, but with Somewhat Lower Poverty. Inter-American Development Bank Research Department Working Paper 454, Washington, DC. June.

Thompson, Henry. 1995. Free Trade and Income Redistribution in Some Developing and Newly Industrialized Countries. *Open Economies Review* 6(3) July: 265-80.

Tybout, James, and Daniel Westbrook. 1995. Trade Liberalization and the Dimensions of Efficiency Change in Mexican Manufacturing Industries. *Journal of International Economics* 39(1-2) August: 53-78.

Tybout, James, Jamie de Melo, and Vittorio Corbo. 1991. The Effects of Trade Reforms on Scale and Technical Efficiency: New Evidence from Chile. *Journal of International Economics* 31(3-4) November: 231-50.

Wood, A. 1997. Openness and Wage Inequality in Developing Countries: The Latin American Challenge to East Asian Conventional Wisdom. *World Bank Economic Review* 11(1) January: 33-57.